The Need for Enemies

ALSO BY F. G. BAILEY

Caste and the Economic Frontier, 1957
Tribe, Caste, and Nation, 1960
Politics and Social Change, 1963
Stratagems and Spoils, 1969
Gifts and Poison (ed.), 1971
Debate and Compromise (ed.), 1973
Morality and Expediency, 1977
The Tactical Uses of Passion, 1983
Humbuggery and Manipulation, 1988
The Prevalence of Deceit, 1991
The Kingdom of Individuals, 1993
The Witch-Hunt, 1994
The Civility of Indifference, 1996

F. G. BAILEY

The Need
for
Enemies

A Bestiary of Political Forms

CORNELL UNIVERSITY PRESS

ITHACA AND LONDON

First published 1998 by Cornell University Press.
First printing, Cornell Paperbacks, 1998.

Printed in the United States of America.

Library of Congress Cataloging-in-Publication Data

Bailey, F. G. (Frederick George)
The need for enemies : a bestiary of political forms / F. G. Bailey.
p.   cm.
Includes bibliographical references and index.
ISBN 0-8014-3470-X (cloth : alk. paper). —ISBN 0-8014-8474-X (pbk. : alk. paper)
1. Political culture—India—Orissa.   2. Orissa (India)—Politics and
government.   3. Rhetoric—Political aspects—India—Orissa.   4. Opposition
(Political science)   5. Enemies (Persons)   6. Political psychology.   I. Title.
JQ620.O759B35   1998
320′.954′1309045—dc21   97-38676

Cornell University Press strives to utilize environmentally responsible
suppliers and materials to the fullest extent possible in the publishing of its
books. Such materials include vegetable-based, low-VOC inks and acid-free
papers that are also either recycled, totally chlorine-free, or partly composed
of nonwood fibers.

Cloth printing   10 9 8 7 6 5 4 3 2 1

Paperback printing   10 9 8 7 6 5 4 3 2 1

Contents

vi

CONTENTS

Acknowledgments

For their comments I thank Eva Bagg, Roy D'Andrade, Sara Dickey, Dan Doyle, and Mary K. Gilliland.

Preface

It is a bad habit to say another man's thoughts are bad and ours only are good and that those holding different views from ours are the enemies of the country.

—Gandhi, *Hind Swaraj, or Indian Home Rule*

It is always possible to bind together a considerable number of people in love, so long as there are other people left over to receive the manifestations of their aggressiveness.

—Freud, *Civilization and Its Discontents*

We live now in a period of sustained nastiness, when American politicians and their congeners methodically evade the golden rule, both in words and in deeds: they do to others what they surely do not want done to themselves.

Political commentators are no less offensive. On radio talk shows, hosts and the callers they select exhibit a degree of insolence and malevolence that is dismaying; the speakers having neither ordinary human decency, nor a proper sense of their own insignificance, nor any attachment to the truth, nor any concern for the evil their words might occasion. What they do have—or present themselves as having—is an appalling moral certitude. They deal in absolutes and their minds are closed behind the impenetrable ramparts of bigotry. Secure in their identity, supremely arrogant, knowing their own essence, they assume that no one else could be as perfect. They alone are virtuous; they alone know the truth; they alone have the right to pass judgment. As if they were gods! Along with this self-assured moralizing goes a pervasive disrespect for all public figures, except those taken to be true believers in the appointed scripture. Nonbelievers are presented as lying, cheating,

ix

lecherous, self-interested, power-hungry, unscrupulous, insensitive, stupid, vaporous, and about as trustworthy as that icon for American untrustworthiness, the person who sells used cars.

How to explain this? Why don't people use their heads? Whatever happened to reason? Why must there be a victim? Why is it not enough to assert one's own excellence, relying on a record of achievement or a program? Why is there so little trust, so little regard, so little charity? Why is it confidently assumed that a single negative counts for more than a bundle of positives? What generates the malice and the menacing assertion of a faith? Why is the debate so personal?

One answer might be that there is nothing to explain, because in mass politics things could not be otherwise. The nature of a mass audience precludes genuinely reasoned step-by-step arguments about issues or institutions, or even about achievements. A simple *argumentum ad hominem* is infinitely more persuasive, not only because it is easier to follow but also because the spectacle of human virtue and human wickedness sets our political hormones raging in a way that issues and systems—mere abstractions—cannot do. Arguments addressed to the mind, moreover, since they use the conditional form of "if *this* is the case, then so must *that* also be true," by their very structure invite listeners to contest the premises, the logic, and the evidence. But, suitably revamped by rhetoric, an argument can be made to bypass the mind's critical faculties and appeal straight to the passions. Issues themselves can be manipulated in this way, but much the most effective tactic is to sideline issues altogether and talk about virtue (ours) and wickedness (theirs). Politicians are like lawyers: they rate victory higher than truth.

The problem may lie deeper than the exigencies of communication; it may be at the very heart of the political process. In politics leaders compete for power; they are rivals, and by definition rivalry entails antagonism. Therefore there is nothing to explain; to ask why politicians are antagonistic would be like asking why water is wet. I think that is the case, but not the entire case. Certainly the current virulence is nothing new; politicians have been saying mean-spirited things about each other since politics began. But there is still something to be explained: the level of virulence within any particular political arena is not constant. I do not mean simply that it rises and falls to match elections, when bad-mouthing is at a premium. There is a wider context that controls both the frequency and the intensity of mean-mindedness. That context is my target.

Madison, writing in *The Federalist*, went a step further and made such antipathies part of human nature. "So strong is this propensity of mankind, to fall into mutual animosity, that where no substantial occasion presents itself, the most frivolous and fanciful distinctions have been sufficient to kindle their unfriendly passions, and excite their most violent conflicts." He was a pessimist: "The latent causes of factionalism are thus sown in the nature of man." He went on to identify contexts that favor or disfavor animosity and saw only two remedies, either the removal of liberty or homogenization, "giving to every citizen the same opinions, the same passions, and the same interests." The first solution (the removal of liberty) he found unacceptable. The second he considered a fantasy; it could never happen (Beloff 1948, 42–43).

He was wrong, in two ways. First, he spread the net too wide. If we do have a propensity to fall into "mutual animosity," that propensity is enacted only when someone has taken the trouble to kindle our "unfriendly passions"—in other words, to politicize us. Animosity is a feature of the political person, the one engaged in a contest for power, not of the whole person. The default condition for ordinary people in their ordinary lives more often is political indifference (benign, we can hope).

Second, there are occasions sufficiently compelling to homogenize passions and make people put aside not only rivalries but even liberty. If a cause can be made to command their true belief, they may sacrifice not just their interests, but even themselves. Things in fact happen that way; people can be persuaded to unite for a cause and then, for a time (and in the context of that cause) every citizen has "the same opinions, the same passions, and the same interests." But later, it would follow from Madison's premise, when the crisis has been surmounted, human nature (in its politicized mode) becomes itself again and people fall to bickering over "frivolous and fanciful" issues.

It is indeed the case that without something substantial to hold them together, people in politics tend to maneuver each other into quarreling. But the judgment of what is frivolous and fanciful is Madison's, made from a distance, and I do not think it reflects the way the contenders themselves see what they are doing. On the contrary, each faction defines its own cause as substantial, and the vast energies expended in attacking other causes (which are likely to be branded frivolous and fanciful) demonstrate exactly the strength of that true belief. What counts as substantial (in my conceptual framework) is what the people concerned, not Madison, are persuaded to treat as substantial. When people are rendered of like mind and heart, accepting the same definition of the situation, then the occasion is substantial and likely to manifest a harmony of opinions, passions, and interests. The harmony, it should be noted, does not do away with animosity. Anger is still there but focused on an outside target.

This book reviews certain ideas about political morale and its relation, on the one hand, to true belief (a religious or moral certitude that disregards reality) and, on the other hand, to doubt, uncertainty, questioning, and the acute awareness that actions have consequences. Mostly I have deduced these ideas from observing what politicians do and say, less from what they claim, because politicians frequently have an interest in concealing the truth, and because they, like everyone else, are often unaware of what their actions imply.

Their actions suggest that high morale in a collective endeavor, when people are manipulated into sinking their differences and are ready for self-sacrifice, must go along with an animosity that is cultivated and *focused on an external enemy*. The animosity has the effect of making people single-minded true believers; it enchants them, it intoxicates them, it hardens their identities, and it renders them incapable of saying, "On the other hand," or "Maybe they have a point," or "Have we thought about the costs?" It is, of course, a commonplace that people close ranks against outsiders. It is less a commonplace (although perfectly obvious from the venom in political rhetoric) that people are expected *not* to close ranks *until* they are induced by leaders or would-be leaders to believe they have a common enemy. In politics the normal route to uncalculating solidarity, the readiness to give one's all for the cause, is not so much love of the cause; it is the propensity to hate those who are presented as the cause's enemies. Animosity is the fuel; without it, leaders and their causes are on the way to being extinguished.

But hatred is not always directed outward. When *in a single political arena* there are many different definitions of how things are and how they should be, and no one of them can be made to command the field, and contenders for power vie with one another to identify sources of evil, then their efforts intensify uncertainty and provoke an unfocused scattershot nastiness *directed inward*, which in turn creates disenchantment with politicians and the political process.

I also will argue, however, that antagonism directed inward and the resulting disenchantment may function as a social antigen. Scattershot nastiness feeds on itself and expands, and eventually factional extravagances and the threat of violence become palpably unbearable and begin to produce antibodies. That situation may stir the ambitions of a would-be savior and a return to true belief, or, if God is kind, room is made for pragmatic people to come forward and argue that reason, calculation, and compromise will make public life less destructive.

The process does not stop there. The cycle continues, and eventually the pragmatic politicians, who see themselves as serving the public interest, drift away from bread-and-butter politics (making things work through bargaining and compromise) to a political marketplace where the general good is subordinated to sectional or personal advantage. Then politicians do not devote their energies to compromise for the sake of a cause but, instead, serve themselves and their friends. That situation is readily identified as corruption, and then the stage is set for a savior, and for an eventual return to true belief, to an ethic of ultimate ends that directs people to do what they are told is right and not to think about benefits or costs.[1]

Those are the issues—they are very much around us—that in part prompted me to write this book. I use limited material from a particular place at a particular time, and mostly I will reproduce narratives told by the various discordant voices that I recorded in Orissa, a state in the federal republic of India, in 1959.[2] I have set the inquiry in that context partly because I have control over the particulars in a way that I could not have in a wider contemporary context, but also because I wish to memorialize the place and the time, and to celebrate the people (unheroic though most of them were). I will write about their particular predicaments and their confusions, about their world as they saw it (so far as I, an outsider, can do that).[3]

[1] The contrast between true-believing politics and the politics of compromise is Weber's distinction between an "ethic of ultimate ends" and an "ethic of responsibility." See 1948, 120.
[2] Focusing on that one year, and the history deposited in it, I cannot exemplify the full cycle outlined above. The light will be directed on the stage at which disenchantment appears and then gives way to pragmatism.
[3] Some of the events this book uses to make its argument were presented in *Politics and Social Change* (1963). I saw the world differently then. One incident, the formation of a coalition government, is also described between pages 57–62 of *The Prevalence of Deceit* (1991) and used to make an argument that is not repeated here.

The framework that is constructed from this narrowly focused examination is offered, however, at least as a candidate for universality, and the book is, to that extent, a treatise on political morale. I am aware that a general proposition is not much validated by a particular example; but it might be negated. There is that possibility; the political culture of Orissa and of India generally from about 1920 onward was deeply penetrated by the ideas of Gandhi, who unbendingly rejected the presumption that animosity is inevitable. I think he was mistaken and in the concluding chapter I will explain why I think so. But, right or wrong, I would be content to have raised a question, even if I cannot consolidate its answer.

Reading about others can be its own reward; it also helps us see ourselves more clearly. We too live much of our lives in conditions of moral and political uncertainty, and from time to time we all are caught in the same net of disenchantment that makes politicians and those around them seem undeserving of trust.

F. G. BAILEY

Del Mar, California

The Need for Enemies

1

The Babel Sound of Politics

Antitheses

Dr. H. K. Mahtab was chief minister of Orissa from 1946 to 1950 and again from 1956 to 1960. In 1955 he was serving as governor of what was then Bombay State.[1] By his own account, he got along well with the chief minister of Bombay, Morarji Desai, like Mahtab a hero of the "freedom fight" in which India won its independence from the British. Desai was a puritanical man and a fanatical prohibitionist, given to boasting that Bombay, under his rule, was dry. Mahtab, having heard that alcohol was readily available, went out and watched his aide-de-camp buy a bottle of "foreign [imported] liquor" from a policeman, who kept a stock under the stand from which he directed traffic. Mahtab told this to Desai, who promptly called a conference and invited Mahtab, as governor of the state, to preside over it. Mahtab listened while "speeches were delivered eloquently as to how drink habit had been given up." He wrote: "Throughout the ages the Indian mind has been tuned to profession of high moral values to such an extent that it refuses to accept realities [that contradict] these professions" (1986, 111). A favorite word to condemn such willful disregard of reality was "humbug." Alternatively, if that seems hard on Desai, one might say that he was concerned more to show his support for high and noble causes than to make things work.

---

[1] Bombay State was partitioned in 1960 into the states of Gujarat and Maharashtra.

On certain occasions fantasies of perfection are appropriate, and everyday reality may properly be swept under the rug. Here is a well-constructed figment of the ideal society, delivered by the then governor of Orissa at the 1955 celebration of India's Independence Day, which is August 15, and printed in that month's issue of the *Orissa Review*.

> Our policy is based on the dignity of the individual, and on the unity of the country. The citizens are all assured of perfect social and economic justice, as also full freedom of thought, expression, belief and faith, befitting the secular character of our polity. Equality of status and opportunity to become all that any one is capable of being has also been vouchsafed to the children of the Motherland. We have been busy, too, with the revitalizing of the nation's economy, making up for the neglect we suffered in the past, and it is a cardinal faith with us that every endeavour should take us nearer to the goal of establishing a Welfare State in India through the raising of the people's living standards and through the eradication of inequalities of every kind.[2]

I spent 1959 in Orissa, most of it in the town of Bhubaneswar, then being constructed to be the state's new capital. Bhubaneswar—the new town—was built across the railway tracks and a mile away from a medieval city of the same name, one of India's great centers of pilgrimage, a "City of Temples around the sacred lake . . . which for twelve centuries has lifted up its thousand towers and pinnacles" (Hunter 1872, vol 1, 97).

India won its independence from the British in 1947. Elections—for the first time with a total adult franchise, the illiterate and the poor now included—had been held in 1952 and again in 1957. Fourteen and a half million people lived in Orissa at that time, almost 96 percent of them (all but six hundred thousand) in rural areas.[3] They elected twenty members to the House of the People (the lower house of the Union parliament), which met in India's capital, Delhi. Orissa had its own legislative assembly, and in 1957 the people voted on 507 candidates to choose its 140 members. From 1946 until

---

[2] The sentiments (and some of the words) in this address were boilerplate in India at that time. They echo, for example, what is written in the Preamble to the Constitution of India.

[3] These figures are from the 1951 census. The 1959 total would be about fifteen million.

1959 the state was held by the Congress *party* (successor to the Indian National Congress, the *movement* that had led the fight for India's freedom). The main opposition from 1952 onward was provided by a party called Ganatantra Parishad, in uneasy alliance with two small left-wing parties, CPI (communist) and PSP (socialist). The alliance was fragile, since Ganatantra was a party of the right.

The governor's 1955 oration suggests, as no doubt he intended, a foundation of hope and confidence, a brave new world in the making. But not everyone discerned a new world, still less a brave one. Here is a paraphrase of what another man, N. K. Chaudhuri, an elder statesman retired from politics, saw going on around him in 1959.

> The years after 1947 were a deep disappointment. People had been led to believe that freedom would be a millennium that would bring them a new and benevolent kind of ruler. But in fact the new system was beyond their understanding. Equally the Congress workers were out of their depth. They found that with the British gone the system still survived, and they were powerless to bring about the changes they desired. (I speak of those who really did want change, and had been sincere in their promises.) Then they made a great mistake: they did not take people into their confidence and explain what was going wrong and why it was going wrong and why they were helpless. They just went on making more promises. They humbugged the people. Ministers went on tour and showed themselves to the people, and told them that the people themselves were the rulers. But even ministers were powerless in the grip of the machinery.

Then, quite abruptly, the sympathetic image of politicians and ministers helpless in the system's iron cage is replaced by stern disapproval.

> The average politician is not interested in local government. If people want a new roof for their school, or a well, they come to me, a social worker. They could get it themselves if they had an efficient local government. But if they had that the politicians would lose power and influence. Nor do the administrators bother themselves about local government. It is not so much they fear being out of a job but because they think the people are incapable of running their own affairs. People, they say, spend all their time in factions

and party politics. But the truth is that the people only do that because they have no power.

This book is built around an assortment of antitheses: Mahtab's realism against Desai's idealizing fantasy, systems blamed against individuals held accountable for their lack of virtue, and, third, that stark contrast between Chaudhuri's tale of disenchantment and the robust true-believing certitude of the governor's oration. Those antitheses, and others that follow, capture the regulating function of opposites. As events flow by, any position that we notionally fix, and so can identify, is in reality not fixed at all, not standing still, but is always in the process of being replaced by one or another negation of itself. Heraclitus called this process enantiodromia (running toward the opposite).

The third antithesis, the happily optimistic governor and the frustrated Nabakrushna Chaudhuri, opens my inquiry. A time of hope gives way to a failure of nerve; confidence loses out to mistrust in one's ability to cope with the future. The disillusion takes a variety of forms. For an individual it may be the devastating end-of-a-lifetime sense that nothing worthwhile has been accomplished, a feeling of impotence that may (or may not) go along with indiscriminate rage. A few of those whose lives and conduct I will document could have been diagnosed in that manner. But in fact failures (mostly other people's, as you will see) were more readily attributed to a lack of virtue than to a fragile psyche. The disheartened, moreover, were politicians, and they were not in the habit of revealing inward uncertainties, least of all to an outsider who came from that "ruling race" from which they had only recently freed themselves.

Assuming I saw the matter correctly, which may not be the case (I will come to that later), I want to explain how it happened that a generation of people, apparently living in and for a brave new world, quite suddenly seemed to realize that their future presented them with far more problems than they had anticipated. As a consequence they began to lose confidence in their ability to conquer adversity, as they had so recently done in the freedom struggle. Certainly, in 1959, they were not at ease with themselves or with each other.

The governor's manifesto is presented as one-piece, comprehensive, and internally consistent, founded on the rights of the individual to political freedom and material welfare. In fact it is a some-

what unlikely meld of political philosophies that do not sit well together: eighteenth-century liberalism (a government accountable to
its citizens and respectful of the individual's right to liberty) combined with mid-twentieth-century socialist notions of a state-
planned economy. This mixture was the official creed at that time,
the established political religion of free India, and, up front, accepted by all the political parties in Orissa, including the right-
inclined Ganatantra. But the people of Orissa, to whom the manifesto was presented, while few of them would have wasted time
arguing against freedom, equality, and material well-being, in fact
spoke with many different voices about the nature of the good society. These voices were not consistent. People disagreed with one another both about what should happen and about what was happening. More than that, one and the same person might invoke values
that could not have been consistently followed, and—another layer
of confusion—the values that people lauded were not always those
that guided their conduct.

This manifold diversity had much deeper historical foundations
than the recently acquired and rather thin integument of party-
based democracy and party ideologies. I want to explore that larger
babel, make sense of the different responses that people and politicians had to their brave new world, and investigate the various
rhetorics the politicians used to contest, sometimes openly, sometimes covertly, often unknowingly, the official rhetoric that is exemplified in the governor's speech. I aim to recapture the reality of
that new world, not in the glorious unity that he portrayed, but as
an arena where values fought with one another. True beliefs (another name for religions, things taken on faith, celebrated, propagated, and never questioned by believers) competed both with each
other and with reason (and with interests) to define reality. That
competition and the uncertainty it produced were one source of the
prevailing disenchantment.

Animosity and Its Sources

Looking back through my notes, newspaper cuttings, and interview transcripts, I fancy I could arrange all that material according
to the level of rancor that the different pieces reveal. At one end
would come a tempered analysis of well-intentioned failure (not
many of those), then plain tales of incompetence, and, at the other

end, vicious, mean-spirited essays in character assassination, plain hatred.

I do not think I invited this. Although I did encourage certain people to tell the story of their lives, I was definitely not on the look-out for malice and disparagement. On the contrary, in 1959 I wanted analyses of institutions, of how the political system worked, of how representatives and candidates communicated with voters when there were no effective mass media; and I was delighted when—on rare occasions—I got such analyses. Certainly I was not hungry for negativism; far from it. I went there to see how the egal-itarian institutions of representative democracy adapted them-selves to a society that was hierarchical, authoritarian, and pater-nalistic at every level—family, village, traditional "feudal" rulers, and the authoritarian bureaucracy that had sustained British rule for more than a century. I was confident, in those days, that I would find statesmanlike leaders, who devoted themselves sincerely, un-selfishly, and intelligently to the common good and the building of a new social order.

I was not entirely disappointed. There were such people, or, at least, some who deserved that accolade more than others. A few, I think, qualified as villains. But I am not sure, because out-and-out rascals were revealed only in what people said about them, not in anything that I knew for certain they did. Sometimes the wrongdo-ers remained anonymous and only their misdeeds were talked about. Then the tale might be told with humor (because what had been done was brazenfaced enough to be funny) or sometimes even with admiration for the ingenuity displayed. Most often, having identified the transgressors by name or by the party they belonged to or the way they made a living, people freely vented the contempt they claimed to feel for anyone who would stoop so low. But these were opinions, backed at best by anecdotal evidence, which itself was hearsay. In other words, my villains are all presumptive. The same applies to saints and heroes.

As I said, I routinely directed my attention at systems and insti-tutions, not at personalities. I know that I did not behave like an in-vestigative reporter digging into the dirt. But I was given it, time and again. The volume of complaint about human wickedness was loud and large. What does that volume signify? Clearly, to say it again, it is not a direct measure of actual corruption, cheating, or any of the other ingenious flim-flammery that I heard about. Proverbs about smoke and fire notwithstanding, what is being measured is a feature of the *discourse* then current about politicians (as it is preserved in my notes, interview transcripts, and various printed sources). It may not have been so salient a feature of political behavior itself. I also think—I cannot be certain—that what I heard and read is an indication of what people *thought* about politicians and civil servants and about their own society. But again I am unsure, because everyone involved with politics (myself included) speaks with an eye to an audience, to persuade, rather than always and only to convey some objective truth. Obviously, no general statement would make sense at this point. When it seems appropriate (and possible) to penetrate the rhetoric and ask how closely any particular discourse corresponded with actual practice, I will do so.

A great deal of the rhetoric was inflammatory. One would expect this of politicians; but civil servants often talked the same way, not least when dumping on politicians. The rhetoric portrayed a world that had a few heroes and a multitude of wrongdoers, and much of the talk was not about how to change the system to make it work better, but how to punish the wicked and remove them from the scene. Then, it was assumed, the world would right itself. The discourse, in other words, was anything but dispassionate; most often it was moral and directed at persons: if things go wrong, it is because people are no good, especially those who wield power or would like to do so.

I think I caught Orissa's leaders in 1959 at the pass that separates the politics of ideals, enthusiasms, and "the cause" from the unexciting bread-and-butter compromise-stuff needed to sustain existence. They were making that transition in the second half of the fifties, and for many of them it was a wintry coming to an unwelcoming land. They were like refugees straggling across a border, escaping from a culture of true-believing unreality that once served them well but now threatened to make life unlivable. Many brought that penchant for unreality with them (and in the seventies and afterwards lived by the dictates of other enthusiasms, less admirable than those of the freedom fighters).[4] They kept their old ideals and even their old expectations, and so they were dismayed and angered by what they experienced in the new world of the fifties. They still hungered for ideology, for something fixed and certain to guide them, for a principle that would help them instantly separate

[4] I refer to Mrs. Gandhi's populist politics of the late sixties and early seventies and to the fundamentalist Hinduism that grew stronger in her day and now seems set to barbarize Indian politics.

right from wrong, would spare them the labor of calculating the likely results of their decisions, and would make them feel good about themselves. They mistook bread-and-butter politics for self-serving, and they assumed dishonesty and base motives in all who did not share their true belief. Others, more responsible people who perhaps had been gifted with a workaday mentality all the time (the managers and organizers of the national movement, rather than its inspirers) looked over their new terrain with the eye of practical reason and stood ready to adjust policy to reality. They would have agreed with Bismarck that politics is the art of the possible. For them, living now on the pragmatic side of the pass where compromise was becoming the political norm, displays of blind enthusiasm (when they were sincere) were a mark of irresponsibility, of fools who did not realize that stubborn faith would be their own—and everyone's—undoing.

Faith in one's cause and in one's own ability to make it victorious grows out of a readiness, when difficulties stand in the way, at least to put the blame on fools, and more often to excoriate evildoers. In this philosophy nothing can ever be accomplished without an enemy. The world that had no adversary would be incomplete, a half-world; it also would be inert, because without enemies one cannot identify, let alone exercise, one's own virtue, and so nothing can ever be done. For such true believers problems that might be solved by compromise and cooperation do not exist; there are only enemies to be defeated and exterminated. Sceptics (or even cynics), the undoctrinal realists who have the courage to compromise and who make doubt and questioning their methodological credo, are the better people, not least because they are relatively compassionate; unlike most true believers, they are not fueled by anger.[5] Self-restraint, especially when it masters antipathy, is surely a virtue.

A Plurality of Cultures

I intend this book to be evocative of the period, calling up an ambience, an ethnography of the beliefs, values, customs, and tactics of those people at that time. I want to convey their assumptions about the conduct of life. These assumptions were not, as I see

[5] The hesitation implied in "*most* true believers" is in deference to Gandhi. I will come to him later.

them, sui generis, a distinctively Indian or Hindu or Oriya way of construing the political world. Certainly distinctive features are found in any political culture. The people I talked with in Orissa (some of them) took for granted ideas that to me seemed bizarre: for example the belief that a leader's ascetic life-style directly influences events in the world.[6] They also had fixed ideas about other cultures, prominent at that time being the notion, undoubtedly a legacy of imperialism, that public affairs in Britain were conducted with a wholesomeness that, unhappily, lay beyond their Indian reach. But to identify and privilege only those designs that are distinctively "Hindu" or "Oriya" would be to commit the exotic fallacy—that nothing should interest us except the "otherness" of other cultures.

My focus is not on the distinctive features of a specific culture but on the mélange of different cultures that went into the working of a particular social and political system at a particular time. I want to understand what people who had power (or sought it) did and said in Orissa in 1959. I want to know how their minds worked, to find out their designs for living. Max Gluckman, referring to troubles in the Copperbelt region of what then was Northern Rhodesia, said that no one should forget that an African miner was also a miner. That universalizing sentiment (benignly intended to counter racist assumptions in Britain and the Rhodesias) is hopelessly out of fashion in this relativistic phase of our discipline, but it does capture a reality that I want highlighted. The Orissa parliamentarian was also a parliamentarian, and what he or she did was a function not only of Hindu categories but also of Westminster categories and of a myriad other designs for politicking and for living. That is precisely the point: there was no single design for living, and if we want to understand what went on in Orissa in 1959, we have no choice but

---

[6] That word *bizarre* reveals my "orientalist" tendencies, at once essentializing the Other as odd and betraying my sense of effortless superiority. But the idea that human spirituality influences the course of nature is not all that exotic. We pray for rain and do other things that would certainly seem bizarre if we did not do them ourselves. Mysticism attaches particularly to a leader, and the idea that his (occasionally her) conduct and well-being have a cosmic fallout is not confined to divine kings on dark continents. I was a visitor on the campus of an American university when John Kennedy was assassinated. The reaction among students surprised me: it seemed less to manifest outrage than a deeply regressive need to be reassured that the world was not falling apart, that they had not been pitched into the infinite abyss.

to acknowledge that Westminster models, Hindu models, models of class antagonism, anarchist models, expected-utility thinking, colonialist assumptions, feudal attitudes, orientalist attitudes, post-colonial confusions, cultural chauvinism, regional chauvinism, even village chauvinism, and many other designs were all there, ready for use and variously used.

The people in the story are principally those who, at the time, were Orissa's leaders: politicians such as the MLAs (members of the legislative assembly), would-be members, party officials and party workers, and an array of civil servants. They stand at the center of my stage. I will reconstruct their views of the world, together with whatever I saw in the life they lived that might make sense of those views. The common people will rarely find a voice in this account. When they do appear, mostly they wear the masks that their leaders chose to fasten on them. In one rhetoric (for example, the governor's) the people's voice is the voice of God; in another (that of the elder statesman) their voice is wrongly silenced; in other rhetorics the common people have no voice, no right to have their opinions taken into account, at best sheep protected by the shepherd's crook, at worst mere instruments, usable things.

I will not iron details out of the story. Many small uniquenesses are as fresh now as they were thirty-five years ago, and they will serve to ornament the bare generality of the argument about failing morale and its (sometimes benign) consequences.

The following chapter sets the scene, not in the form of a comprehensive and systematic description, but through vignettes of places, people and events. These vignettes will serve to indicate that the politicians of Orissa were not of one persuasion. Later chapters take off from this setting to analyze assumptions about political conduct that underlie the diverse values and opinions people voiced and the actions they took.

2

Bhubaneswar New Capital

The Tented Eatery

When a person of consequence went out for a meal, perhaps to have a discreet conversation with another such person, and, as a bonus, to get as near gourmet eating as was then possible in Bhubaneswar, there was only one place to go. Its name and the name of its proprietor—widely reputed to be a good contact man—now, thirty-five years later, escape me. The restaurant was located on a patch of waste ground, alongside the railway line that separated the new town from the old, in a tract set aside on the new town's fringe for private housing. It was a pioneer establishment; it had no building, and one dined under canvas in an enormous rectangular marquee. A section at one end was closed off by a shoulder-high canvas screen that ran the width of the tent. Behind this the cooking was done, and the tent's apron was raised to let the acrid charcoal fumes escape.

The place was dirty. The waiter who served us the first time I went wore stained khaki shorts, was shirtless, and his feet were bare. A sacred thread, suggesting twice-born status—that is, high caste—was looped over his left shoulder and across his body. The remnants of the last meal, scraps of food and broken toothpicks, littered the table; when we complained, he flicked a soiled towel off his right shoulder and energetically wiped the table, leaving fresh curlicues in its layered grease. It was a popular place, one of the few—the tea-room in the legislative assembly building was another—where men of importance or would-be such men (rarely a woman) went to gossip, make contacts, do deals, and be seen by other men of importance.

The tented eatery was a monument to private enterprise, although no one ever remarked on that fact. Good meals could be had, excellently served on impeccably clean white tablecloths by waiters in white drill uniforms, in the State Guest House. But that establishment was patronized by tourists, or officials from international development agencies, most of them Europeans or Americans, or the occasional foreign businessman. (I once met an engineer there, a German, sent down from some distant place to oversee the fixing of the chief minister's Mercedes. He had complimentary things to say about his Indian subordinates. "Good as Germans?" I asked. "Maybe," he said, "in about a hundred years.") More than tolerable cheap meals, very cheap in moderately hygienic surroundings, were available at the railway station restaurant, but that was for functional eating (satisfying hunger) rather than for social occasions. There was another restaurant, run by Sindhi refugees from Pakistan, in a shop in a modest mall built by the government in the center of town and rented out. I knew no one who ate there.

Both the State Guest House and the railway cafe were government enterprises, not part of the private sector. The tented eatery, when I look back now, presents itself as an allegory of private enterprise in the then scheme of things: none too clean but significantly used and popular; something needed, but its importance carefully unemphasized, leaving the front stage free for the state and its socialist ideals. What counted officially was the public good, not private profit.

Optimism and the Third World

In 1959 and the early sixties the climate of scholarly opinion about Third World countries (not yet politically emasculated as "the South") was still robustly optimistic. The world could be changed to our own design. Discourse about those countries and their economic growth, and about such transitions as I planned to study in Orissa (replacing an authoritarian colonial regime with a parliamentary democracy) was dominated by a positivist framework and in particular by the economists' expected-utility model. Social systems were natural systems. People everywhere, it was assumed, in whatever country of whatever culture, made rational choices and, by providing the appropriate structure of incentives, their behavior could be guided and the world could be made better. Rationality was translatable between cultures; it was a universal concept, accurately descriptive of the way people's minds worked anywhere. More than that, not just their mental processes but their wants, too, were for all practical purposes universal. That framework is nicely caught in a sentence written in 1962 by an economist, who had this version of our human essence: "Many countries have indeed attitudes and institutions which inhibit growth, but they will rid themselves of these attitudes and institutions as soon as their people discover they stand in the way of economic opportunities."[1]

That level of brassy confidence was not commonly found among anthropologists. We were made uneasy by such bold essentialism. We knew for a fact that understandings varied from one place to another, and that what was an "incentive" in one culture might not be in another. Cultures differed; indeed, that difference was our professional entitlement. We also knew that values and beliefs were often quite resistant to the kind of "rational" calculation that economists took for granted. We wondered how they could ignore a fact that so clearly limited their model's usefulness. "Utility," we knew by experience, was a domain of diverse values that did not readily trade off with one another, as economists assumed all values did, and the economists themselves had no theories about how utility was constituted; they behaved as if none were needed. But at that time many anthropologists, myself included, believed that positivist frameworks had merit, that the expected-utility model was the best we had for understanding growth and change, and that the anthropologist's task (in that particular context) was to educate economists and planners about value formation by demonstrating that people sometimes had in mind other objectives than exploiting "economic opportunities."

In 1959 my attitude was determinedly scientific. I saw Orissa as a particular instance of a general problem. My task was to identify features or properties that were generalizable, and to provide evidence that these properties really existed and were not my fantasy. Intuition, speculation, and other such imaginative activities were, of course, a necessary part of the procedure; but they remained mere intellectual games—albeit enjoyable—unless backed by evi-

[1] W. Arthur Lewis, a distinguished and influential West Indian economist, later a Nobel laureate and the recipient of a knighthood, wrote this in the foreword to Epstein 1962.

dence, the collecting of which was hard work. I intended to ascertain the true facts and then explain why progress towards growth—and towards democracy—had gone only so far. I would identify what stood in the way of further progress. *Progress* was then a respectable, indeed, a compelling idea, even in anthropology. At that time it had not been undermined by relativism, the present disdain for positivist discourse, and the peremptory rejection of the concept of objectivity.

Scientific ambitions notwithstanding, I was in fact anything but detached and dispassionate. I admired what I thought was being done in India and in Orissa. I was not so naive as to assume that the transition from authoritarian rule to democracy would be smooth, but I did think there would be, even after the mere twelve years that had elapsed since independence, discernible progress. I was not negatively inclined, not pessimistic; this was not the worst of possible worlds. I believed that *development* (like *progress*, a magic word at that time) not only was possible but was in fact taking place. I was appalled—vicariously offended—by that redneck engineer who thought it would take Indians a hundred years to reach German standards of industrial efficiency. The presentday cynicism, or despair, that habitually (and often justifiably) colors attitudes toward the Third World and its endeavors had not yet taken hold. Neither do I recall (at least among people of my generation) the patronizing imperialist assumption that Indians were by nature passive, childlike, and responsive only to compulsion exercised by superior people. Indeed, particularly in academic circles, an abundance of goodwill was manifested in the mostly unquestioned notion that the leaders of that world were not only strong but also effective, men moved to honest endeavor by noble intentions. When failures occurred, it was politically correct to blame them on the colonial legacy or on neocolonialist entrepreneurs. A certain amount of hardihood was required for an academic, especially a foreign one, even to talk about corruption or naked ambition for power, unless these vices could be attributed to the former colonialists or their surviving lackeys. Such explanations were the stock-in-trade theodicy of the Orissa Public Relations Department, the part of the Devil being variously played by "feudal remnants," the departed British, or the communists, who were considered agents of Russian imperialism. In academic circles this rhetoric of colonial exploitation had its roots in Marxist commentaries, but it was not theirs alone; at that time it was rarely questioned. The same rhetoric has survived the demise of positivism and now, focusing less on economic exploitation and everyday brutality than on literary productions and cultural performance, has become a mainstay of contemporary anthropological moralizing.

These assumptions about human nature in the Third World went along with a corresponding faith in planning, which I shared. One did not talk about "the free market," except to make fun of the American-financed *Forum for Free Enterprise* or the few neoclassical economists who came to tell Indians how to bring their economy to the point of "take-off" (as they have been doing recently in Poland and Russia). America's presence was large and in the public eye, but it was not directly a businessman's market-oriented presence. It was managerial and bureaucratic, manifested not only in the various institutions of the United Nations (including the World Bank), but also in the Ford Foundation and the Rockefeller Foundation and the funds they provided. These funds were disbursed not according to the principles of a free market economy but by planning, and at the time it seemed a nice irony that money accumulated "by the nastiest of men for the nastiest of motives" should finally be used "for the good of us all," and, moreover, not directed there by Adam Smith's "invisible hand" but by the hands of managerial bureaucrats and socialist-minded Indian politicians. (As you will see, there is a further layer of irony, because in fact the pattern of disbursement was substantially influenced by a political free market—more on that later.)

Along with most of my contemporaries I took it for granted that socialism—the planned society—would not only guarantee distributive justice but also, in good time, would make India prosperous. For sure, a brief acquaintance with the new order's aesthetic productions, described below, convinced me that socialism had not yet found a way to combine civic elegance with material prosperity and social justice. But elegance was a secondary matter, immaterial in both senses of that word. Frills and good taste could come later. In short, I went to Orissa in 1959 with the expectation, more or less taken for granted, that I would find a brave new world, populated by heroes (and some heroines), all pointing themselves toward the future, youthful in outlook (even when not in years), innovative, enterprising (but not entrepreneurial), public-spirited, and selfless in their vocation.

The New Capital

Orissa's new capital (officially styled "Bhubaneswar New Capital," handily abbreviated to BBSNC) was being constructed to a perfectly rational and determinedly functional design that was a compromise downward from the vision of a renowned architect and town-planner, Otto Koenigsberger, toward a reality defined by Orissa's politicians and bureaucrats. Cuttack, the old capital, founded in the tenth century, was about eighteen miles to the north, on low-lying land where the Mahanadi (the "great river"), flowing eastward to the Bay of Bengal, begins to open itself into the many channels of its delta. The town was built on a wedge of land between the Mahanadi and, to the south, its first main distributory, the Katjori. Cuttack was protected by gigantic masonry-faced embankments, sloped and stepped like the side of a pyramid, several miles long and above twenty feet in height. During the monsoon, when the rivers were in flood, parts of the town were below the water level. At that time the views from the embankment across the mile-wide swirling expanse of the Katjori were enchantingly beautiful, distant hills to the west standing dark against a cloud-swept sky.[2] But that also was the time when the drains worked backwards and the open rat-infested sewage ditches, which lined the town's older streets, overflowed. At all times the smell was formidable, but not, as I recollect, entirely disagreeable, a mixture (characteristic then of small towns in India, especially in the still air of sunset) of frying food, woodsmoke, and kerosene, all overlaying a whiff of sewage. Cuttack was crowded. Its wedge-shaped site between the river arms had little room for expansion, and the elevated water table would have made high-rise building, requiring deep foundations, difficult. It had, as I indicated, drainage problems and the place was reckoned insalubrious, being conducive to the two endemic scourges of that region, malaria and the dysenteries.

The decision to start again on the dry plains adjacent to old Bhubaneswar therefore was quite rational, arising out of a practical necessity. It was also in accordance with the spirit of the times, for in 1947, the year India gained its independence, there was a great

---

[2] The river's name ("plank brook") suggests a stream that could be spanned by a single wooden board. Evidently it had grown. A mid-nineteenth-century report speaks of the river widening by one third over a period of fifteen years. In the dry season the bed of the Katjori was a vast expanse of sand, on which, in March 1921, Gandhi addressed an audience of fifty-thousand people.

reaching out for modernity, for a new start.[3] (There was some opposition to the move from what might be called the "Cuttack lobby" and from some of the more austere statesmen who saw the new capital as an unbecoming exercise in political grandiosity, squandering resources that could be better spent elsewhere. I will come to that later; it was one among many indications of incipient disenchantment.) Bhubaneswar's foundation stone was laid in 1948 by the prime minister of India, Pandit Nehru. By 1952, when I first saw the town, segments of the government had already established themselves there. By the end of that decade most government offices had made the move. So had some parts of the university, including the newly established department of anthropology, in which, when I first arrived, I found a place to live.

At that time the new capital was quite small. I could walk across it from one end to the other in about forty minutes. The old town of Bhubaneswar, more compactly built, and seeming always dense with people, was even smaller. This was the great "City of Temples," the domain of Shiva, who is "Lord of the Earth" (which is what the name *Bhubaneswar* means), begun in the fifth century A.D. and completed in the seventh. Walking there, both in its crowded streets and on the barren red-gravel plain beside it, enjoying the form and texture of the many deserted temples, was a frequent pleasure. I went there most mornings (except in the rains), very early, while the sun was rising and the shadows were still long, sometimes encountering brisk and amiably talkative middle-aged men with walking sticks, like me taking "morning exercise." If I walked in the new town, it was out of necessity, not for recreation.

Bhubaneswar NC was not built to be a city like London or Paris, a fully-equipped metropolis where everything that is wanted is to be found, and the past is melded into the present and the future, and the institutions of government, commerce, the arts, the fourth estate, religion, and whatever else, all coexist within the same civic boundary. Old Bhubaneswar had a very long history, but the new capital had none; at least it had no visible legacies, no buildings from the past to blur and soften its harsh modernity. Furthermore, the town was unambiguously monolithic in function, built for a single purpose, which was to be a seat of government and administration. It was to be Albany in New York or Sacramento in California

---

[3] The proposal to move the capital to Bhubaneswar was first made in 1945. See Grenell 1980, 32–33.

or perhaps Washington, D.C.—there was a ring road, which, were I there now, I might call the "Beltway." Even making it the location of Orissa's university and various other educational and research institutions, and (some time in 1959's future) a center for culture and the arts, would not radically change the town's character, because all these activities were themselves state-sponsored and state-controlled. Manufacturing, some of which was in the private sector of the economy, the planners consigned elsewhere, much of it to new industrial suburbs constructed on the plain to the north of Cuttack across the Mahanadi river.

In short, like Chandigarh in the Punjab or Edwin Lutyen's New Delhi, Bhubaneswar NC signaled, somewhat arrogantly, a break with the past and a venture into modernity. It also, as befits the seat of government, very firmly symbolized order and regularity. Indeed it did; after living there for a month I could identify bungalows type II through type VIII (peons and low-level clerks in type II and cabinet ministers or very senior civil servants in type VIII), and therefore I also could estimate the monthly salary of a bungalow's occupant.[4] I lived half my stay in Bhubaneswar NC renting a room from a professor (type V), and the rest as the guest of a somewhat Spartan MLA, who lived in a bedbug-infested type IV.

The different areas of the town were identified as "units," each measuring one square mile, separated from one another by wide thoroughfares, and distinguished by number. If these areas had names, no one used them. Koenigsberger, in accordance with the town-planning ethic of the post-war world, intended neighborhoods to be mixed, and in a sense they were. But communitarian values were observed more in the letter than in spirit. Hierarchy prevailed; the high and the humble were not segregated into separate colonies, but they were marked by visibility. High-status residences (detached) fronted the wide main roads; the meanest dwellings were crowded in neat barrack-like rows along narrow unpaved lanes, hidden inside the units. (Koenigsberger ceased to be associated with the project in 1951.) My memory also is that, apart from one or two crescents, where public buildings were constructed, and the ring road, and two roundabouts, the grid pattern prevailed; everywhere there were parallel lines and right angles, and no road in the residential areas had a bend in it.

The partial exception to all this uniformed regularity was that

---

[4] I have no recollection of type I quarters. Logically they must have existed.

small tract of land, running along the railway line (this is the main line that connects Calcutta with Madras), where the tented eatery was pitched. Small clusters of mud and thatch huts housed the capital's humblest inhabitants, the rickshaw pullers and casual laborers. To the south of the intersection of the New Capital's main avenue and the railway line, on the western side, land was available in plots for private sale. Housing was in short supply, and from about 1956 onward some other areas in the new capital were zoned for private development. I believe that many of those who bought property and built houses at that time were higher-ranked public servants, who benefitted from low-interest government loans. Then, continuing to occupy their subsidized official residence, they would rent out the new house at market rates, perhaps to a government agency or to a businessman wanting a base in the capital. Plots were small and the architecture tended towards the compact, houses built to fill the site, and some of them two or three storys, unlike the one-story design of all but the highest category of official residence. Ornamental iron railings and a variety of stucco colors, absent from official dwellings, made a half-hearted statement about individuality. But in fact the variation came out of a quite narrow range of ornamentation (the iron railings and doorways and wall paint), a bid for nonconformity that in the end said no more than "not quite government."[5]

There was, it must be said, a certain aesthetic vacancy about Bhubaneswar NC. It was tidy and orderly and quite well-maintained and had no slums and no evident squalor (except for the squatter settlements beside the railway line) and it did have effective sewers. But it utterly lacked character; its architecture was standardized; it had no history; it had streets that were thoroughfares rather than public places. There also were many inconveniences. In the monsoon there was a lot of mud; the roads were paved, but most of the sidewalk space in residential areas was not. For the same reason the summers were dusty. Hot weather everywhere makes people torpid or bad-tempered, and Bhubaneswar had several features that made them more so. Houses had ceiling fans, but they depended on a very erratic supply of electricity. No house that I knew was air-conditioned (which also, of course, would have been at the mercy of the power station). Furthermore, the architect, so people said, had

---

[5] In the sixties the government began to build multi-story apartments. As I remember, there were none in 1959.

managed to orient the streets in such a way that it was virtually impossible for the onshore evening winds to ventilate a house and drive out the day's baked and stale air. (The Bay of Bengal was about thirty miles away. From February through June, when the rains broke, a distinct, and very welcome, evening breeze blew.) There was also a conspicuous lack of trees, understandable in a place so new, built on laterite,[6] much of it without any covering of fertile soil, and forever troubled by water shortages. A flower garden or a vegetable plot in the fenced yards that fronted all but the smallest bungalows would have been hard work, and most householders did not even try. Five capitals had failed at or near that site for lack of water, I was told by someone educating me on local history. The present one was only saved by running a pipeline from the Mahanadi at Cuttack (about twenty miles). There had been several stands of old mango trees, the same man said, but a housing contractor made short work of them; it saved him time and money to root them out and, besides, he made a profit on the lumber and the firewood. How much truth there was in all this foundational mythology, I do not know, but the telling reveals a mistrust in the efficiency of government and its ability to curb unscrupulous entrepreneurs. I do know that water was short, available from the tap for only a brief period each morning; I also know that there were frequent electrical failures; and I know that the only trees to be found at that time (with a few exceptions, one overhanging the tented eatery) were in the well-watered gardens of types VII and VIII bungalows, and in 1959 none of them was more than about fifteen feet high. Bhubaneswar NC, in short, at that time was drab and uniform, without charm and without grandeur, characterless, and surely a bleak and boring place to live.

Its bureaucratic inhabitants certainly professed to find it so. They complained about Bhubaneswar, younger ones more vigorously than their elders, perhaps because the elders had lived through postings to really jungly places, far in the back of beyond. Several district headquarters in Orissa were in that category at that time. Bhubaneswar was different, not jungly. It had schools and a hospital and paved streets and piped water and sewers and electricity

---

[6] Laterite varies from a "sandy clay," through a "loose gravelly condition" to firm rock that is "largely used as building stone, having the peculiar but important property of being softest when first cut, and of hardening greatly on exposure" (Hunter 1872, vol. 2, 165). Laterite blocks were the common building material in both the old and the new town.

and other modern amenities. It also had in 1959 a population that had grown over a ten-year period from under seventeen thousand to almost forty thousand.[7] (Cuttack then contained over one hundred and forty thousand people.) But this was not a real town, the complainers said. Where were the bazaars? True, there were a few shops near the center of the town, in a building then under construction and officially designated a market, but at that time there was nothing more than a place for selling handicrafts to foreign tourists, along with a restaurant that no one patronized, and a dry goods and provisions store (run by a Sikh) charging prices high enough to make most people take the bus and do their shopping in Cuttack. In fact the complaint was not about provisioning. That was not a problem, because every day the peon's wife or the cook in a type III-and-up bungalow was visited by hawkers selling vegetables and other perishables. If taking the bus to Cuttack was inconvenient, one could find the basic domestic necessities—rice, flour, sugar, tea, soap, cigarettes, kerosene, and the like—in unobtrusive roughly built mud-and-thatch shops near the railway or put up here and there (illegally) on vacant lots in the new town. There were also tea stalls and cobblers' stands and people who could mend bicycles and the other street-side conveniences that grace an Indian town.

The everyday necessities were available. What the grumblers professed to miss was the animation, the verve, the vitality that, they insisted, goes with life in a big city (in this case, Cuttack). Bhubaneswar had no life. There was nothing to stimulate, no excitement. Admittedly, the Burmah-Shell gas station (I can remember only one petrol pump in Bhubaneswar) sold liquor from an Aladdin's cave (a shed) round the back. (The liquor was bootleg except for people who had registered themselves as alcoholics and been granted a permit.) But that was a drop in the ocean. What the place needed, the grumblers explained, was a temple or two (which, of course, were legion in the old town), along with resident holy men, and ayurvedic clinics, and rows of shops that sold cloth and jewelry and books and patent medicines and religious knick-knacks and all the other variegated goods and services that made it a pleasure to stroll through Cuttack's twisted malodorous streets.

The Kala Vikash Kendra ("A Centre of Culture"), located in Banka–

---

[7] This figure includes inhabitants of the old town and some nearby villages. My guess is that about two-thirds lived in the New Capital.

bazar, Cuttack, in 1958 put out a "souvenir" publication of articles on dance and music in Orissa. It was printed in Cuttack. It contains advertisements from suppliers of the following: sanitation fixtures, diesel and electrical engines, ceiling fans, paints and varnishes, pharmaceuticals (an Ayurvedic cooperative), cast-iron pipes, steel furniture, cycles and rickshaws, stoves and lanterns, steel safes and other products, more cast-iron goods, tubewell pumps, more sanitation fittings, barbed wire and agricultural implements, laboratory instruments, automobile accessories, cement, sports goods and children's playground equipment, and various other things. There was an advertisement from an "Eye Clinic and Optical Home;" an announcement for a sweepstake in support of the Orissa Red Cross; and two appeals, one for the Centre's own building fund and the other for its Distressed Artists' Fund. All these enterprises carried addresses in Cuttack.

I cannot recall if there was even a regular cinema show in Bhubaneswar NC. My memory is that people went to open-air showings in the old town. One civil servant, a young man, identified the consequence of all this aridity: "This forsaken hole! Officials' birth rate is going up and up! What else to do?" He was married, and childless.

The Framework

Time is like space. Now, after thirty-five years, I see things that I could not see then. That is not surprising; look at the trees, the proverb says, and you miss the form the forest takes. Many of the details I still recall, but now they make patterns that were not there before.

Knowledge beamed over a long hindsight is likely to be general, whereas what is more immediately known cannot so readily escape the form of particulars. Those who look back, therefore, more or less willy-nilly commit sins that are now fashionably deplored: abstractionism, reductionism, essentializing, totalizing, systematizing, annihilating what is unique. In fact, of course, they are not sins at all, any more than breathing is; they are procedures that must be followed if one is to survive by understanding how the world works. How else does one communicate an idea except through an abstraction or an image, both of which reduce a confusing complexity to a simplicity? What explanations could there be if phenomenal experiences were not first reduced to categories and models? The unique is inherently inexplicable.

Of course that is not the whole story. The complaint about essentializing and the like is not only that it violates the persons essentialized by reducing them to one-dimensional objects, but also that it is often done with a hegemonic intent. Abstraction may be used not to better discover the truth, but to conceal it, and thus more effectively persuade, control and coerce; what purports to be only an analytic tool then becomes an instrument for domination. The question is complicated, involving not only the rhetoric of those (now mostly dead) Oriya politicians, but also the rhetoric of scholarship and research prevalent both then and at the present time, and, of course, the rhetoric that I am using to make this presentation.

My rhetoric will reveal itself as the presentation continues. Some features of it, no doubt, are still unknown to me. But I am clear, I think, about the conceptual framework that I intend to use. It is simple, and by no means novel; I have used it before (1960). It models the way individuals cope with the world and with each other; in other words, it models their designs for living. Here it is, in bare outline (with its terminology somewhat updated).

First, it is impossible to understand the world without assuming that there *is* a reality, a hard objectivity. We experience it most sharply when we do something, anticipating one outcome, and encounter consequences that we did not expect. Experience continually reminds us that the world is more than we define it to be. In 1959, before relativism, antiessentializing, and the cult of the decentered consciousness began to invade our discipline, that would have gone without saying.

Second, we cope with this real world by simplifying it, by making definitions, by generalizing, by constructing models that strip away many of the features that, because we experience them, we know are part of reality. We select what we judge is essential for the purpose we have in hand; we highlight what we have selected as the *essence* of the situation or of the culture or of the persons involved. In everyday life we mostly do this by habit, not giving a thought to the discarded features and the complex reality they represent, until things go wrong.

When things do go wrong—more accurately, when someone decides things are going wrong or are likely to do so—the models cease to be second nature and become objects of critical scrutiny. We are driven to realize that the essential features we selected are in fact not the essence of the situation. The error in essentializing is not when we do it—we can do no other—but when we do not admit the contingent nature of *essence*. In other words, an essence is a feature in a model. Critical inspection of a model results in some essences being discarded and others inserted. In this way, models are revised or replaced; we experiment with a different set of essences.

Such models are designs for living. They guide our actions and they satisfy our craving for making sense of things. The social world can then be construed, from the point of view of any individual in it, as a menu or repertoire of designs for living. There is no single design but, rather, several competing ones that define the world differently and enjoin different courses of action. People choose between them and argue with each other about their applicability and their moral worth.

The choices people make are not necessarily their own, in two senses. First, to a considerable extent people are unaware that their conduct conforms to one or another design, and, by the same token, unaware that there are alternatives. In the strict sense, people do not make decisions or choices, even if, from the point of view of an informed outsider, what they do is a de facto choice that excludes other courses of action. The "choice," so to speak, is determined by the prevailing culture.

Second, designs for living may be used not simply to guide one's own conduct (or not, as the case may be), but also to manipulate other people into accepting (or rejecting) a particular design, and, in that way, control them. As leaders see it, the varying definitions of reality and the associated designs for living are resources that can be used to elicit attitudes and, consequently, actions that will serve them (the leaders) in the struggle for power. In that respect, the task leaders set themselves is to politicize people. At any one time the aggregate selection that both ordinary people and their leaders make may result in one or another model dominating and the rest being subordinate, or else there can be uncertainty because all designs are equally contested and none prevails.

In 1959, when I thought about what was happening around me, I modeled the situation in two linked ways, one cultural and the other social, both of them being commonplace conceptual frameworks of the period.[8] In the cultural model, traditional values were

---

[8] In the intellectual parish in which I lived at that time, the term *culture* was barely respectable. Values were considered epiphenomenal, by-products of a

giving way to (or putting up a resistance against) modernity. In social terms, a framework of rights and duties that inhered in small
communities (caste and village and small face-to-face political communities) was now in competition with larger social formations—
class divisions, urban and rural interests, and so on—that were the
product of political and techno-economic innovations. From the
point of view of government and politics, I was witnessing the progressive (in both senses) replacement of an authoritarian bureaucratic regime by a parliamentary democracy.

The model of choice-from-a-repertoire remained somewhat un-
developed, the result, in part, of my consorting with number-happy
economists and political scientists, and relying uncritically on a
simple expected-utility framework. That framework, as it was in
practice used and as the quotation about "economic opportunity"
demonstrates, did not seriously accommodate *moral* values; "utility" bespoke only material, usually pecuniary, advantage. In particular I did not sufficiently explore the moral imperatives that underlay authoritarianism (both bureaucratic and traditional), nor did I
perceive the extent to which authoritarianism survived as an habitual choice to guide political action. I did not, in other words, take
sufficient account of Gramsci's "hegemony." Nor did I appreciate
the volume and diversity of designs for living offered in the repertoire. All models require abstraction and simplification; I was cava-
lier and came to closure much too quickly, and, propelled by expected-utility thinking, came near to caricaturing the situation. I felt
close to the world of practice and policy, and to have insisted continually that matters were much more complex than anyone admitted would have seemed like a betrayal, an admission that one
had nothing useful to say to those who might want advice. Con-
fessing to perplexity, being tentative, acknowledging that there
might be no solution, were out of accord with the prevailing opti-
mism of the times. The dark shadow of intellectual nihilism, which
is the terminal stage of aporia, still lay some years into anthropology's future.

I was not out of fashion. Marxists, who come to any problem already equipped with the answer, had a short way of dealing with
complexity, which they shared with social engineers, neoclassical

---

material reality, of little use when social processes were to be explained. That
dictum is a large sinkhole for an anthropologist; we avoided it, disingenuously,
by using the word *custom*.

economists, and other single-template intellectuals. Values that did
not accord with the approved framework (because they were
clearly not universals) were sidelined as epiphenomena, obfusca-
tions of reality, mere superstitions that did not count. Complexities
that got in the way of the favored solution were not allowed to
overthrow the regnant theory. In the nineteenth century people
were slightly less disingenuous and would have invoked "disturbing causes."[9]

The repertoire model that guides me now still has an expected-
utility form, but I think of utility as more than material benefits.
Certainly, I assume, people can be rational; they do not (always) act
at random. Sometimes, to the best of their ability and within the
limits of information available to them, they calculate the consequences of possible courses of action, most often in the quick form
of identifying a situation and linking a course of action with it. *The
incumbent is a corrupt person; therefore I will not vote for him.* Alternatively: *The incumbent may be corrupt but he belongs to my community
and therefore it is my duty to vote for him.* Yet again: *I have been offered a
bribe and will vote accordingly.* Or simply, reducing calculation to its
minimal form of habitual action (still rational because it is in principle open to justification): *I always vote socialist.*

At a more abstract level, designs for living may be ordered, made
articulate, and packaged as ideologies, such as socialism or free enterprise. Such ideologies may then be condensed into phrases that
are marked as sacrosanct, for example "the dignity of the individual" or "the unity of the country," which occur in the governor's
address. Kenneth Burke, in *A Grammar of Motives* (1969, 105) writes:
"In any term we can posit a world, in the sense that we can treat the
world *in terms of* it, seeing all as emanations, near or far, of its light."
He is referring to models, designs for living, sets of assumptions,
ideologies available to make sense of our experience and guide our
actions. *Terms* are the labels that identify those ideologies; he names
them "God terms." The ideologies themselves could then be called
"God frames," since, purportedly, they are applicable everywhere
and always, supplying all needed answers. He also refers to them
as *formulae,* a wonderfully wide-reaching word that covers rituals
and recipes and mathematical rules, and sometimes suggests slav-
ish, unintelligent, and unquestioning adherence to conventions.

[9] Nineteenth-century economists rearguarded the deductive method by looking, a posteriori, for variables that, not being built into the model, limited its application. These variables were called "disturbing causes."

Burke goes on to give this canonical advice: "Such reduction to a simplicity being technically a reduction to a summarizing title or `god-term,' when we confront a simplicity we must forthwith ask ourselves what complexities are subsumed beneath it." In other words, behind the title is the frame, and hidden in the frame are its entailments, which are to be brought into the open.

God frames (ideologies) are persuasive, would-be coercive, things. The persuasion may take the form of explicit argument; at other times the salesmanship is camouflaged, even to the point where the sellers see themselves not as salesmen but as messengers conveying a simple and indisputable truth that must sell itself. Unpackaging the terms reveals hidden assumptions, entailments, and sometimes contradictions. What is presented on the front stage, in other words, is often at variance with the backstage performance. The front-stage socialism of the governor's address in the practice of everyday politics went along, in varying degrees, with the spirit of free enterprise, with feudalism and paternalism, and with the still formidable remnant of Gandhi's anarchic religiosity.

To state the point again, these God frames that pretend to exclusivity in fact do not have it, but exist as alternatives, antagonists in an arena where leaders, who see an advantage in promoting one God frame or feel a moral imperative to do so, take pains to open up to public scrutiny the backstage performances of their rivals. In this way any God frame is exposed to two kinds of attack. First, its opponents are ever ready to reveal the skeletons of inconsistency and hypocrisy that are hidden in its closet. Second, it must, sooner or later, survive the test of objectivity: Does it in fact deliver what it promises? These two forms of assay feed into one another to produce a complicated and usually acrimonious critical discourse.

My task, in short, is to describe the competing models in all the relevant complexity (front stage and back stage, articulated and taken for granted), to identify the selections made between them, and to say what are the consequences of making one or another selection.

Past and Future

In some ways it is odd that the denizens of the new capital should have displayed such resolute ennui. The grumblers were living in the capital city of a state of more than fourteen million people. They

were citizens of a country that only twelve years earlier had freed itself from foreign domination. Even for a bureaucrat this should
have been a brave new world. There were certainly many attempts
to define it so, if one can judge from the material put out by the
Public Relations Department. These publications, many of them issued both in an English and an Oriya edition, were designed to enhance and fortify pride in past achievements and confidence for the
future.

Oriyas were urged to feel good about their long and glorious and
distinctive past:

> Orissa had been a prosperous land ever since the beginning of the
> Christian era . . . The magnificent temples and caves are silent wit-
> nesses of the glorious days of Orissa which was one of the last
> kingdoms of India to lose its independence to the foreign invaders.
> It was only in the 16th century that the king of Orissa lost his free-
> dom.
>
> Orissa was not only a land of prosperity. It was also a land of
> peace. Two thousand years ago on this soil Asoka realized that not
> war and conquest but peace and prosperity of the people were
> what the emperor should strive for. Orissa was the meeting ground
> of the pre–Aryan and Aryan cultures. In Orissa evolved a synthesis
> of the two cultures which is symbolized in the cult of Jagannath.
> Waves of dynasties from the north and the south came to Orissa
> through successive centuries and have got assimilated in the re-
> gion to form a people great in art and literature. These men of
> peace have left imperishable marks in history, in the rock-hewn
> caves of Khandagiri and Udayagiri and in the temples of Bhu-
> baneswar, Konarak and Puri.

They were reminded also of their past martyrdom and urged to
rejoice in adversities surmounted and in the heroes who made that
victory possible:

> Ever since the early part of British rule, however, Orissa became
> dismembered and a major portion of the State lay scattered in the
> four neighbouring States. As a result, development of the region
> and welfare of its people was long neglected. This led to a move-
> ment for the amalgamation of the Oriya-speaking tracts and for-
> mation of a separate Orissa Province. After this agitation lasting
> for about 35 years a separate Province of Orissa was carved out in

1936 with areas from the then provinces of Bihar and Orissa, Madras and C.P.[Central Provinces]. It was, however, in 1948 that the dream of Greater Orissa was realized and a major portion of the Oriya-speaking people came together under one administration, thanks to the genius of Sardar Patel, the then Home Minister of India, and the untiring efforts of Dr. H. K. Mahtab, Chief Minister of Orissa.[10]

Recent struggles against the British were remembered too. The chief minister, Harekrushna Mahtab, hero of the freedom fight and leader of the Congress party in Orissa, edited a four-volume *History of the Freedom Movement in Orissa*.[11] It was published on August 15, 1957, the tenth anniversary of India's independence. Many freedom fighters were still active in public life, some directly in politics and others in social work. To have taken part in the freedom fight was a hallmark of political respectability. Here, for example, in the January 1958 issue of the *Orissa Review*, is part of an obituary of a former minister of education in the Orissa government and, at the time of his death, a Congress party member of the Union parliament. In 1921, at the age of twenty-seven,

> he resigned his post [he was a lecturer in Sanskrit at a college in Bihar] to join the Non-cooperation Movement. Since then he took to a life of service and sacrifice and threw himself into the struggle for freedom of the country and courted persecution at the hands of the authorities of law and order. He was jailed in 1930, 1932, 1940 and 1942 in connection with the Freedom Struggle.

Those whose career in the freedom movement might have been less notable also had their representation. One special category was that of "political sufferers," comprising people who could claim to be disadvantaged now, as a result of their contribution to the freedom fight, and therefore deserving of support. There was an agitation to give them pensions, like ex-soldiers.

A bright future awaited the people of Orissa, if they seized the opportunities available to them. Here is a broadcast speech in 1949 from the then governor of Orissa:

---

[10] This and the preceding quotation come from a government of Orissa publication: *A Handbook of Orissa*. 1958, 1–2.

[11] A fifth volume appeared in 1959, advertised as a "supplement" to Volume IV, the writer of which had since died. Judging from the tone of the supplement, it was intended to counter the relative even-handedness of the earlier volume.

In respect of its resources in land, forest, rivers, waterfalls, mines and maritime potentialities put together, Orissa is next to none of the major provinces . . . [it is] a paradise of planners . . . and . . . Nature's favourite whose highest potentialities have been preserved for thousands of years for timely development. (*Orissa 1949*, 1)

Here is a cabinet minister, also in 1949:

Orissa is a virgin country with immense potentials awaiting human energy and skill for exploitation . . . Destiny is calling and those who are not afraid of pioneering will not only build their own fortunes but will be building that of the generations to come and of Mother India. (*Orissa 1949*, 47)

The governor, addressing the Assembly in 1950, had no doubts about the goal and the way to reach it:

If the material and cultural poverty of the toiling masses is to be effectively abolished within a given time, a scientific plan will have to be drawn up and a determined drive will have to be initiated to execute it according to plan. (*Orissa 1949*, 51)

Of course all these are speeches on public occasions, windy things, depictions of the brave new world, exhortations, sermons, pep talks, rhetoric that the skeptical can pass over as mere cultural performances, orations that leaders make because a politician, even when not up for election, likes to gratify an audience. But, speeches and the *Orissa Review* and the Public Relations propaganda apart, there were many substantial and visible achievements for the inhabitants of Bhubaneswar to contemplate. Every day their town was growing and expanding, new buildings rising, new roads built, and new tracts laid down. In Sambalpur district, at Hirakud, an enormous dam was being built, to provide irrigation for the western regions of the state and electricity everywhere. On the coast, where silt deposited by the rivers and the sand-bearing tides and the currents of the Bay of Bengal make landing and loading facilities difficult anywhere south of Calcutta, a new port was being built at Paradip in Orissa. It was opened in 1959, and in January that year the *Orissa Review* carried an article entitled "A Year of Unbroken Progress in Orissa." By that time Hirakud was supplying power to the new steel works at Rourkela, to a new cement factory, to a new ferromanganese factory, to paper mills, and to Cuttack, Puri, Sam-

balpur, and other towns. Five industrial estates were being ex-
panded or newly opened.

It would be unrealistic to expect these achievements, or the
rhetoric that celebrated them, or the rhetoric of exhortation, to gen-
erate a condition of continuous enthusiasm. Events of this kind do
not immediately and directly enter the everyday life of ordinary
people, and the most that one could reasonably anticipate in the
way of authentic emotion is that from time to time, in moments of
reflection, the bureaucrats and the politicians might experience a
quiet pride in what was being accomplished. But there were other
events and issues that did sometimes penetrate everyday life and
fire the emotions of politicians, of the common people, and even of
bureaucrats. The emotion that was kindled was usually anger. One
such issue was Oriya nationalism.

Oriya Nationalism

I noticed in 1959 among many educated Oriyas a thinness of skin
in the way they talked about certain other Indians. They displayed
sensitivities not unlike those found at that time in Indian attitudes
toward the British. Most Oriya-speaking tracts had until 1911 been
governed from Calcutta, as part of the Bengal presidency; Bengali
was the language of government. It also was the language of the intelligentsia. Oriya intellectuals experienced the provincial discomfort of being fascinated with Bengali metropolitan culture and at the
same time resenting it. Sambalpur in the west was then in the Central Provinces, where Hindi was the dominant language. Districts
in what is now the southern part of Orissa, Ganjam and Koraput,
had been part of the Madras presidency (northern Madras was Telugu-speaking). There are obvious disadvantages for those who do
not speak the language of government and administration, and
there is, therefore, a strong incentive for the intelligentsia to learn
that language and to have their children educated in it. The fashion
drifts downwards until eventually, even in elementary schools, the
politically dominant language becomes the language of instruction
and pupils are punished if they use the language of the home. Until
early in this century, that process of attrition was the fate of the
Oriya language in the border areas. In Midnapore district, for example, now part of West Bengal, Oriya-speakers declined from
572,789 in the 1891 census to 181,801 in the 1911 census. W. W.

Hunter, the indefatigable chronicler of *The Annals of Rural Bengal*, reported, "The children in some village schools of Midnapur District learn Bengali in the morning, and Uriya in the afternoon" (1872, vol. 1, 314). He added, in a footnote, "Our system of Public Instruction is rapidly destroying such local distinctions."[12]

More than language was involved. Appointments in the administration went to Bengalis to such an extent that Oriya protesters called them an "intermediate ruling race." Bengalis also became landholders, often by devious means. In the three years that followed the extension of Bengal regulations to Cuttack district, slightly more than one-third of the estates (measured by the tax they paid) were sold at public auction for arrears of revenue. There was, I heard from one man (a senior civil servant and by no means a fervent Oriya nationalist) a "sunset law." Land revenue had to be paid in three installments—say, January 15, February 15, and March 15. If it was not paid promptly (by "sunset") the estate would be put up for auction in Calcutta, often without the knowledge of its owner. It would go for a song to a Bengali family, perhaps related to the clerk who had arranged for the sale. This maneuver would be repeated, and the family would eventually become a substantial landlord. The countryside in three coastal districts, Cuttack, Puri and Balasore, was "littered with the decaying palaces of these people." (My informant was himself related through his mother to one of these domiciled Bengali families.)

Subordination to outsiders had a longer history than this. The last independent king of Orissa died in battle in 1559. Thereafter the province was under the control of Muslims, and then Marathas (from about 1753), and then the British, who took control in 1803. Hunter described the subordination of the Oriyas (vol. 2, 125):

The Bengalis, Lala Kayets [originating from Bihar and northern India], and Musalmans monopolized the principal offices of State under the Muhammadan and Marhatta governments, and continued to do so after the province had passed under British rule, until the vernacular of the country was substituted for Persian as the language of public business and of the courts of law [a gradual

[12] William Wilson Hunter was superintendent of public instruction in Orissa between 1866 and 1869. A statistician educated in Glasgow, Paris, and Bonn, he was twenty-six years old when appointed to the post in Orissa. In 1871 he became director-general of the statistical department of the government of India and was responsible for India's first census in 1872.

process, begun after 1837].[13] This change enabled the Uriyas to compete with the strangers for official employment, and almost simultaneously it was authoritatively laid down that, in selecting candidates for Government service, preference should be given to natives of the province, if they possessed equal qualifications. The Uriyas thus obtained a fair chance, and the lower ministerial offices [he refers to messengers or clerks] are principally in their hands. The higher executive posts, such as those of Deputy Magistrate and Collector, are still, however, monopolized by Bengalis and other immigrants. This is little satisfactory to the natives, but the latter generally admit that the Bengalis have had the start of them in education and enlightenment. In 1869 an attempt, fortunately unsuccessful, by some of the Bengali party to get their language practically substituted for Uriya in the schools gave rise to some bitterness.

The proposal to make Bengali the language of instruction in schools (on the grounds that there were no textbooks in Oriya) was made by a Bengali, an "antiquarian scholar." The opposition, speaking up for Oriya, also was led by a Bengali, domiciled in Orissa. Public life in Cuttack during the nineteenth century, the author remarks, was dominated by Bengalis (Pradhan 1990, 133). Bengalis also took both sides in a more academic version of the conflict, a dispute about the status of the Oriya language. In 1870 one Kantichandra Bhattacharya, a domiciled Bengali teaching in a school in Balasore district, intervened in an exchange that was going on about the relative poverty of Oriya literature with the claim that the Oriya language was not a language at all, but merely a dialect of Bengali. This assertion was indignantly rejected by other domiciled Bengalis and by a senior English official,[14] John Beames. The proposition was, he wrote, "profoundly destitute of philological arguments." Other critics pointed out that precisely the same evidence could be used to brand Bengali as a dialect of the Oriya language (Mahtab 1957, vol. 2, 135).

This long history of exploitation and denigration of their culture

[13] The revised edition of O'Malley's *Cuttack Gazetteer* (1933, 211) states that as early as 1805 (two years after Orissa was taken from the Marathas) "orders were passed that in all written communications with the natives of the Province the subject should be written in Oriya as well as in Persian." Most of the clerical jobs that this order produced apparently went to immigrant Bengalis.

[14] *Official*, used as a noun and not qualified, refers to a civil servant or a bureaucrat.

perhaps justifies what at first I thought to be a mild paranoia among Oriyas, a feeling that other Indians, especially Bengalis, did not respect them and made jokes about their passivity and their lack of sophistication. My Bengali friends delighted in telling jokes about Oriya servants in Calcutta. They mangled the Oriya sentences to make them sound rustic, in just the way people in England used what they took to be a bog-Irish accent to tell Pat and Mick jokes or Americans perpetrate a plum-in-the-mouth voice to mock the English.[15] I recall overnighting at a travelers' bungalow in northwestern Orissa with a Bengali friend. The other suite was occupied by a young official, with whom my friend struck up a conversation. "Extraordinary!" he said later, "That fellow is an Oriya but he speaks the most chaste and elegant Bengali!" Perhaps the words are harmless; the tone, however, conveyed amazement that anyone who began with such a handicap could yet rise to such heights.[16]

I can trace the reputation for passivity—from another point of view it is spinelessness—back to 1911, during a debate in the House of Lords, when Bihar and Orissa became a province separate from Bengal. Lord Curzon said, "The interests of the Oriyas have been sacrificed without compunction . . . because the Oriyas are a non-agitating people."[17] Compared to what had been going on in the previous decade in Bengal and among the Marathas, Lord Curzon may have been correct. There was a political association, the Oriya Union Movement (Utkal Sammilani), founded in 1903, a very re-

[15] The old Oriya servant advising the young one: *jeteku sunilo/damoyu! bolila/ totoku bujilo/ bipodo ghatila.* (When you hear him/ Say "Damn you!"/ Then you know/ You are in danger.")

[16] Hunter (1872, vol. 2, 139) notes a saying popular with "the acute inhabitants" of Bengal: *As stupid as an Uriya.* O'Malley's *Gazetteer* (1933, 211) has this: "Orissa was described as the Boeotia of India, and its people as equally stupid and ignorant." Catch the tone of a Bengali historian, in a book published in 1930: "The average Oriya . . . is usually dwarfish in stature and brownish black in complexion." (Banerji 1930, vol 1, 136–37.)

[17] Some scholars place the origins of this alleged passivity back in the 16th century. Banerji, explaining "the loss of all military instinct," wrote that it was "intimately connected with the long residence of the Bengali Vaisnava saint, Chaitanya, in the country. . . . Considered as a religion Indian 'Bhaktimarga' is sublime, but its effect on the political status of the country or the nation which accepts it is terrible. The religion of equality and love preached by Chaitanya brought in its train a false faith in men and thereby destroyed the structure of society and government" (1930, vol. 1, 330–31). What Banerji made of that later purveyor of equality and love, Gandhi, I do not know. Banerji died in 1930.

spectable "non-agitating" middle-class organization, employing paid propagandists ("missionaries"), supporting Oriya schools in outlying areas, giving scholarships to Oriya students, and submitting "memorials" to the government, the goal being to bring all Oriya-speakers together in their own province. That province was formed in 1936. Many Oriya speakers were still adrift in Bihar, Bengal, the Central Provinces, and what was then northern Madras (now Andhra Pradesh), but in those years (until 1947) the Oriya movement was in the shadow of the greater struggle to achieve freedom for India.

In 1959 I kept hearing about Saraikella and Kharsawan. These were two small kingdoms that had been under the jurisdiction of the British Political Agent for the Orissa feudatory states. Large areas, particularly in the western upland region of Orissa, had been royal domains, ruled by dynasties that claimed at least five hundred years of history (in one case more than three thousand). After 1803 their rajas governed under the tutelage of British civil servants, and the kingdoms were styled "feudatory states" or "tributary states." There were twenty-seven of them and they varied greatly in size, from (in 1947) almost a million in Mayurbhanj down to twenty-six thousand in Tigiria. They also varied in the enlightenment of their rulers, ranging from a man who (it was said) kidnapped girls off trains, where the line ran through his territory, to others who were careful and conscientious administrators, fiscally responsible, interested in the health and education of their subjects, and in economic development. On the eve of India's independence several of these rulers got together with others from neighboring provinces (the term *state* came into use after 1947) and attempted to form an Eastern States Union that would be part of the new India but not under the jurisdiction of any of the new states. The move was quickly blocked by the Union government in Delhi (in the person of Sardar Patel) and in Orissa all the rajas, save one, quite soon "acceded to the Union," thus losing their kingdoms and their right to govern, receiving in compensation certain perquisites and a privy purse. Many of them were the owners of substantial private properties.

Saraikella and Kharsawan were allocated to Orissa when the princely states acceded to the Union at the end of 1947. But there was a noisy local agitation against Orissa (organized, Oriyas said, by Biharis coming from outside Saraikella and Kharsawan) and the two states were made part of Bihar, possibly on the soon-to-be-disproved assumption that Oriyas were still a nonagitating people.[18] That decision was made easier because between those two domains and the rest of Orissa lay the large kingdom (now district) of Mayurbhanj, and the raja of Mayurbhanj held out for a year, refusing to accede to Orissa. For doing so he received, so the bitter scuttlebutt had it in Orissa, a telegram of congratulation from the President of India, who was a Bihari. A year later the raja gave in and Mayurbhanj became a district in Orissa. But nothing more seems to have been said or done about Saraikella and Kharsawan at the time.

In 1952 a Telugu social worker, Potti Sriramulu, fasting to make the Union government bring Telugu speakers together in a new state (Andhra), died. There was an outburst of violence and the new state came into existence the following year. In 1955, anticipating violence elsewhere, the Union government set up a States Reorganization Commission (SRC), charged, among other things, to redraw the boundaries between states so as to minimize the problem of linguistic minorities. In 1956 a States Reorganization Act was passed. The commission's report, on which the act was based, infuriated Oriyas, principally because Saraikella and Kharsawan remained with Bihar. Oriyas then set about proving Lord Curzon wrong by showing they could be as agitating as Bengalis, Biharis, or Marathas. The tone was struck by a student leader in Cuttack, who had been designated to propose a vote of thanks to the chief minister of Orissa on the occasion of the latter's address to the student body.[19] No vote of thanks was proposed. Instead the student delivered a tirade on the subject of Saraikella and Kharsawan and the Orissa government's failure to stand up to the Union government. He gave me this account of what later took place.

Members of the SRC came here and there was a general expectation that we would get justice. We did not expect to benefit at others' expense. But the report was very opportunist. When they talked of other states they used one principle; when they came to Orissa, they used another. They thought we were weak and the others strong.

[18] The region contains iron ore. India's first iron and steel plant was built there, in 1908, at Jamshedpur.
[19] At this time the chief minister was Nabakrushna Chaudhuri.

On 17th evening [January] the news came and twelve hundred students marched on the house of Kanungo, because he was a minister in the central government. Next two days there was a general strike.

On 19th, when there was a procession of protest, there was some provocation by the police. People were manhandled.

On 20th tempo rose. There was some disturbance at a public meeting. Some fifteen thousand people assembled. Some Congress people there attempted to break it up by causing strife, and almost succeeded. For half an hour there was chaos and pandemonium. But we students saved the meeting. We brought it to order and formed a council of action for all Orissa. We decided to picket central government agencies; railway, post office, All-India Radio.

On 21st we began picketing. Some leaders were arrested. We picketed the anicut [an irrigation dam carrying the main road north from Cuttack across the river Mahanadi] where they were going to send police to Bhadrak. We expected firing, but we gave no provocation and the police withdrew. Then we went to All-India Radio. The superintendent of police mishandled the situation and the students broke down the gates. There was firing with blanks.

Next morning students went there again. Gurkha military police had come down from Delhi in thirty airplanes. They broadcast warnings and then they used tear gas and the people threw stones at them. There was some firing and people were hurt. The crowd took these people to hospital. On the way they found the Congress [local party] president and beat him up and he had to go to hospital. In the hospital they found the wife of the chief minister [Maloti Chaudhuri] and they seized her and dragged her to All-India Radio.[20] She cried for help and the police opened fire and that was when Sushil De was killed.[21] He was only a bystander. I was there at the spot and saw what happened.

There was also firing at Puri as a result of provocation by the Orissa Military Police.

There was indeed a general strike. At Bhadrak, in northern Orissa, the trains were held up for a week and students, who were the picketers, organized canteens to feed the stranded passengers. At Puri the railway station was attacked and burned; the police

[20] Other versions insist that she was leading the protest.
[21] The name indicates someone of Bengali descent.

opened fire and killed one of the crowd.[22] The young man killed at Cuttack became a martyr and featured in the election the following year, when Congress representation in the legislature shrank from sixty-seven (the 1952 election) to fifty-six in 1957. Leaders of the main opposition party, Ganatantra, and members of the left-wing parties courted arrest by defying the ban on public meetings, following exactly the precedent set by Congress in its defiance of the British. Nehru, it was widely rumored in Orissa—the tale told with a somewhat smug indignation—had said Oriyas were *goondas* (hooligans). "Would he have dared talk like that about Andhra people?" they asked.

I saw nothing like this in 1959. I listened to several people talking about the 1956 *sima* (boundary) riots, in particular the young man who had taken a leading part in them and who gave me the account reproduced above, and it was like listening to old men reminisce about the First World War. There were tales of heroism and fatuity, ingenuity and brutality, but, after only two years, the telling seemed to have lost its immediacy. More than that; there was not much passion on display. I thought I perceived a detachment on the part of the tellers, even a sense that they had worked out what would be the effect of the story, and how best to tell it to that audience (myself). Probably, I thought, they would cast it differently for a different audience. The tactics mattered; what the conflict was about had become secondary. The events seemed to have lost whatever intrinsic value they once possessed and to have become mere stuff for rhetoric.

It is hard to know where to draw a line. I am sure that many of the people I knew, politicians and others, were genuinely infuriated by what they saw as the persecution of Oriyas and the disvaluing of Oriya culture. My host, the MLA, was a man of letters. He liked to expatiate on the magnificence of Oriya literature, and never failed to lament its imminent demise. But somehow, for most politicians by 1959, talk about the issue had become calculated and accommodated to other considerations, the principal one of which was power in the state and in the legislature.

The Coalition

When the tributary states acceded to the union, a few princes took themselves elsewhere, the sybaritic ones to the fleshpots of

---

[22] Rumor had it that the stationmaster was a Bengali and the superintendent of police a Bihari, and that both would be replaced by Oriyas.

Calcutta. Some remained "just sitting" on their estates. A significant number of the more energetic royals entered - or reentered—the political arena and set up Ganatantra Parishad, the political party that, in a precarious alliance with socialists (PSP) and communists (CPI), constituted the opposition in the legislatures elected in 1952 and 1957.

In the 1957 election, in a house of 140 members, Congress did not win enough seats to govern as a majority. They had only fifty-six members, and to form a government with a working majority they needed allies. Five members from northern Orissa, bordering Bihar state, belonged to Jharkhand, a tribal party based in Bihar. They voted with Congress. In addition, a number of people who had been elected as independents (six out of seven), and even some who had been elected on a Ganatantra ticket (eight out of fifty-one) were persuaded to cross the floor and join the Congress. There was much scabrous gossip about motivations. As people do in those circumstances, MLAs maneuvered—wheeled and dealed—to get what concessions they could, sometimes for themselves, sometimes for their constituencies. Where a politician's loyalties should lie—self, family, ethnic group, constituency, party, state, nation—is a difficult question, and I will come to it later. Moral judgments are therefore hard to make, but not, perhaps, in every case. One MLA, it was said, crossed the floor from the opposition to the government benches in return for an Austin A-40 motorcar, which, of course, would better enable him to keep in touch with his constituents and so serve their needs.

The traffic was not all one way. Some, whose demands were not met, crossed the floor in the other direction or declared themselves independent. By the early spring of 1959 Congress was kept in power by three votes, seventy-one government to sixty-eight opposition (the total is 139 because by convention the Speaker of the house does not vote). The survival of the government was clearly uncertain, a situation, one might have anticipated, that would cause anxiety and heighten emotions. On February 23 I watched the government being defeated on a motion to introduce a bill concerning a disputed election. Depending on the circumstances, such a defeat may require a government to resign.

I will describe this event, as I saw it, and its outcome, because I want to convey what, on reflection, I now see as a strange cloud of uneventfulness hanging over the whole affair; even the protagonists behaved like tired actors in a drama long gone stale. From another point of view, their actions and their pragmatic attitudes might be called hypercivilized. However described, the scene was a world away from railway lines blocked, police firing into rioting crowds, and Gurkha soldiers flown in to protect government installations from a mob. On that day in February I witnessed the opening act of a cultural performance that celebrated hardheaded practicality and the foolishness of excessive enthusiasm.

The performance also marked, I now realize, the end of an era in which the freedom struggle had dominated politics in Orissa. The movement's legacies, mainly an ethic of resistance to authority coupled with Gandhian antistatist values, now were grinding against other foundational philosophies, particularly paternalism and self-interested individualism. (All these will be described in subsequent chapters.) The resultant upheaval at the surface not only put an end to the rule of the Congress party in Orissa, unbroken since independence, but also displaced from center stage the philosophy of the freedom fight itself. Gandhi's values receded; so also did the notion that resistance was the only correct posture in the face of authority. From the perspective of history, those are not small developments; they are foundational shifts. The occasion, however, was managed in a way that signaled none of the trepidation that one might have expected; rather it seemed to me to demonstrate a somewhat weary wisdom in the ways of the world, not so much apathy or boredom as a rather mundane common sense. The politicians heated up their rhetoric, as politicians do; but the actions they took indicated cool-headed calculation (in some cases miscalculation) and a sufficient control over their passions.

The everyday parliamentary performances in the Orissa legislature, including the language used, were at first sight perfect Westminster, highly routinized, and rarely dramatic. Consider the following extracts reporting the debate that followed the presentation of budget estimates in 1959. They were reported in the *Amrita Bazar Patrika.*

The leader of the Opposition, Sri Singh Deo agreed with the Chief Minister Dr Mahtab's sentiments and observations regarding Paradip, but regretted that the Second Plan had made no provision for this port.

Sri Singh Deo characterized the surplus . . . as mere speculation . . . He accused the Government of having discriminatory attitude in the allotment of development projects.

Sri Rabindramohan Das, leader of the PSP in the Assembly . . . said that the correct appraisal of Orissa's needs was lacking.

Sri Lokonath Chaudhuri (Communist) made an allround criticism of Government activities.

Sri Aintu Sahu (Ganatantra Parishad) characterized the budget provisions as "penny-wise and pound-foolish."

Sri Bejoyananda Patnaik (Congress), welcoming the budget, said the opposition members participating in the Debate were indulging in party politics . . . they blamed the Government with partisan spirit.

Language and procedures, at least in this reporting, are all very parliamentary. The leader of the opposition initiates the attack. Members of the other opposition parties take their turns in making their criticisms, and replies from the treasury benches (that was their name in Orissa, as well as in London) praise the government's accomplishments, and, using that riposte found universally in democratic settings, accuse the opposition of being less concerned with the general welfare than with the interests of its own party.

Most of the time the atmosphere during sessions was relaxed to the point of being casual. The etiquette and procedures of the mother of parliaments were in use and so were the conventions of a gentleman's club. Ministers could be seen working at their files (unobtrusively, since this was reckoned a breach of decorum) while speeches were made from the back benches. Other members conversed quietly with one another or sent each other notes. Occasionally people would cross the floor to stand near a member of the other bench to chat, quietly and apparently amicably. Members entered and left the chamber at will, pausing only to bow perfunctorily in the direction of Mr. Speaker.

At question time the benches, government and opposition together, on a normal day contained about ninty to one hundred members. Debates at other times, especially in the afternoon, might see the number shrink to forty or so. There were numerous attendants at hand, their job being to convey files to the ministers or to carry notes from one member to another. Everyone who sat on a front bench had a microphone, but the rank-and-file members were rationed, and there was often a delay while an attendant shifted a microphone from one place to another. In a debate, those who wished to speak stood in the hope that the speaker would select them. Speeches were time-rationed, a bell being rung halfway through the allotted time, and another to indicate when to finish. It was obeyed on the instant, even the most loquacious members seeming to have the art of silencing themselves in mid-sentence. Prepared speeches in English were read (usually rapidly and without oratorical flourishes). Speeches in Oriya were apt to be more declamatory. Questions in English were answered in English, but for supplementaries the exchange often shifted to Oriya, interlarded with technical expressions in English. Some of the Jharkhand members made a point of using Hindi, and this was accompanied by *sotto voce* mocking repetitions of Hindi words from the less well-mannered among the Oriya speakers.

The visitors' gallery was always filled. I had a pass to the distinguished visitors' section, often having it to myself. Senior civil servants or their deputies, come to hear how their minister fared in question time and to help him out, had their own box to the right of the speaker. During question time on February 23, the day the drama opened, attendance on the floor was thin, about thirty people on each side of the aisle. When question time ended the opposition benches suddenly filled, until about fifty opposition members were present. There was no matching influx on the government side. The Congress whip was not even in the house at that time.

The Minister of Revenue and Excise then rose and asked leave to introduce a bill. The speaker asked for those in favor. There was a languid murmur of "Aye." He asked for the "No" vote and there was complete silence. He announced that the ayes had it.

The minister rose again and asked for leave to introduce another bill. When the speaker asked for those in favor there was the same lackadaisical chorus of "Aye." Then he asked for those against and there was a stentorian bellow, in unison, from the opposition benches of "No," followed by chuckles and self-congratulatory grins all round on that side of the house. The speaker stared at them for a moment, in evident surprise, and then said, tentatively, "The ayes have it." That provoked an uproar and loud shouts of "No! No! No!" "Do you want a division?" he asked and was given a loud "Yes!" So the bells were rung and government supporters rounded up from the lobbies and the tearoom and the library and there was a division and the government lost by fifty-one votes to forty-three. The ruse had worked: The government had fallen into a trap and had lost a vote on the floor of the Assembly.

But there was no resignation. The chief minister later announced that this had been a "snap vote;" it therefore signified no loss of confidence in the government, only that, for various reasons, government supporters had been away from the house at the time.

Therefore there was no reason for the government to resign. A petition was filed next day "under Section 226 of the Indian Constitution" by the secretary of the PSP (the socialist party) that "writ of *quo warranto* or order or direction be issued on chief minister of Orissa, restraining him from assuming office or continuing to hold the same." On February 26 in Cuttack the Orissa High Court dismissed the petition. Next time the house met (the government benches were predictably full) the speaker was asked to rule on a motion by a PSP member that a vote of confidence in the government must be held before the house could continue with its business. He ruled against it. After that nothing more concerning the defeat was done in the house, although opposition members continued to make speeches outside the house insisting that it was in the best interests of Orissa that the government should resign.

About the middle of March there was another episode in the series of theatrical events that led up to the fall of the Congress government and the formation of a coalition. In a remote area in northern Orissa a steel plant had been constructed beside a village called Rourkela. That plant, like the Hirakud dam, was a source of pride and self-congratulation for Orissa's modernizers. Steel is the beginning of industrial development; without it there are no bicycles, no sewing machines, no machine tools, no bridges, no technical modernity (vintage 1959). India had three foreign-sponsored steel plants at that time. Bhilai (in Madhya Pradesh) was built by the Russians, Durgapur (in Bengal) by the British, and Rourkela by the Germans. There were also several indigenous steel plants, the earliest, owned by the Tata enterprises, built in 1908 at Jamshedpur in Bihar.[23] Orissa's new steelworks was sited at Rourkela because there were generous deposits of iron ore in the vicinity. But to get at the ore and build the plant, a number of villagers had to be displaced from their homes and farms. The local MLAs, some of whom were Jharkhand (the party that helped to keep Congress in power), took up the cause of the displaced persons.

They did so after a social worker went on a hunger strike to protest the displacement. He began inside the Assembly building on March 16, at the door of the speaker's room, but the Assembly's own police ("Watch and Ward") removed him and dumped him outside the gate of the building. When I first saw him he was sitting in the road, clinging to the gate, and several subinspectors and po-

---

[23] Otto Koenigsberger prepared a development plan for that town too.

lice constables were standing around him, looking puzzled. Later I saw him lying two yards from the gate, covered by a white sheet, under a shelter constructed of placards, and utterly still. There was no one near him—no spectators, no police, no crowd, no excitement.

But inside the house he made his presence felt. On March 19 the opposition moved an adjournment so they could discuss the issue that he represented. The speaker refused, on the grounds that the question had already been considered and the chief minister had arranged for representatives from both sides of the house to go to Rourkela and inquire into the condition of displaced persons. The opposition, adopting a Gandhian tone, replied that the present issue was not Rourkela but the welfare of the person starving himself to death at their gate. The speaker again disallowed the motion, saying the starving man and the displacement issue were one and the same. Thereupon the opposition began to raise points of order, and kept it up for about an hour until the speaker told them trenchantly that if they continued to be obstructive, he would adjourn the house. A brief pandemonium followed and then the leader of the opposition rose and walked out, followed by all the Ganatantra members and their left-wing allies.

Two days later there was another walkout, but this time two of the Jharkhand members went with the opposition. That same afternoon the government announced that demolitions and displacement would be stopped at once, pending the results of the inquiry. The hunger strike—the first man had been joined by three fellow-travelers the previous day—was then called off.

Newspapers—the main English-language ones circulated in Bhubaneswar and Cuttack were the Calcutta dailies, the *Statesman* and the *Amrita Bazar Patrika*—made the most of those seemingly dramatic events. But in Bhubaneswar there was no noticeable tension, not even around the man starving himself in front of the Assembly. The apparently dramatic walkout from the Assembly came across to me as staged and orderly, like a negative vote but heated one or two degrees. The element of performance dominated. When the chief minister made a public offering of coalition, the leader of the opposition, as the newspapers reported it, "did not seem surprised. He made a suitable reply."

The event that did eventually break the government's will and induce the coalition was not a matter of high drama. On April 2 five Congress members resigned from the party. They did so on the grounds of "regional partiality." The government, they claimed, had acted unfairly in allocating Orissa's second medical school to Sambalpur in the west of Orissa. All five of them represented constituencies in Ganjam district, which is in the coastal region, where the existing medical school was situated (but in Cuttack district, not Ganjam). Two days later three of the defectors returned to Congress. When it seemed certain that there would be a coalition, the two holdouts were expelled from the party. On May 22 a coalition government was sworn in. Now, the new government said, everyone could stop playing party politics and get on with implementing the plan.

Inconsistencies

That was the place and those were the events in 1959 that I have chosen to highlight. They are enough to start the inquiry, for they indicate clearly that different voices were making themselves heard at that time: Oriya nationalists, left and right in politics, the archaic call of princely ambition, and many others. These were not Madison's *factions*; loyalties were too diversified to make single-minded factionalism possible. People who were allies in one cause, were enemies in another. These were *voices*, a babel that invites an ordering based not on particular loyalties and adherences but on underlying assumptions about the nature of the political process and the political person. It was not simply the "system" inherited from the British that caused people to be "out of their depth." The root cause was a basic incongruity between certain fundamental socio-political philosophies and the incapacity of any one of them to dominate the field.

In the following chapters I will look more closely at the people involved and at what might have been in their minds to make them behave the way they did. Their logic is not self-evident; whatever it was that guided them contained numerous inconsistencies. For example, the metaphor that is built into the new capital's architecture—control, order, and rationality—was made real in many other contexts, in which there was an overt acceptance of the need for "a scientific plan." The virtue of "muddling through," which once inspired some British Tories (they gloried in it), was nowhere in open sight. But concealed behind the structure of routinization and predictability was another edifice, in which common sense and muddling through were the reality, perhaps even, on occasions, the intention. That subaltern philosophy was symbolized (for me) by the lived-in confusions and cherished disorders of Cuttack, where spontaneity ruled and you could never be sure what was round the next corner. Chapter 3, which is on paternalism, takes up this topic.

Close to that contradiction, but not quite the same, was the tension between duty to the collectivity and the interests of its lesser units. This was manifested, for instance, in the choices that faced MLAs. Whose interests should they work for: India's, Orissa's, the party's, their constituents', their family's, their own? From the perspective of each upper level, those below it represent potential chaos, confusion, and partisan interests. From below, each higher level means betrayal masked as concern for the public interest. The same antithesis was evident in the strong undertow of private enterprise, pulling back against the tide of socialism. Its icon in Bhubaneswar at that time was the tented eatery, the pleasant, acceptable, but unobtrusive face of capitalism. But, more than that, the elevation of private gain above public interest was generally assumed to be the statistical norm, not just a businessman's vice. Everyone was like that; to be acquisitive was to be human. Chapter 4, which is about the rhetoric of business, will examine this view of the world.

Then there was that curious contrast between the languid proceduralisms of the Assembly and the zestful violence that showed itself in the riots of 1956. Indeed, if one looked more closely at the Assembly members, the contrast was present in their conduct too. Despite their apparent relish for parliamentary maneuvering and respect for the rules, they often refused to play the game at all; they walked out and went off to Cuttack or some trouble spot to organize a protest meeting or arrange a strike or a violent or nonviolent protest in defiance of the law. Of course they did; their leaders, who were their role models, and many of the rank and file themselves, had matured during the freedom fight when those methods were respectable and often the only ones that were effective. Chapter 5 is about the rhetoric of struggle.

There remains an antithesis that has not emerged clearly from the events I have chosen to represent Orissa politics in 1959. Alternatively, I might say that it pervades them all. Does the good society function as a single unitary moral entity, or can there be many incompatible moralities, making choice possible and therefore compromise a necessity? That question is considered in chapters 6 and 7 in an extended discussion of Gandhi's adamantine philosophy and its antithesis, which advises attention to reality and to the consequences of action, and accepts the need for compromise.

I will endeavor to make sense of this diversity not by homogenizing it, reducing it to a structure of ideas that are consistent with one another, but rather by presenting it as a set of alternative values. Or, since I think I am dealing as much with rhetoric as with internalized guides for conduct, what I will present is an array of alternative vocabularies available at that time for justifying or condemning what was done or said.

The first to be considered is the rhetoric of paternalism and the quite complex set of values, not all of them consistent with one another, that guided Oriyas in their attitudes toward government and other forms of authority.

CHAPTER

3

The Rhetoric of Paternalism

Look to Government

A neighbor, a bright-eyed old man, would sometimes drop by for a chat in the evening. I met him through his younger daughter's husband, the official who joked about official birth rates, and he took it on himself to keep me abreast of the faults and foibles of the capital's politicians and officials. One night, when the lights went out, as they often did, the old man broke off what he was telling me and began to laugh. The failure reminded him, he told me (not without pride), that the previous evening, when the outage happened earlier than usual, his eight-year-old grandson exclaimed (in Oriya), "Grandfather! Electricity already gone!" and then added sententiously (in English), "We must look to government to do the needful."

I heard that phrase many times: "Look to government." It is equivocal; it may be keyed either to responsibility (governments are like servants to be reminded of their duties) or to power (government, the *raj*, is an all-powerful master whom one approaches as a supplicant). The governor, in his 1955 address, when he spoke of individual dignity and equality of status, inclined toward the former meaning, or perhaps to the more elusive idea that we ourselves, the people, are the government. But throughout the year spent in Bhubaneswar and the two earlier years in the village of Bisipara, I rarely heard, except from the mouths of politicians making speeches, voices raised in praise of equality. Not that people spoke against it; they simply did not mention it. The framework they used to make sense of their world and their interactions with each other was overwhelmingly patterned as hierarchy. In that ambience the phrase "look to government" is not equivocal; it indicates the posture of a supplicant, one who requests a favor, not one who asserts a right. That framework I will call paternalism.

The celebration of deference goes on at the front of paternalism's stage, where hierarchy is the main theme in the drama. But equality also has a place. At the back of the stage the performers demonstrate that inequality can on occasion be neutralized. People are then free to do, within limits, what they wish; so long as they stay off the front stage, they can be their own masters.

Reserved Seats

One MLA I interviewed represented a two-member constituency where I had lived between 1952 and 1955. I did not know him then. Bisipara, where I stayed, was in the highland part of the constituency, and he came from a village on the plains along the upper reaches of the Mahanadi river. I will sketch his background, so that the reader may begin to understand the varied assortment of people who in 1959 inhabited Orissa's new political world.

His constituency covered about 2000 square miles and had a population of 250,000. That produced an electorate of 125,000, of whom 65,000 cast valid votes in the 1957 election. This was a two-member constituency. There were fifteen candidates, two standing for the Congress party, two for Ganatantra Parishad, and the remaining eleven were independents. The two Ganatantra candidates won. Of the remaining thirteen hopefuls all but one, a Congress person, forfeited their deposits. A deposit was required of each candidate and it was returned only to those who polled a stipulated fraction of the valid votes (one sixth in a one-member constituency and one twelfth in a two-member constituency). Fifteen candidates competing for two seats suggests a degree of unfamiliarity with the electoral process.

The electoral system was intended to ensure that disadvantaged categories were represented in both the Parliament and the Assembly. These categories were scheduled castes (untouchables) and scheduled tribes (adibasis).[1] Three-quarters of Orissa's tribal popu-

---

[1] What criteria should be used to identify an adibasi (formerly called *aborigines* or *tribals*) has never been agreed upon. In broad terms, adibasis are those who

lation lived in the hill districts in the western part of the state; the untouchables were more evenly spread through the hill and coastal regions. (The general population was almost equally divided between the hills and the coast.) In two-member constituencies one seat was reserved for whoever among the reserved-seat candidates polled the highest number of votes. Once that seat had been filled, the disadvantage provision was removed and the second seat went to whichever of the remaining candidates, scheduled category or not, received the highest number of votes. In one instance in 1957 that procedure returned two reserved-seat candidates, one for Ganatantra and one for Congress.[2] Thirty-nine seats in the Orissa Assembly (140 seats in all) were in the two-member reserved category. A further fifteen constituencies had single-member reserved seats. In sum, more than a third (38 percent) of the MLAs were either scheduled caste (twenty-five seats) or scheduled tribe (twenty-nine seats). Since, at that time, untouchables and tribal peoples together made up 39 percent of the total population, it seems that the governor's promise of "equality of status and opportunity" was being fulfilled, at least so far as concerned parliamentary representation.

In the 1957 election Bisipara, which then had a population of around seven hundred, fielded no less than three Assembly candidates. Two were scheduled caste persons. One of them, the Congress candidate, forfeited Rs.125 (about four months wages for an elementary schoolmaster, which is what he had been before entering politics). His name was Balunki Sahani. The other, standing as an independent, likewise forfeited his deposit. He was Gondho Sahani, a retired police constable. The third, Basu Pradhan, not privileged as an untouchable, forfeited Rs.250. I asked people I knew in Bisipara if they had voted for their own Bisipara men. They had not. The candidate for the general seat was considered untrustworthy, no longer a man of the village, being too much involved with

---

live far away from the metropolitan centers of civilization and who are less "advanced" than the rest of the population, and who, as a consequence, are worthy of special treatment by government in order to improve the quality of their lives and to protect them from exploitation by more sophisticated people. Whether they were to be considered Hindus by religion, or Hindus "who have lost touch," or Animists ripe for conversion, was a matter of contention both among scholars and politicians.

[2] Both members came from the one royal family in Orissa that (to my knowledge) was formally recognized as adibasi. Royal status evidently mattered more than party affiliation.

government and bidding for government contracts. One reserved seat candidate was rejected because he stood for Congress and most villagers had more faith in the leaders of Ganatantra. In addition, although they had no particular liking for the Ganatantra reserved-seat candidate, they voted for him rather than either of their two fellow villagers because he came from a region where, so they believed, untouchables still knew their place and were not as uppity as those in Bisipara.

The failed Congress candidate from Bisipara, Balunki, became a Congress party organizer and from time to time visited Bhubaneswar. He came to see me at eight o'clock one morning and brought along his successful rival, the sitting MLA. (I discovered later that Balunki's wife was a distant kinswoman of the MLA.) The latter seemed in very good spirits. The meeting was clearly his idea, not Balunki's, who had little to say. We spent about half an hour sitting under the ceiling fan (it was March and already hot at that hour of the morning) while he made jokes about the visits they were going to pay me in London and saying catty things about his colleagues. "That one! Hooked on opium! That's what belonging to Congress does to you!" I asked him about another man, also Ganatantra, who had defected to Congress and received a minor appointment in government. His Oriya was too fast for me, and when I tried to get him to repeat what he had said, he could not at first speak for laughing and finally stumbled out a phrase in English, "political death!"

I did not understand the hilarity. It was apparently still there five days later when I interviewed him. He professed to be afraid of the recording machine. There were no small tape recorders at that time and my wire recorder, although relatively inconspicuous, seldom went unremarked. "Turn that damn thing off!" another man remarked, "and then I can tell you the truth." On this occasion the MLA suggested that I might be a spy or a policeman to own such a thing. But neither that thought nor the machine itself seemed to inhibit him, and he talked quite freely. He seemed excited, his tongue running away with him to an extent that was unusual in formal interviews with MLAs.

He was twenty-eight, he thought. He once had a scholarship, but they cut the stipend in the middle of the course.

> I was not a success as a student. I couldn't study. Then I applied for training in welfare and they sent me to Koraput. But I found I

couldn't do the work well, neither the studying nor the labor. I was getting headaches. Then I made an application to X [a junior minister] to be trained for Village Level Worker. But he tricked me. [I suspect this means he paid a bribe and did not get what he wanted.] Then one teacher in our area did some dirty work and I got his job. Then my health went bad again. I went to hospital for two months. I came home and they made a lot of trouble for me because I was earning nothing. I had lost my job.

I applied to the Depressed Classes League [an organization for untouchables], asking for a job, but they turned me down. So I became an honorary worker for them, and became popular. Then the Kalahandi Raja [the former ruler of Kalahandi] called me and invited me to work for his party [Ganatantra] and said he would help me to be a candidate at election time. I defeated all the others. I am a popular man.

I asked him what Assembly committees he was on. He named three and added:

They don't take me for select committees. I make a lot of criticisms. That's why they don't take me. Officials listen and agree but then they don't do what they say. They just do what the Congress government wants. No government department works well.

Should there be a ceiling on land? [I had asked him.] Yes; there should. That's what All-India Congress says. But what about Orissa Congress? There's a lot of landowners among them. They won't do anything, except maybe a few left-wingers.

He was proud that he had stayed with Ganatantra and resisted inducements to change parties. But the sense of insecurity and inadequacy, and the projective contempt for others, stood out. If other untouchable politicians were like him, I thought at the time, the new order evidently still had a problem with its minorities, reserved seats and headstart-like programs notwithstanding. His surname was typically found in the Gauro (Herdsman) caste, but people in Bisipara said he was unambiguously an untouchable. In the past some Gauro must have consorted with an untouchable woman. They added that Ganatantra publicists had told everyone that the party was passing off a Gauro for an untouchable seat, but no one believed them. Stories like that could hardly have enhanced the MLA's self-respect.

He was the only one of the twenty-six scheduled caste members

with whom I recorded a formal interview. In all I have forty interviews with MLAs, the notes and transcripts ranging from a mere
five hundred words to one, prolonged over several meetings, of
twelve thousand words. I have only two recorded interviews with
scheduled tribe members. Out of fifty-four possible interviewees to
have gleaned only three from the reserved category seems a poor
showing, and it has led me to think about the nature of the contacts
I made with politicians and others during that year. There is something to be learned from it, perhaps, both about the society into
which I was intruding and about the forces controlling that intrusion.

I went to India armed with visiting cards that listed the degrees I
held and the university in Britain that employed me. A person of
consequence, if an official, had his door guarded by a uniformed
peon, who took the card to his master, and in due time one would
be invited into the room. This was the only way I knew to gain ad-
mittance to a senior person without previous introduction. It usually worked because the combination of being a foreigner and an
academic made one a novelty and, moreover, made it clear that the
encounter was not going to be yet another argumentative exchange
over a permit or a license. Even if the official was busy, he would
usually either come out, or admit me for a short time, and suggest
another occasion for a meeting. It was not done to call in the same
way, unknown and unannounced, on officials in their own homes.
Household servants were trained to say *babu nahanti*, which means
"Master's not here."[3]

Sometimes a senior official would have one or more of his juniors
in the room, and would either suspend or quickly conclude whatever business they had been conducting in order to converse with
me. The juniors functioned as an audience, remaining silent unless
invited to comment by the master. More often, if there was a junior
present, he would be dismissed before the official began his conversation with me. But that was not the way with politicians. Their offices were crowded with people, important ones sitting on chairs
and near the boss, lesser people squatting on the floor, further away
from him, some of them engaged in menial tasks (like sorting

---

[3] Except in the offices of senior people (and occasionally their homes) tele-
phones were not generally available at that time.

Babu, used as a noun or a title, is respectful, equivalent to our "gentleman" or
"mister." The mildly derisive Anglo-Indian usage, connoting "half-educated
and pretentious," is not applicable here.

through papers or running out to fetch tea or a chew of betel), none of them talking to each other except in occasional furtive whispers. In the early days I did attempt to make initial contacts through the visiting card and without prior introduction. If the politician had some degree of eminence, there would be a man guarding the entrance to the room, not a peon in a uniform but a hanger-on. I would be invited in and given a chair and the politician would involve me as yet another of the satellites revolving around him, the sun. It was not a matter of joining in *the* conversation because there were multiple conversations, connected systematically by their common focus on the only person in the room whose presence counted. He decided whether to involve the newcomer in an ongoing exchange, or to start a new one. Remembering that superhuman multivocality, I think of Nataraja, the dancing Shiva and his many arms.

For me these occasions were certainly informative, but more on style and custom than on content. The people spoke both in English and in Oriya, switching occasionally even in mid-sentence, which sometimes caused me to lose the content even of the conversation in which I was centrally involved.

Eventually I used the visiting cards only when travelling and paying a courtesy call on senior officials in whatever district I was visiting. In Bhubaneswar I came more and more to rely on go-betweens, people who, prompted or unprompted, were willing to introduce me to someone else. Also, as will become clear, I made my own contacts by hanging around in the Assembly tea room, or the library, or the office of the assistant secretary of the Assembly. The card would still be used when I went to see someone, but he (occasionally she) had been forewarned of my coming. If there were not too many other people present, or if they were of relatively low status, the person of consequence would sometimes allow me to set the agenda, or at least attempt to do so.

Why did they consent to talk? I can only guess, for it never occurred to me to ask directly why they should agree to spend time talking with someone who obviously was in no position to further their careers or the causes they represented, who did not even have a vote, and who, on first being noticed as a regular attendant in the Distinguished Visitors' Gallery of the Assembly, had been labeled in the scuttlebutt as a Russian, probably a communist spy.[4]

[4] At the time this was incomprehensible. Later I recalled the advice given me

Some of them talked reluctantly, and minimally, probably only talking at all because someone whom they respected had asked them to do so. I think that was the case when I interviewed the wife of an ex-ruler (more on him later; his hobby was handcrafting leather). She was a very shy lady. Her husband had consented to the interview, and he was present throughout and answered many of my questions himself. She did volunteer, however, when I asked about committees, that she was on the family planning committee; they both blushed. Such diffidence in a person of that high standing was unusual. Two other women MLAs, both from royal families, sophisticated, educated by tutors, fluent in English, one Congress and the other Ganatantra, were articulate and trenchant and clearly accustomed to speaking their minds. It was a pleasure to watch one of them, during question time in the Assembly, make life uncomfortable for one or other minister.

There were a few who saw me and my recording machine as their avenue into history, one of them taking the trouble to have a clerk type out the main dates in his life story and send it to me afterwards. I invited this biographical format, asking about their background and family and childhood. The tale usually turned into an apologia, a defense of what they had done with their life, the story of their successes and, less often, of their failures. Then I would try to lead them into topics that concerned me in 1959: how elections were won, what contact they had with their constituents, what was their relationship with officials, what development was going on in their constituency, and so forth. The technique serves my present purpose well enough: Even those who used the occasion primarily as an exercise in autobiography could not help but convey, if sometimes indirectly, how they saw the world then, how it had been, and what they would like it to become.

Some—not many—understood precisely what I was trying to do and subordinated their egoism and their personal histories and the deeds of individual heroes and villains to the analysis of social, economic and political forces. They put a slant on what they said, of course; that is inevitable. But they conversed; they did not harangue me as if they were addressing a meeting or talking to the press. Some of them were old men, freedom fighters, schooled in the Gandhian mode of the civilized exchange of views. Others belonged to the small parties of the extreme left, the CPI (communist) and the

---

by a senior colleague in London: "Shave off your beard, dear boy! They'll take you for a communist or, worse, a Muslim."

PSP (socialist). All told, among the forty MLAs I interviewed, persons who entered into a dialogue and displayed a penchant for analysis numbered hardly more than half-a-dozen.

Obviously there is a bias, not in my deliberate selection of a small number of reserved-seat members for interview, but in the sample that actually was interviewed; it was a mere 5 percent of the possible universe, and less than one-tenth of those interviewed. I fell far below the one-third representation that the electoral system achieved. But in fact, although I thought about it from time to time, I never made a serious effort to get proportional representation; to persuade anyone to sit for an hour or more in front of the recording machine was triumph enough. Why, then, did it happen that way? What were the forces that directed me to that particular sample?

I often had occasion to visit the office of the assistant secretary of the Assembly, to ask him questions or to pick up whatever documents were available to the public. One morning I was waiting in his office for him to arrive, when two men came in. I knew their faces from having seen them sitting on the government back benches. One of them, a well-fed man in early middle age, at once introduced himself and began a conversation with me. The other remained standing until urged by his companion to take a chair. Then he sat down. He did not introduce himself, nor did his companion introduce him. He said nothing. The assistant secretary came in and the talkative man at once launched into a brisk, confident, and very businesslike statement to the effect that his companion had been overcharged on his rent and would like a refund. The records were checked and the secretary concurred, and the two MLAs left, but not before the talkative man had suggested to me that he should be interviewed. His companion had remained silent throughout, only nodding his head when the secretary put a question to him.

The silent man was a scheduled caste member from a double constituency. The open-seat member, who shared the constituency with him, was a well-educated former cabinet minister, a lawyer and reputed to be somewhat unapproachable. (I did not manage to interview him.)[5] The talkative man represented a neighboring constituency in the same district, and had come along, as a favor, to explain to the secretary what the other MLA evidently felt incapable of explaining, although it did seem a simple enough matter. A

---

[5] Sometimes, it seems, the relationship was more familiar. I heard one reserved-seat member, an untouchable, referred to as the open-seat member's "coolie."

week or so later I conducted a long recorded interview with the talkative man (some of it is presented below). I had no contact at all with the other man.

What does one conclude? My method of making contact biased me in the direction of the confident and the articulate. Some of them came to me. I was steered to others, because my friends knew they would talk and enjoy talking. The confident and the articulate tended to come from the ranks of those who were relatively well educated and who had been successful in politics or in business or in the professions. In other words, they were not the disadvantaged, mostly not the MLAs who filled the reserved seats.

I do not know why my local MLA volunteered himself. Perhaps he was tired of being ignored by officials and the other politicians and wanted someone of status to listen to him. Perhaps he was just curious, and Balunki's presence allowed him to follow the village custom of having a sponsor when contacting a person of high status. For him, despite his position as an MLA, I was higher, because I was educated and belonged to the former "ruling race" and associated relatively freely with the present rulers. I was uncomfortably aware, even at that time, of my own status and its ambiguities. It was not, as might have been expected, the matter of my belonging to the former ruling race. In 1959 a spirit of Gandhian magnanimity prevailed, and, whatever was going on inside people's minds, I cannot recall a single instance of *overt* hostility on that score. What gave me pause was the assumption—to which, nonetheless, I clung resolutely—that, despite being relatively young (thirty-five), and a junior academic, and a foreigner, I had the right to trespass on the time of people who, in varying degrees, controlled the destinies of more than fourteen million people. I expected to be able to talk with chief ministers. In fact I did, one of them being extraordinarily helpful, the other less so. I imagined an Indian university lecturer, visiting London, and wondered whether he would get the same privileges from Harold Macmillan, and I knew at once that he would not. Why did such people accommodate me? Obviously, there was an imperialist hangover of some sort; I did represent the (ousted) ruling race. Magnanimity is another part of the answer; another is their regard for learning. They were politicians, too, and for them publicity is oxygen; and the more prominent among them were accustomed to giving interviews. An important element, I am sure, was that great respect for social engineering, current at the time, combined with a somewhat vague and surely (as now is painfully obvious) unrealistic notion that my work would in one way or another way contribute to the grand design.

That acceptance from on high, once known, made others more ready to permit my intrusions. I was, so to speak, certified as a person of good will. That sentiment was probably responsible for one of the scheduled tribe MLAs allowing himself to be interviewed. He belonged to the Congress party, and had been introduced to me by the talkative MLA, who, I suspect, put some effort into making the arrangement. The adibasi MLA came half an hour late for the appointment (in the Assembly library) and told me that he had been talking with the other MLA, probably, I guessed, having his doubts brushed aside and his arm twisted.

> I read up to matric[6] and got plucked [failed the exam]. I worked as a forest guard. My eldest sister is married to X [one of the few tribal persons prominent in the Congress party] and he persuaded me to become a Congress social worker. Then I stood in 1957 and was elected.
>
> Our development work is not going as well as I want. There is strong opposition from other parties. They do not cooperate. They sabotage. Here in the Assembly the Jharkhand members vote with Congress. But in the constituencies they work against us. Communists also sabotage our efforts; and there are always delays on the official side.
>
> *Gram panchayat* [local government] works well only in a few places, because there is too much party. Adibasis are simple people, without education, and they believe the party people who come to the constituency and tell them lies about us.
>
> [I asked if people voted according to caste or tribal affiliation.] No; that is not how people vote. Most of us are Santals, anyway.[7] Nor do people vote for party, not much. It's individual; they vote for the person they think will do the work.
>
> Last year we tried to get all the adibasis and scheduled caste members into an all-party group to work for development. But the opposition leaders put a stop to it. We have no organization.

For sure, this was a party line—things go wrong because opposition politicians sabotage them—but I had the impression of a sin-

---

[6] This is the high school examination that qualifies those who pass to proceed to tertiary education.

[7] Santals are a tribal people, most of them living in the Chota Nagpur area of Bihar.

cere man, not entirely wrapped up in his own career and achievements, as so many others were. But, like my local MLA—and despite being in the ruling party—he gave the clear impression of someone who considered himself ineffective and out of his depth.

This was not so in the case of the other scheduled tribe MLA I managed to interview. I talked to him in his constituency, in his own home, on May 23, when the monsoon was beginning to break. The recorder did not work well in humid conditions and on this occasion I did not use it. The following is a selection from notes written after the interview.

A mile off the main road is an adibasi village. There is a wide street which will be a quagmire in a fortnight's time when the rains come properly. The houses are in a straight line and under one continuous thatched roof, the length of the street. The eaves are low and the doors are hardly more than five feet high. At the end of the street is an alleyway which gives into a courtyard, where there is a tall house with a large varnished seven-foot-high door that has chromium-plated handles. In front of the house is a deck and on it, near the door, a telephone. In the corner of the courtyard is a pylon carrying a power line. Everything says "prosperity."

The family are agriculturists and they are prosperous. The area grows sugar cane. He is thirty-four. He was a union organizer in the processing factory. Congress was looking for a strong candidate and he was approached by the chief minister and two other ministers. Reluctantly, he agreed. After his work in the factory the voters thought he must be against Congress, and he did not try to undo that impression. The voters did not like Congress, because they were not getting the development they wanted. He won. His Ganatantra opponent was literate, but not much educated, and had a bad reputation as a spendthrift and a troublemaker. Big men came down to speak for his opponent but only one Congress person of standing came to talk for him; he won the seat on his own, because he had many friends and contacts in the constituency. That was in 1952.

He did not want to stand in the 1957 election, but again he was persuaded. He even had a call from a minister in the Union government in Delhi. He was not really interested in politics. It was all just meddling. If the party would let him he would leave politics and go back full time to agriculture. Until then, he would work for his own area. He was a member of the DCC [District Congress

Committee] but didn't bother to attend their meetings. Congress has no organization in his constituency. What counts is his personal popularity.

[I asked about cooperatives.[8]] He said no one would give up their land to a cooperative. That was just fantasy. Even loan cooperatives don't work because people fiddle the money. People look after themselves. The trouble is they do not understand the principles of cooperation. They think it just another government organization that can be cheated when you get the chance.

The following day I talked with the district Congress organizer. My path to him ran through his brother in Bhubaneswar, not through the MLA. Congress, he said, got a lot of help from the processing factory. When he, as party organizer, needed money locally, that was where he went. But he had to do so through the MLA, because the factory owners trusted him. It was their backing that made him powerful and their money that got him votes. He was lazy and never toured in his constituency. The management of the factory liked him because when there was some trouble five years back he had tricked the union into doing what the management wanted done.

That MLA, by descent certainly adibasi, had clearly moved out of the tribal world into the arena of the political bourgeoisie, where he was evidently a not unskilled competitor. Unlike my local MLA or the former forest guard and social worker, he belonged in actuality, rather than as a token, to Orissa's minor political elite. It was rumored that for the next election the party would set him up for a seat in the Delhi Parliament. To that extent—equality of opportunity—he qualified for the governor's brave new world, although it seems unlikely that the governor's vision was of a person reputedly so self-centered and devious.

Attitudes to Authority

The officials I knew well in Bhubaneswar, young and old, enjoyed complaining, as people do everywhere, and "government" was everybody's target. Complaining was a sport, a conversational interchange, one story of official ineptitude capping another, some-

[8] The 1959 Congress meeting at Nagpur had passed a resolution: "The future agrarian pattern should be that of cooperative joint farming, in which the land shall be pooled for joint cultivation."

thing to laugh about. ("Did you see the report on the number of compost pits dug last Plan period? Put them together and they cover the entire state, including the Chilka lake." The instance is well-chosen, given what goes into a compost pit.) Even though they worked inside the government, officials had bad things to say about it (usually about other departments). Most countries, even those with repressive governments, have a program in their culture that allows the expression of mistrust in the capacities or the honesty of those who wield power. But it seems to me now that, both in that year spent interviewing politicians and civil servants and earlier when I lived with village people, I was listening to a style of griping that was subtly different from that heard in British or American politics. The style indicated a philosophy of government that belonged less with an impersonal bureaucracy—and even less with a democracy in which the people believed they were the rulers—than with the familial style of ruling that I am calling paternalism. It reminded me of troopers grumbling about regimental life.

The griping style had two features. First, the target was government in the abstract, not particular persons but institutions. (When personalities came on the scene the tone changed.) Second, the criticism was relatively bland, frequently humorous, and usually resigned. Along with a stern demand that government live up to its paternal responsibilities would go an indulgent certainty that even if government did set out to fix the problem, "they" would inevitably get it wrong again, anyway. It was a self-contradictory theodicy: The ruler is infallible, but things go wrong and misfortune requires an explanation, blame has to go somewhere, and government comes in handy, even if government is the ruler and therefore infallible. This kind of discourse was not one bit revolutionary. There was no notion that radical institutional change was needed, not even the intermediate step of "throw the rascals out." All that people did was complain that the rascals ought to do their job better. Soldiers grumbled that way about military life. Legitimacy was not anchored in performance; it floated free. It also reminded me very much of the villagers and their identification of the raj (government) as *ma-bap* (mother-father), both parents combined in a single nurturant protective role, owed loyalty, and, even if incompetent, best tolerated because also inevitable—God's design, so to speak.

The attitude of habitual disrespect, almost affectionate and certainly tempered, was well ingrained. Notice its direction; one complained *about* government, not *to* it. This was the way of the villagers too; tales of official idiocy and incompetence were told behind the official's back, not to his face. Complaints were also made directly, but in that case another kind of speaking altogether was employed, using not the vocabulary of ridicule but of a petition, a formal and respectful request for redress. (Again I am reminded of regimental life.) The language of such written documents (or sometimes spoken addresses) could be quite forceful, providing a reminder of duty and legal obligation and thus designed to constrain official addressees with their own official regulations, but always framed as a request. The petitions were not in the mode of bureaucratic impersonality; they went to the official as the *person* who, if he so wished, could set things right. Nor were they in any way like the threatening letter that a lawyer might write; quite the contrary. The tone and form was always that of the supplicant, the person bent to touch the master's feet, speaking upwards, as a respectful child would in the presence of an esteemed parent.

Notice another difference between private grumbling and public petitions. It seems likely that the private grumbling accurately reflected an attitude. It might involve some posturing, but it surely was not entirely a pretense. That was the way people really felt about their rulers. They were somewhat disrespectful, but at the same time they thought of their rulers as the only ones they had. It went without saying that someone had to be in charge, otherwise life would be intolerable. *Disrespect* nicely catches the attitude; *outrage* would be too strong to fit the private grumbling that I heard.

But public petitions were different. They were not couched in common speech, the vernacular, the language of the ordinary people who are the subjects. They were in a form that the rulers had decreed would be acceptable to them. If the petition did not use that form, then it would not be heard. In 1952, on October 2, the day on which India celebrates Gandhi's birthday, I rode in a cavalcade of cars—about five—escorting a cabinet minister on tour to inspect projects appropriately visited on that particular anniversary. My invitation came from the collector (the principal administrator) in whose district the projects were located. One of them was a half-completed village school. The minister made a speech—he made several that day—and as he finished a man of middle age, a villager, somewhat brusquely asked a question. I had been a month in Bisipara and my understanding of Oriya was miniscule. The collector translated for me; the man was asking about the supply of cement and "some bribing." The minister, evidently disconcerted at being questioned at all, turned to one of his retinue, who gave an answer that was not well received. The villager persisted and before long he and the minister and the official were shouting at one another. Eventually a policeman, part of the cavalcade, took the villager away from the meeting. "There is a real grievance," the collector said, as we walked back to the cars, "but he could not be allowed to speak to a minister in that disrespectful way." Speaking one's mind from mighty to humble was culturally acceptable; the other way round was not.

Things unspoken, however, were surely in their minds. The form of a petition did not accurately reflect the common people's sentiments. When a villager addressed a high official as *Huzoor* (The Presence) that did not mean that he felt reverential awe. When the peasant said *ma-bap*, it seems improbable that he felt for the official the veneration and affection that is properly felt for parents. These were manipulative devices, obviously so. Their point was to remind the superior persons of the obligations they had towards those they ruled. Of course the form, even if known to be used with at least some degree of insincerity, did have a clear significance both for the petitioner and the superior person: it was an acknowledgment that power lay undisputably with the superior. Any calculations about the use of power started from that fact as a given, inescapable, unshiftable premise. The king was the king. The game for the underling was not to seize power from the masters, nor to openly contest their right to use it, but to constrain them into using it in a way that would least harm and most benefit the underling.

That political philosophy, paternalism, is caught precisely in the expression the boy used, "Look to government to do the needful." I heard it many times in various forms in the years I spent in Orissa, but always with the same essential meaning. The philosophy of power epitomized in the phrase is that of Hobbes: an orderly society is the first need, and order is constructed and maintained by a Leviathan, an authority that has legitimate power and alone has power. The problem, as every politician and official in Orissa would have been ready to point out, was that rulers sometimes abused power and served their own interests. On this subject the villagers in Bisipara had a clear mythology. They thought very senior officials, like their British predecessors, were not on the take; everyone else, officials, politicians, even their fellow villagers, anyone having access to public funds, habitually cheated.

People I knew in Bhubaneswar, being themselves insiders and often knowing the persons they talked about, were more discriminating and liked to sort out individuals rather than deal in whole categories. But I did several times encounter a generalization about local princes, both from the princes themselves and from their enemies. The opinion was that, although there were some "profligates and fools" among them (people liked to tell the tale of the raja who had trains stopped so that he could abduct pretty girls), rajas as a class, when coming into politics, were more likely to be honest than other politicians. When I asked why, the rajas said that rajas were accustomed to carrying responsibility, had a sense of *noblesse oblige*, and, anyway, that was the way a raja was brought up to behave. Their opponents had a different explanation; rajas tended to be less dishonest, at least around money, because they were already rich.

The Royal Style

Twenty-two out of the 140 members elected to Orissa's 1957 legislature belonged to royal families. Seven were independents, seven Congress, and the remainder Ganatantra. That is how the session began. By 1959, all the seven independents had attached themselves to one or the other party, mainly Ganatantra. The royal MLAs all represented constituencies that more or less coincided with their former kingdoms, and only one royal candidate was defeated on his own territory by a commoner. Former princes, evidently, were successful campaigners.

In fact they did not need to exert themselves. When I interviewed MLAs I asked them about campaigning. Orissa at that time had a very low literacy rate, there were few radios, there was no television, rural constituencies (that is, all but a handful) were large and roads were few and poor. For most people the first occasion to vote had been 1952. No candidate, except in a few areas, could count either on habitual loyalty to the party or on an efficient party machine. But one category of persons did not have this problem: those fortunate enough already to have name recognition. A few of the more distinguished leaders of the Congress movement had this because their efforts in the freedom fight had given them fame, and, in some cases, the kind of contacts that are the product of "nursing" a constituency. The other people whom the voters already knew were the rajas. They—at least the enlightened ones—had been nursing

what now had become their constituencies for years, if not generations.

The nature of this tie between ruler (*raja*) and subject (*praja*) revealed itself in some of the interviews:

> Most kingdoms were small and everyone could get to the ruler.
> Suppose a house burned down. That very day the ruler would
> sanction money for rebuilding and the work began at once. Now it
> takes an age and innumerable steps before you get things done. It
> is the same with court cases. The ruler settled things easily and
> quickly; now there are endless delays.
>
> The people think that by putting their rulers in power they will
> get back the old kind of direct paternal rule. Of course, there is also
> a lot of personal loyalty.

The following is from a defeated Congress candidate:

> The raja was a remote and respected figure before 1948; the rani
> [the raja's wife] was even more remote. He was respected for his
> wealth and his position. But when he stood for election he came
> out and visited the houses and begged the people for their votes.
> The rani—wonder of wonders—did the same. People thought a
> vote a small thing to give, and they sympathized with him for the
> difficulties that must beset his new life to make him come and beg
> from their hands.

Another former ruler, elected (as was the first) on the Congress
ticket, said this:

> As an ex-ruler, even a bad ex-ruler, you still command the affection
> of the people. Some of my people like the Congress; a lot don't.
> They say they'll vote for me as their ruler, but they wouldn't vote
> for any Congress wallah.[9] One of the problems is this absurd delay
> in doing things. A boy comes to me—that is, when I was a ruler—
> and asks for two hundred rupees to pay his fees at Ravenshaw [the
> college in Cuttack out of which Orissa's university grew]. I tell him
> to come to my office in an hour. My accounts officer is two yards

[9] Wallah is an Anglicized form of the Hindi suffix *-wala*. It denotes a person
connected in some way with the noun preceding it. Here it is best glossed as
"chap" or "fellow" and carries with it a small signal of contempt, as with our
"type" or "specimen."

behind me. I get the boy to put his case. Then I tell the accounts officer to look into it and then, if it's good, beat him down to one
hundred rupees. The boy agrees to the one hundred rupees. I tell
the accounts officer to keep the treasury open an extra half hour.
The order is typed and I sign it and the boy gets his money and is
on the bus back to Cuttack that evening and next day pays his fees
and starts the term on time. How long would it take now? About
nine months! I was a minister in the last government. You won't
believe where my accounts officer was! He was in Ranchi, in another state [Bihar], not even in Orissa!

Two of those anecdotes make a virtue of efficient action, decisions
taken rapidly by leaders acting on their own responsibility, not im-
peded by, or, which would be worse, not taking refuge in, or (worse
still) personal profit from, bureaucratic regulations. That sort of person has virtue, in one sense of the Greek word *arete*, which is what
heroes have; they are bold, unafraid, decisive, men of action. The
word refers to prowess on the battlefield, to what once was called
manhood, and it is derived from the name of the god of war, Ares.
The Latin word *virtus* similarly denotes the quality of a man, *vir*.
Arete later came to have, alongside its first meaning, a moral sense,
being applied to a virtuous person, one who behaved according to a
moral code, one who, in other words, was just and honest.
   Both these qualities, courage and fairness, are likely to be claimed
by any leader in any kind of political regime. But paternalism dif-
fers from certain other philosophies, which I will consider later, in
that it makes no regulatory provision for dealing with a defective
ruler, one who lacks virtue. It is left to God or some equivalent *deus
ex machina* to set things right when the ruler goes wrong. Wickedness on the part of the underlings is not a problem; the ruler exists
precisely to correct them and restore order so that ordinary people
can once again trust the system and cooperate with one another. But
in paternalism, as in any principal-agent series that assumes rational self-interest as the prevalent motivation, the top is vacant. There
is no ultimate watchman whose job it is to watch the last watchman.
What this means is that the system can provide a sense of security
only if there is faith, if people believe in it enough to do their duty,
from which it follows that rational self-interest cannot be the only
motivation. Quasi-mechanical externally sanctioned supervision,
which bureaucratic and legal rules provide, must in the end be con-
verted to an internal supervision. In other words the system works

to the extent that it commands moral assent, to the extent that people follow its rules as a matter of conscience.

When the system is in good shape, the ruler and the regime are seen as part of the natural order of things, to oppose which would be not only foolish and self-destructive but also sinful. But even when the system is not in good shape, faith may remain because people can imagine no legitimate alternative. Is this not what led them to vote even for bad rulers? Here is someone who led an agitation against the raja of one of the tributary states:

> The ruler went to England and when he came back his head was turned. No one was allowed to wear a moustache like his. He alone could wear a white dhoti; everyone else had to wear a mud-colored one. Money was extorted for offences done long ago, when they probably weren't offences. For example the ruler's men would demand a permit for the roof timbers of a house built twenty years before, and then fine the owner if he could not produce the paper. Every man between fifteen and thirty had to join the boy scouts and buy two pairs of khaki shorts. Yet, when that same ruler stood for MLA and was opposed by a man who was sincere and educated and had every good quality, they returned the raja with a thumping majority. I have decided people are no good.

That particular raja, when I interviewed him, said that he did not do any campaigning or make any speeches. He added that if he had put his elephant up as candidate the people would have voted it in. Perhaps he was recalling Caligula; he was a somewhat bookish person. He also was the one whose hobby was handcrafting leather, not a recreation that one would expect for a high-caste Hindu, and all the more unexpected since, as raja, he was responsible for the upkeep of temples and for the organization of the main rituals in his kingdom.[10] Dassera, the great autumn festival, brought him back every year from Calcutta, where, for some years after 1948, he had gone to live.

I interviewed him in his quarters. His wife, the MLA on the family planning committee, had the other half of the duplex. He was small and round and very amiable, not at all the ogre one would imagine from his detractor's account. He remarked (correctly) that

---

[10] Leather, the hide of a cow, is polluting and work on it is done only by untouchables.

the leather briefcase I carried was German-made, and he talked about his travels in Europe. The room did not have the monastic bareness of most MLA quarters. The bed was piled with books and reports. There was a filing cabinet. Two or three well-brushed dogs hung around the place.[11] He began by getting out an album of photographs. One of them, taken in the garden of his town residence in Cuttack about the time of the first world war and somewhat faded, showed a line of children seated on deck chairs. He was in the center, about ten years old. He identified one naked infant as the present leader of the opposition (related to him as his mother's brother's son) and another as his wife, the MLA and the sister of the leader of the opposition. The twenty-seven royal houses certainly believed in close breeding. I never met one royal politician who did not have a multitude of royal "cousins" throughout Orissa, both Congress-affiliated and Ganatantra. (They also were quick to mark the boundary. "Him?" another raja's wife said, when I asked about an MLA usually styled *raja*, "No! Not royal, only a zemindar [landlord].")

I went to the chiefs' college—like an English public school, with some military training and education up to about senior Cambridge. Then I went into the service for one year's administrative training. After that I did economics and history for two years at Ravenshaw college and got a degree. Then I returned to my state and worked in all the departments: the prisons, the hospital, the forest, revenue and settlement, and so on. I also went through the ranks of magistrate—third class, district, judge, sessions judge, and so on. That all took two years. I could be trained there because my state was manned by Europeans who had retired from the British services.

[He talked about Congress agitations in his state, saying they were instigated by a disgruntled man whose career he, the raja, had forwarded.] It started in my state because the education level was high. A man from my state stood first in ICS exams. The first lady to write a book was from my state. Perhaps we had highest standard of education anywhere. I had the best boy scout movement. We had a good forest department and a fine police department, one of the best in the province.

---

[11] They were a mark of aristocratic eccentricity. Bhubaneswar's bourgeoisie rarely kept dogs in their houses.

I was the first ruler to sign the merger [of his state into Orissa]. I left my state five days before the merger and lived four years in Calcutta. I went to England in 1951 for some treatment and while there I received telegrams asking me to be a candidate. Both my wife and I sent our nominations but owing to some trickery they were not accepted. Coast Oriyas had come in to run my state and they treated my people like slaves and negroes. There were risings and troubles and that is why Ganatantra came into being.

My wife, who is very sensitive and very emotional, developed the idea that we had left the people to their fate and had run away like cowards. In 1954 she became district president for Ganatantra, and in 1957 we both were elected.

[I asked about the time in Calcutta.] I was coming down every year for some pujas [religious festivals]. Always the Dassera; I still do that every year. I am like a religious chief in the state, although I no longer have administrative powers.

I do things now as MLA that I used to do when I was ruler. I consult with important people in the villages about what should be done. Difference is we never faced these lies and conspiracy and betrayal and treachery and injustice and unfairness. Cheating and giving false promises do not pay; Congress is beginning to find that out. [This was one week after the coalition government was sworn in.]

They need people like us in their administration. There is no discipline. Once an officer learns something [discreditable] about the minister, he does what he likes. I would like to be a minister and put the fear of god in those officials, the way I did in my state. They were terrified of me. One subinspector was discharged from Bonai [a tributary state] and I gave him a job, saying no bribery or oppression. Three months later he was stretching out his hand to take a bribe and did not know I was standing near. When he saw me, he fell senseless and I had to take him for saline injections. It is all this delay that makes people give bribes. In three months I could stamp it out.

Their people knew them, the rulers said, and they knew their people, and the Congress politicians, coming up from the coast, did not. Here is the younger brother of another raja:

We have been for generations the choice of the people. In this state they are nearly all adibasis. We are their religious leaders. Raja starts *nua khia* [first-fruit ceremonies]. At coronation an adibasi is first to bind the turban on the raja. We intermarry with them, sometimes a token marriage, sometimes real. My great grandfather took a Kond woman as his third wife.[12]

In this philosophy the person of the ruler is sacred, not a god in himself, but someone who embodies the orderliness that God has ordained. Leviathan-like, he takes precedence over rules and regulations, since he is their creator. Thus a king is a person and if one can reach the king, things that in the world of impersonal bureaucratic regulations would be impossible might come to pass, as miracles, so to speak. Personal contact is effective, it is believed, and rules are feeble things that by themselves offer no real protection. Kings held *durbars* (audiences or levees) where their subjects could present themselves and make their needs known. In 1959 the more influential politicians, ex-rajas and others too, held durbars of just that kind. They sometimes spoke of this institution as *direct democracy*, because it allowed the common people to have their say.

But the "say" they had was limited. If one "looks to government" and petitions the ruler or presents oneself at his durbar, one does not engage him in debate about first principles. The issue is never one of the eternal verities, such as the structure and values of the society, but practical things that will yield to a solution that is rational exactly because the premises are not in question. A subordinate official has been going in for "bribery or oppression." The harvest is poor and the peasants need a tax remission. A boy needs money to pay his college fees. A house burns down and a new one must be built. Such requests are all framed in a pattern of established rights and duties, and ultimately in a structure of society that is fixed and beyond question. New arrangements are seen as dangerous, perhaps even sinful. The philosophy of look-to-government, as should already be clear, does not cater for radical change, for revolution, a sudden turn in a new direction, not even for debate. On the contrary, both underlings and rulers assume that the main features are permanent; indeed, it is unthinkable that they should not be. A debate, in place of a petition, would be the first step towards revolution.

[12] Cobden-Ramsay's gazetteer has this entry: "[The Raja] must marry a Khond girl. This marriage ceremony is performed by presenting a girl to [the Raja] who immediately returns her to her parents and the tribe by the Khond system of divorce, whereby a fine is paid by the husband to the tribe for divorcing his wife" (1982, 202–3).

This notion of permanence, I realized as I began to work over some of my interview transcripts, had somehow strayed out of its institutional setting into everyday life. Even elected officials confused themselves with the permanency of their office. Politicians in their sixties spoke as if they were just reaching maturity; they seemed to think themselves nonrescindable. Even though the constitutional framework formally challenged the notion of a leader's permanence, as when it required periodic elections or the resignation of a government that lost a vote of confidence, and even though it catered specifically for succession through the concept of a "loyal opposition," the politicians I encountered still seemed to plan for the very long haul and sometimes to assume that their tenure in office would be unlimited. I have notes of a conversation with a sixty-year-old leader who was sketching out his plans for exercising *his* powers over the next twenty years. (He lasted one year more. Much later Mrs. Gandhi's regime put the unfortunate man in prison.) Several others in office talked in the same way, as if time had no stop for them. They knew, of course, that this was not the case and they worked constantly to secure their political base. Nevertheless, there seemed to be an underlying sense that true leadership could not be time-limited. The line that separated the godlike image of Leviathan from the mortal person wearing the mask of Leviathan was easily obscured.

Part of this notion of permanence and stability is derived from the conviction that power begins at the top (with God) and flows only downwards; or should do so. Power from below would be unsettling. Power-downwards is the official doctrine, so to speak, of paternalism; it is what is enacted and celebrated on the front stage. But this doctrine, like any ruling orthodoxy, describes only part of what actually takes place. When one looks at what people in fact do, one perceives, in the shadow of "proper" conduct, a performance that is its inverse. The raj is all-powerful, the doctrine says, because without the raj there is no order, and therefore no existence. The raj is part of the natural order of things, the moral order, *dike* for the Greeks, *dharma* for the Hindus. But in reality a vast part of life is lived outside the raj's confines, and what at first sight appears to be a total despotism is limited because there are many areas that the ruler cannot reach (or chooses not to). In other words, unlike bureaucracy and its iron cage, paternalism does not aim to be exhaustive, all-encompassing, all-anticipating; there is a place for freedom, unpredictability, eccentricity, spontaneity, magic, for a system that is the very opposite of the routinized and closely regulated world that Bhubaneswar NC and its civic design symbolized.

In truth, some of those rajas were, socially speaking, free spirits. I do not know whether it is indeed the case that the Raja of X stole pretty girls off trains. Certainly the leather buff was an eccentric, and so were some others. Most of what I saw seemed harmless enough. "I like dancing," one of them said, "I learned ballroom dancing. It's not sex or anything like that. I just like dancing. I like to dress for it properly, too. I don't drink or smoke, as it happens, because I don't like it. And so I say to them if they want me to give up ballroom dancing, then they can give up their *kathak* [a form of classical Indian dance]." I met another raja, a dyspeptic glutton, staying in a Circuit House (a lodging for judges and high officials on tour but available to other persons deemed suitable). I was with three people, two of them Indians. We dined with the raja. That is to say, we sat at the foot of a very long dining table and ate food provided by the Circuit House cook, while the raja sat at the head of the table and ate the food that the cook he brought with him had prepared. My companions tried to engage him in conversation, but he ignored them. He ate a gargantuan meal, swiftly, seemingly without drawing breath, and on everything he splattered Tabasco, enough to make us wonder when he would spontaneously combust. His final course was a two-layered chocolate-covered cake; that, too, got its Tabasco. He retired, still wordless, to take a siesta in a room adjoining the main hall, and through the door we could hear him groaning and breaking wind, in evident and fitting discomfort.

He was a glutton; as the leather-working raja said, the royal houses had their quota of "profligates and fools." In 1870 W. W. Hunter visited

a fair specimen of the old Hindu Raja—a good deal in the hands of the Brahmans, very proud of his domestic bards and genealogists, but destitute of anything like that sense of responsibility to his people which forms so conspicuous a feature of our English Government. (1872, vol. 2, 120)

Neither profligate, nor perhaps a fool, but, in Hunter's eyes, wanting in the qualities that made for a good ruler. Two other princes he visited were of the sensual repulsive type . . . Before they were five minutes in my presence, they had administered to me an artless concoction of truth and falsehood about their poverty, the devastation of their villages by tigers and wild elephants, the wicked encroachment of neighbouring chiefs, and the ruinous state of their Forts. This monotone of complaint they wailed forth in the whining falsetto of men habitually addicted to narcotic drugs, while their glazed eye and absent manner told the same tale. (1872, vol. 2, 120)

The rajas I encountered in 1959 acknowledged a certain amount of dissipation in a few of their peers but did not see it as part of the royal style. Nor, in their interviews, did any of them make much of the pomp and circumstance of their position. The leather-crafting raja described the leader of the opposition (his cousin and brother-in-law) as a "gentleman," who was firm, but always reasonable, and very hard-working—the qualities that make a good administrator and civil servant. The training that he himself had been given—a stint in every department and on each rung of the judicial ladder—bespeaks bureaucratic responsibility. "We are princes but we are not aristocrats," the man who liked ballroom dancing confided, somewhat confusingly, and added, "We are middle class."

But they were not middle class if that phrase means bourgeois in their outlook. They did not have the mentality that shopkeepers are supposed to have, frugal and penny-pinching like the bania, India's merchant class, avoiding display and extravagance. They enjoyed the fruits of conspicuous expenditure. Hunter also visited the leathercrafting raja's ancestor, possibly his great-grandfather.[13]

The Maharaja soon arrived in state, with sumptuously caparisoned elephants and a gilded umbrella. He is a middle-aged man of courteous and intelligent demeanour, speaks Hindustani fluently, and knows a little Sanskrit. He suited his conversation to the supposed tastes of the British Officer, and talked at great length of the 297 tigers which he had shot during his long and prosperous reign. He wore a fine silk tunic interwoven with gold spots, and had a gold-embroidered hat, shaped like a crown, on his head . . . In the European suite of rooms, which are laid out in halls something like those of a Neapolitan nobleman, I was called on to ad-

---

[13] The visit took place in 1870. The maharaja died in 1877, according to Cobden-Ramsay (1982, 165). His grandson was on the throne in 1910. I am conjecturing that the man I knew, who was born in 1904, was the latter's son.

mire a curious medley of the costliest objects of art mingled with the pettiest gimcracks. The drawing-room tables of white marble and polished fossiliferous slabs were loaded with musical boxes, three or four of which the Maharaja set a-going at once, microscopes with beetles fixed in them, chiming timepieces, wax dolls, massive gold Albert chains, and little stucco sheep with black faces and yellow wool . . . costly engravings, side by side with cheap German prints of nymphs combing their hair on the surface of a lake, and pirouetting *danseuses*. But the object of art on which he chiefly prided himself was a microscopic opera-glass which, when you looked into it, discovered a picture of the Queen with the Prince of Wales climbing on her shoulders, and an infant slumbering in her arms. (1872, vol. 2, 105–6)

Hunter speaks from the heights of effortless superiority in matters of taste. (He did, in fact, much admire the Maharaja—"He spoke with pride of his system of dealing directly with the husbandmen . . . No middleman is allowed to stand between him and the peasant . . . the Maharaja gives a fine interpretation to his position . . . ") Nevertheless the stereotype of display and the reaching for magnificence emerges clearly. That stereotype was still in 1959 available for use in constructing the image of a ruler.

Part of this image was that the ruler should be seen. The ruler was the marker of occasions, the person whose presence signified that what was going on was not everyday work but a dramatic celebration of the natural order of society. The ruler was responsible for the upkeep of the main shrines in his domain and presided over the rituals that marked the Hindu year. These were sacred occasions. They were not necessarily solemn occasions, for the ruler was also the provider of entertainment, of spectacles that impressed and gratified his subjects, giving them the chance to enjoy what they called a *tamasha*. The image of self-effacing ordinariness that Scandinavian royal families now offer to their people was unknown and in a princely state would surely have been thought an oddity and a dereliction of duty.

Politicians in 1959, who had nothing to do with princely states, also worked hard to show themselves in public celebrations. Every third page in a year's run of the *Orissa Review* seems to have photographs of big men on big occasions: Nehru at Jharsuguda; Nehru visiting Rourkela; the President of India laying the foundation stone for Utkal University's new building in Bhubaneswar; the chief minister laying a foundation stone for a college in Angul; the governor's wife opening a bazar; the governor visiting a cement factory; the home minister visiting a temple; the chief minister addressing a medical conference, laying a foundation stone, visiting a school, attending a reception for an All-India Writers' conference; and so forth. Democratic leaders, of course, bear a burden that is not laid on princes: they need votes, a good enough reason to keep themselves in the public eye (especially since, at that time, the media could not give them the publicity they wanted). Nevertheless, vote-getting apart, I believe that, still in 1959, leaders were trying (most of them without much success) to do what the princes had done in their states: in some quasi-mystical way to represent the body politic and be the guardian of its well-being.

The task was difficult because there are some crucial differences between an elected ruler and a prince. The princes often had very distinctive personalities but their legitimacy did not rest on a cult of the individual. The office itself provided all the legitimacy that was needed, for, unlike chief ministerships, cabinet offices, and MLA-ships, it was buttressed by ancient religion and ancient tradition.[14] Second—the matter of votes—the prince was not in regular and institutionalized competition with other princes for the loyalty of his subjects. Third, there were stylistic limits. Politicians in free India were expected *not* to be princely in their demeanor. A master performer in that arena where religion and politics and public relations meet was Gandhi himself, and his style inverted that of the rulers, emphasizing equality and humbleness.

In the tamashas I watched in Orissa in the 1950s, politicians in their public performances seemed to stray to and fro across the line that separated princely display from Gandhian humility. On that same trip to celebrate Gandhi's birthday, we came to a village in a former princely state, selected because it had on hand a project to build a connector road, linking the village with the (dirt) highway that led to the district headquarters. The villagers had arranged a reception that was very much in the princely style. A platform had been built and a pandal erected over it.[15] The digni-

[14] Basham (1963, 19), discussing political ideas in ancient India, writes: "The king, the land, the people, the flora and fauna, and even the weather, were mystically interlinked . . . his private virtues were thought to have an unseen effect on the whole order of nature in the kingdom."

[15] An open-sided construction that sheltered those sitting beneath it from the sun.

taries sat on the platform to watch an entertainment put on by the villagers. Two men, keeping time with small brass cymbals and a pair of sticks, beaten together, danced and, taking turns, sang short satirical verses, making fun of government and of their visitors. I could not follow what they said, but evidently they were on the mark, because my translator, the collector, sitting beside me, collapsed into suppressed laughter. But the senior dignitaries who had come down from Bhubaneswar were not amused and after three or four verses one of them peremptorily ordered the singers to desist.

It was now the turn of the dignitaries to entertain the villagers. This they did by making speeches. I sat at one end of the line of politicians and officials (the minister being in the center) under the shade of the pandal, while everyone on the platform, except me and a member of the (dethroned) local royal family, made a speech. Almost without exception the speakers addressed the twin themes of equality and the new role of the raj as servant of the people. Work on the road, one man said—he was a senior official in the Public Relations Department—was no longer *bheti* (forced labor); it was *shramdan* (the gift of work), the people's gift to themselves, the new raj. The people listened, squatting in the dust before the platform, looking patiently upwards, faces mostly expressionless, cotton shawls across their heads and shoulders, in the full heat of the late morning sun. What they made of being told they were now the raj, I do not know.

After lunch and a sleep, we set off, accompanied by drummers and singers, to inaugurate the road. To build a road you fill baskets with earth from the adjoining field and dump it where the road is to be. The Public Relations official took off his shirt and set to work filling baskets alongside the villagers, for a short time (two or three basketfuls). So did some others of our party, but I do not remember who they were. Village women, themselves working or standing nearby, broke out giggling, each pulling her sari across her face, holding a corner of it between her teeth; they were amused or perhaps embarrassed by the gesture's patent insincerity. I noticed that the collector did not join in the work; nor did the member of the local royal family; nor did the minister himself. My final recollection of that day is the village musicians chasing after the minister's car, demanding more baksheesh. He had already given them some, but evidently not in line with what they considered his status required. He rolled down the car window and tossed out a few more coins.

Whether this was seen as Gandhian frugality or the bania's nig-
gardliness, I do not know.

On that occasion I came to realize how much politicians were
given to verbosity. The princes were not. A prince at his durbar, or
attending Dassera puja, did not have to make speeches to center attention on himself, because there was no one to contest his preeminence. But politicians, everywhere and always, felt that they had
forfeited the occasion if they did not use it to orate. I will come to
that issue, talk that hides reality, in a later chapter.

Rajas, in short, were expected to be extravagant and to show
themselves off. They also were privileged to be eccentric. They
could also be gluttonous, like the guest in the Circuit House, and
people would say it was in the nature of rajas—some of them—to
be uncouth and make pigs of themselves; they were still rajas. Even
their exactions (considered later) were part of the nature of things.
Paradoxically, following their natural instincts made them free.
"Here only the Maharajas are free," an MLA (not royal) told me,
"Every other politician must maintain a spotless private life. Otherwise he goes down."

Similar indulgences were not given to a senior civil servant, because civil servants lived in a world that did not permit exuberance
or tolerate eccentricity. The unpredictable Cuttack again provides
the allegory. Much of it was built before the iron cage of bureaucratic planning descended. Every street in the older parts of the
town had its own wild architectural and functional discontinuities.
A row of shops, substantially built and bespeaking bourgeois prosperity, might give way to cheapjacks' wooden stalls built lean-to
against the ten-foot wall of some raja's half-acre garden and palatial
(if sometimes crumbling) town residence. Buildings often had their
individual mark on them. I recall a shop built on a triangular plot
where the road forked and at the apex, one storey up, was a ledge
on which stood a splendidly carved life-size statue of a heavily
moustached soldier with crossed braces, carrying a musket and
wearing a pith helmet. The statue connected with nothing whatsoever around it, and I never discovered how it came to be there;
someone's folly, I suppose. Nothing like that was to be seen in the
new capital. Its standardized construction iconized bureaucracy;
Cuttack portrayed the unfettered and unpredictable style of the
princes. Paternalism, in short, allows a freedom of expression that
bureaucratic principles inhibit.

The same is true of the lives that its underlings live. Paternalism,

lacking the systematic regulatory apparatus of a proper bureaucracy, has a limited reach. Some of the time the underlings are beyond the master's grasp. Certainly they may be conscripted into his
armies when he can catch them, and they pay him rent if he can get
to the harvest before they have hidden half of it away, and from
time to time their lives are made a disaster by his foolish adventuring into wars that devastate the countryside and open the way to
disease and famine. For sure the generalized portrait of landlordism that the British liked to paint was not that of the contented
peasant. Here, again, is W. W. Hunter:

> If a child of the landholder married, the resident husbandman
> paid [a fee to his landlord]. If a child of the husbandman married,
> the husbandman paid. If a landholder died, the resident husband-
> man paid. If a husbandman [bought land from a Brahman], he
> paid a fine to his landlord. [They] paid the landholder for liberty to
> erect embankments to protect their crops. They paid the land-
> holder for the privilege of attending the festival of Jagannath, to
> drag the car. They paid for a licence to grow sugar-cane . . . in ad-
> dition to the high rent exacted for the requisite quality of land.
> They had to pay the landholder for keeping up the embankments,
> and then they had to give their labor free to do the work. (1872,
> vol. 1, 56–57)

Hunter was writing about the alluvial plain to the south and east of
Bhubaneswar, in Puri district. Whether the peasants were in a state
of seething anger and incipient revolt, as Hunter seems to insinuate
he would have been and they should have been, or whether they
saw these exactions in the same way they saw the floods that every
few years devastated their land, I do not know. The money went to
pay a privileged class that included Brahmans.

> The idea of resuming or interfering with religious grants, struck
> the Maharaja as peculiarly impious. It seemed to him quite natural
> that the land which is the free gift of the gods, should pay some-
> thing towards the worship of the gods. (Hunter 1872, vol. 2, 107)

Perhaps his subjects thought that way; perhaps not. They may well
have done. A righteous anger about "feudal" extortions has been a
continuing part of the rhetoric of twentieth-century reformers, but

there is no way of knowing how those peasant farmers saw the situation. My fall-back strategy, which is to refer to the people of Bisipara, here will not work because Bisipara never knew landlordism of that type and on that scale.

Paternalism does not have, in its back stage, anything that signifies revolution. Agrarian issues, certainly seen by the landowners as revolutionary, did emerge in the freedom fight (and afterwards) but they were part of another rhetoric that I will come to later. Resistance there surely was, but it took the form of evasion and trickery, possible because the underlings in the model of paternalism do not live in a world where the boss tells them how and when to work, as happens in modern industrial countries. Paternal rulers and their regulations do not intrude into every aspect of everyday life. Underlings have their own domain, which is theirs and closed to the masters; closed in part as a matter of defiance, of keeping the rulers at bay, but also because rulers may simply not be interested. In any case rulers often lack the means to interfere. So the common people have a private life from which the state is excluded. They have liberty, in one of its senses.

In its other sense, the right to participate in affairs of state, the underlings have no liberty. They merely watch, and sometimes suffer, but do not engage themselves in the arenas of government where decisions are taken and power is contested. There is, in other words, a very marked division between "us" and "them" as moral categories of the person, which nature—God—has made distinct. An underling trying to do what a ruler does or a ruler recusant of his obligations are equally abominations. Once again, of course, reality contains examples that invert this rule. They exist in the free space where paternalism runs in competition with the two other styles that I will examine, resistance and the world of business, both of which make heroes out of underlings who climb to the top. On the other side, some rajas neglected their duties, especially when they became former rajas. Nevertheless, the theme that people have places and should stay in them was still apparent in 1959, albeit not much invoked in public. It certainly was not a feature of the governor's address quoted at the opening of this book.

Thus there are rulers and there are subjects and the prime directive of paternalism is that subjects must do what they are told to do, even when the ruler is bad. This implies several things. First, subjects must have faith in the system, even at times when their experiences with it are uncomfortable. Second, one reason for having faith is an acceptance of the system as morally right, as part of nature, as God's design. The system logically implies that people in the end are guided by conscience. Third, this is in essence a holistic philosophy, at least at the level at which it locates the source of order. Order depends on people doing their duty and following the rules and not questioning these rules. If they do comply, their social world is safe and predictable and unchanging.

But paternalism also has a quite other face. The effective way to survive is not simply to obey the rules, but to find a patron who will make the rules work properly, or who can bend them if necessary. The system works through persons and personal connections, not only through people following the rules. Furthermore, once one gets beyond the range of the prime directive—that this system is divinely ordained and beyond questioning—there is a large territory where freedom is found, together with tolerance, unpredictability, spontaneity, human weakness and human imperfection, and all those other features that are the negation of strictly holistic principles. Thus paternalism has a side to it that is quite amoral, in the sense that people can do what pleases them, either in unobtrusive defiance of Leviathan, or because Leviathan does not care.

The Officials

When people talked about "looking to government," those who were old enough and who had lived in a princely state might have thought regretfully of the ruler with his finance officer a few yards behind him, and of the speed with which things could be done in those days (if the ruler chose to do them). But half of Orissa's population had been under direct British administration since 1803. In any case, the princes were more than a decade dethroned by 1959. In matters such as an erratic supply of electricity, or the insufficiency of piped water, or the low procurement price of rice (it was bought and sold by government agencies at fixed prices), or the scarcity of firewood in towns, the government "looked to" was in effect the bureaucracy. A complaint might or might not go directly to an official—it could begin as a letter to the newspaper, or a request to an MLA to intervene, or a protest meeting—but any remedial action, even if decided elsewhere, was implemented by an official, a bureaucrat.

The people in Bisipara made a distinction between *raj* and *sircar*, roughly corresponding to our *government* and *administration*. I recall asking a friend how he voted and hearing him say, somewhat shamefacedly, that he voted "for the raj" (which meant the Congress, the party in power at the time of the election) because he was employed by the sircar (he was a schoolmaster). He added that he instructed his wife to vote Ganatantra, as he would have preferred to do, but he did not think it worth risking his job; the ballot might not be as secret as officials said it was. Thus the police and the public works department and the revenue officials and the education department and the civil surgeon and the collector himself, the top of the district pyramid, were all part of the sircar. People in the village also were quite clear in their minds that the MLAs and the ministers of government who came touring were not sircar; they were raj. They also knew that raj took precedence over sircar, but at the same time most of them would have thought it a strange state of affairs if told that the almighty collector was the servant of their MLA and of themselves.

In fact their notions of an official, especially a senior official such as the collector or the superintendent of police, were much closer to paternalism than to our idea of a rational bureaucrat. As I said, the claim that these officers were their servants, servants of the people, made no sense. The officers were servants of the raj, and only the raj could punish them for misconduct. One could petition the raj to get that done, but at the higher levels the process was confusing, because the general idea still was that, where there was no prince, the raj could be nothing other than a higher official. In places like Bisipara, still in 1959, those high officials were *de facto* the raj. Appeals went upwards from the junior to the senior official, and even a judge, if the case got that far, was himself an official, with yet more officials above him. Stated this way, raj and sircar lose their difference and meld into one another. But villagers, I suppose, did not work things out that way and worry themselves about the inconsistency. For most of them, on most occasions, the practical incarnation of the raj was the collector.

Certainly the etiquette of mutual interaction that both parties accepted as right and proper supports that interpretation. The collector's style was regal—not a crown and robes, not a "fine silk tunic interwoven with gold spots," but unquestionably the demeanor of one who ruled as of right and commanded deference as the guarantor of natural justice and good government. I will describe such a person, not an actual man but a composite drawn from several I encountered, presenting the role not as the modal reality but as an ideal type.[16] The senior officials I met in districts, in particular the almighty collector, and in particular when dealing with ordinary villagers, in some cases came quite close to this patriarchal caricature.

Civil-servant patriarchs, with the advent of parliamentary democracy and still more of local government, were a vanishing breed. They no longer were almighty. But, knowing what they had been like, one more readily notices that some of these imperial qualities survived in officials, even when they were offering humble and deferential advice to a minister or politely explaining to an MLA why it was impossible for the administration to do what he wanted done in his constituency. I heard complaints of this kind from politicians, and they talked angrily or despairingly about red tape or bloody-mindedness or arrogance or the unfortunate legacies of imperialism. But in fact the self-willed civil servant was a product not only of India's colonial history and of the feudal sentiments implicit in paternalism, but also of a paradox that inheres in the praxis of bureaucracy anywhere. Officials, if they are any good at the job, do not *follow* the rules; they *interpret* them and therefore, in a sense, make them, and are to that extent their own masters.

Let me begin with the regal collector. I was mildly taken aback, when I was first in India, by what seemed to me the ubiquitous and totally unsubtle manifestation of inequality. It was and still is every tourist's truism that in Third World cities men in sharkskin suits and women loaded with jewelry ride in chauffeur-driven cars past naked and deformed beggars. Coming from a culture that professes to deplore such inhumanity, one experiences a sense of socialist outrage. I was also embarrassed by the way people addressed their servants, speaking to them as if they were things, not people—never a hint of "please." Effortless superiority seemed to be manifested everywhere. I recall a fat old man in a dhoti, a customer in a shop in Cuttack, using exactly the same degrading tone on everyone around him, including me (he wanted to know my business in Cuttack) and including a middle-aged man accompanying him, evidently his son (who spoke in the same imperious way to the shopkeeper). Not all manifestations of hierarchy seemed to me offensive. People greeted senior relatives by touching—sometimes kneeling to place their forehead on—the elder's feet. The habit of

---

[16] An ideal type is a nonsatirical caricature, an abstract of essential qualities.

extreme deference was pervasive and I got used to it. I also ceased to be irritated by the haughtiness, when I realized that deferential servants equally dehumanized their masters. These were masks interacting with masks; underneath—sometimes—there was a human relationship.

The habits of grandeur were prevalent too. One scene has stayed with me for forty years. The collector sits behind his desk, working his way through a large ledger-like book, while one servant squats on the verandah, pulling the rope that runs through a hole high in the wall to swing the punkah (a large fan suspended from the ceiling) and, when the collector hits a bell, a second servant bounds through the door to turn the page in the ledger. I also recall in detail the day the collector dropped in to have us to lunch. We lived, seven miles away from the district headquarters, in a small three-room inspection bungalow, made available by the grace and favor of the same collector. The day before, a man on a bicycle delivered a note saying that the collector would be coming to Bisipara and would like us to join him for lunch. By eight o'clock that morning a bullock cart arrived—they must have left Phulbani about five—and two men unloaded a large marquee and began to set it up behind our bungalow. The cart also brought the collector's cook, who took over the kitchen (a shed detached from the main building) and commandeered our own cook to help him prepare the meal. The bullock cart had also brought folding chairs and a table, and crockery and cutlery and table linen. The collector arrived by jeep mid-morning, held court (regal, not judicial) for the villagers, heard grievances, inspected the school, entertained us (no villagers) to lunch, talked anthropology, and departed in the middle of the afternoon. The tent came down and, as dusk fell, the bullock cart set off for Phulbani.

Grandeur, however, was not the essence of the collector's role. Its central feature was a readiness to accept responsibility and take decisions, qualities that are not universally associated with bureaucrats. In law, of course, the collector was a bureaucrat, with defined and limited responsibilities, bound by the rules and regulations, and answerable to superiors. But the collector also was a generalist coordinating the work of several departments—revenue, law and order, education, public works, and everything else. This coordination was itself directed by regulations and established procedures, but, since it combined so many different activities, it was of its very nature complicated, and likely to need constant interpretation and intervention, as situations not before encountered arose. In other words, the position of a collector had some resemblance to that of a feudal chief, likewise not a specialist, and likewise having the right to interfere in anything that went on in his domain. The difference is that the collector had not only a right, but also a duty, to interfere. A second difference is that the feudal chief was not answerable to anyone above him for what was done within his own domain.

In certain conditions a level of local autonomy—freedom to interpret and therefore remake regulations—is a bureaucratic necessity. The center hands down the rules, which in effect are empty forms into which subordinate officials must fit local content. When that content does not fit, the officials must be empowered to stretch the form. The administrative policies of the British in India even before 1857, when the government formally took over the mandate of the East India Company, make this clear. As new areas in India were annexed, various organizational categories were used—agency areas, non-regulation districts, and so forth—to allow the officer on the spot to use his discretion to remake the rules that came down from the center so that they would be appropriate at the periphery. This tradition survived in areas that no longer were on the frontier, and an ethos of personal responsibility pervaded the Indian Civil Service (ICS). The collector in charge of a district was expected not simply to apply rules and regulations, but to interpret them, making sure that they did not lead to an impasse or disorder, and that the letter of the regulation did not overcome its spirit. The collector, in other words, was not treated as an agent whose work must be closely monitored, but as a principal who could be trusted to behave in accordance with the ethical code of the institution. Appoint the right man and give him a (relatively) free hand; that was the policy.

But this was not a free-for-all. Bureaucracies and diversity are adversaries. As more was known about newly acquired regions, the authorities yielded to bureaucratic imperatives and strove constantly to rationalize and simplify administration by eliminating diversity and establishing uniformity. Moreover, as one moved down the hierarchy, officials were regarded more and more as agents, whose work required close supervision and detailed regulation to make sure that they did not put their own personal interests before those of the service. The results of this—it is a process of degradation—are well known. Initiatives were stifled; change was feared and resisted; and, a great irony, the forest of regulations amplified opportunities for bribery and other forms of corruption. At every lower level those who ran the system were inadvertently empowered to make it work for them, which usually, of course, gave them an incentive to resist change.

The concept of the trusted official, in the case of the lower ranks, was thus monstrously inverted. The idea no longer was to find the right man and trust him to do what is right but, on the contrary, to anticipate every possible contingency and provide a rule for it. In that way, so long as the official could be sufficiently intimidated into never disobeying a rule, there was no longer any need for trust or any room for the notion of conscience. The official had become, in the often-used metaphor, a cog in the machine. Or, an alternative metaphor, bureaucratic administration had become a natural system in which the concept of choice did not apply. No legitimate room was left for individuality, for spontaneity, for deliberately doing something that had not been done before. Nor was there any place for conscience. Of course, perfect standardization is never achieved, not even in highly regimented military or religious formations. But to the extent that standardization is achieved, such organizations are effective at doing whatever it is they are programmed to do, and not at all effective when they must adapt themselves to changed circumstances.

A civil service that is charged with keeping things going as they are is least troubled by this paradox of responsibility. There is a simple pair of linked rules for that situation. Follow the precedent, and if none exists, do nothing. But a bureaucracy expected to implement plans for radical social change cannot follow those rules, for it exactly must depart from precedent. But departures from precedent require the frontier mentality, a readiness to take responsibility and to innovate. If the innovations succeed, the pendulum then swings back. The new procedures have to be made solid and stable and treated as a precedent for future occasions. In this way, even those who strive to bring about radical change are themselves constantly pushed towards uniformity and standardization, towards banishing human unpredictability. The result of that is quite predictable: people grumble and resist.[17] The new capital itself, as an exercise in

---

[17] Faced with this problem, Mao emulated King Canute, who dared the tide to come in against his will. Mao instituted a continuing revolution, with results that were calamitous.

standardized civic architecture, and the people's response to it, alle-
gorizes this process.

I turn now to one consequence of hardening administrative arter-
ies: the emergence of those subaltern freedoms that also character-
ize paternalism.

Subaltern Freedoms

The Bhubaneswar eatery had an air of impermanence, unpredictability, irregularity, casualness, and disorder. It was located at
the city's margin, on the periphery, in unplanned opposition to the
stately structures—the (future) legislative assembly building and
the secretariat—that would mark the center of town. The eatery was
canvas, not brick and stone, and surely not part of the town plan-
ner's blueprint. It was filled with people who came there, certainly
to eat, but also to do things they less easily could do in official
places—gossip, intrigue, do deals, get round the rules, and the like.
In a rather grubby way, when set against the official edifices, the
eatery signified the free spirit, the negation of a routinized life. So
also, in a grander way, did Cuttack.

Of course, people did intrigue in official locations. But there was
a strong sense that getting round the rules should for preference not
be done in an official place where the rules were supposed to be
sacrosanct. A wash of propriety seemed to spill over into the domain of rule breaking and rule bending. I was once stopped by a
policeman for a motoring offence that I was sure I had not committed. It soon became clear that he wanted a bribe. I did not offer one
and the policeman took out a notebook and wrote down my name
and the car's number and then let me go. Later that morning, I happened to meet a friend who was an official, and told him about the
incident. He walked me round to the police station and explained to
the inspector that I was a friend of important people and it was to
be hoped that no more would be heard of the matter. This conversation did not take place in the police station. The official first went inside and brought the inspector out, and we stood in the compound,
well away from the building.

There was an official way to do things, and, under its cover, there
was another way that did not entirely coincide with the official way.
Socialism and implementing the plan, as I have explained, were up
in the front. In the shadows moved the businessmen and the touters

(I will come to them later) following their own devices, but only to the extent that they could work on the blind side of the regulations. As the incident of the policeman should make clear, this coexistence of back and front was not something peculiar to socialism and the planned society, something that appeared only in 1951 when the five-year plans were introduced. Paying respect to a front and doing something quite different behind it is, for sure, a universal mode of behavior. Anywhere and anytime order exists, people live Janus-faced, looking two ways: upwards to what the rules say, and downwards to what in practice can be done. It must be so, inasmuch as rules are general and the situations in which they have to be applied are particular.

The relationship between front and back, moreover, is likely to be dynamic; the front and the back influence each other, often in the mode of positive feedback. The more those in charge think their rules are being evaded, the more severe and detailed they make them. It is a perfect example of expected-utility thinking: the greater the penalty, it is supposed, the greater the incentive not to break a rule. From the other direction, however, the more detailed and constricting the regulations, the narrower their range of application and the more chance they have of being impractical. The result, then, is that either the rules are constructively disobeyed or, if they are obeyed, stagnation and, ultimately, chaos result. The reason for chaos is obvious; the world sometimes moves in ways that no one has foreseen and the rules have to be adapted to new situations. Again we encounter the great paradox of social life. Rules, which ensure order, taken to the extreme will ensure chaos. Rule breaking, which creates disorder, is required if the ultimate chaos is to be avoided.

Certainly people who break rules do not do so to avert "the ultimate chaos." They usually do it because they think it will pay them. Their actions also signal that they see no point in "looking to government," because government is either being obstructive in the matter or is indifferent to their wants.

The Complexity of Paternalism

I am unfolding the varied assumptions that people in Orissa in 1959 made about the conduct of their political life. The structure of the present chapter may suggest that my strategy is to set out the goals presented in the governor's address, and then mark failures to attain them, or sometimes even to seek them. That is not my intention; to do so would be to privilege the official "God frame." Something has to come first, and the governor's statement is conveniently brief, clear, and abstract. It serves as a background to point up values of a different kind. The governor highlights individual dignity, social justice, equality of opportunity, freedom of thought, and various other assorted values that are derived both from liberalism and from socialism. These values, however, are not the measure by which other rhetorics are to be judged good or bad. Rather they stand as one set among others that guide conduct or, perhaps more often, serve as a rhetoric to justify or condemn what is being done or being said.

Some of the terms that the governor used are extremely vague. (One could hardly expect them to be otherwise, given the occasion and the need for grandiloquence.) Consequently, it is not a simple matter to contrast his brave new world—let us call it modernity—with the more or less feudal values of paternalism. For example, the governor speaks of *dignity*, and in my portrayal of how servants are used, it seems clear that in the mode of paternalism their dignity was no one's concern. But that is too easy, because it assumes modernity as the standard; there is no evidence that the servants felt their dignity violated. Dignity means a sense of self-worth, and servants are not precluded from feeling that being a servant is a worthy calling.

Similar problems arise with the concept of *social justice*, which clearly must be relative to whatever rhetoric is active at the time. Consider the implications for the concept of justice (and dignity and equality) of what Hunter saw when taken on a tour of the maharaja's jail.

I found the gang [of prisoners] divided into two sections, each of which had a shed to itself . . . The one shed was monopolized by ten men, whose light complexion declared them to belong to the trading class, and who lolled at great ease and in good clothes in their prison-house. In the other shed were crowded the remaining fifty-nine, packed as closely as sardines, and with no other clothing except a narrow strip around their waist. On expressing my surprise at this lighter treatment, and asking whether the ten gentlemen who took their ease were confined for lighter crimes, the Maharaja explained: "On the contrary, these ten men are the plagues of the state. They consist of fraudulent shopkeepers, who receive stolen goods, and notorious bad characters, who organize robberies. The other fifty-nine are poor Pans and other jungle people, imprisoned for petty theft, or as the tools of the ten prisoners on the other side. *But then the ten are respectable men, and of good caste, while the fifty-nine are mere woodmen;*[18] *and it is only proper to maintain God's distinction of caste.*" (1872, vol. 2, 109. emphasis in original)[19]

The governor speaks of "equality of status" and the "opportunity to become all that anyone is capable of being" and "the eradication of inequalities of every kind." But the testimonies of two out of three of the reserved-seat MLAs make it quite clear that their "equality of status" was no more than a token equality, and that one reason for their sense of inadequacy in the parliamentary arena was the entrenched paternalist assumption that the world is made up of superior people and their inferiors. Recall the use of the contemptuous epithet *coolie*. The same message appears to come no less clearly from the ex-rulers and their equally entrenched assumption of their own natural preeminence. Paternalism, in short, emerges as an implacable contrary to "the eradication of inequalities of every kind."

But so also does the governor's brave new world, once one begins to open the package. "Revitalizing the nation's economy" and "establishing a Welfare State in India" could not be done without a bureaucracy. *Bureaucracy* is not a good word for celebratory rhetoric, and so it does not appear in the governor's speech. But a welfare state and the socialist version of economic growth then envisaged in India necessitate bureaucracy. If bureaucracy is to be effective, inequality is entailed. More than that: if the bureaucrats are committed to innovation, there must be among them persons with *arete*, leaders who, like a raja, do as they see fit, whether or not the rules allow it. In Orissa in 1959, this logical requirement of bureaucratic praxis must have been helped out by the imperfect distinction, in many minds, between the feudal and the bureaucratic modes of government.

The governor also talks of freedoms of "thought, expression, be-

---

[18] The word, I conjecture, does not refer to their occupation but is Hunter's alternative for "jungle people," that is, the unsophisticated.

[19] In 1859 the raja of Banki was in Cuttack jail, serving a life sentence for murder. He "occupies most profitably a whole ward in the jail and has more servants than he needs and deserves in confinement" (De, S. C. 1990, 194).

lief, and faith." At first sight paternalism would negate most of these freedoms, because no one but the ruler—Leviathan—is free in that sense, and all others must express themselves in a manner that will not offend the ruler. Notice that the phrase *freedom of action* does not feature in the governor's list. It cannot do so because the governor speaks from the front of the stage, and, by the nature of the occasion, cannot take account of rhetorics of evasion that might be active at the back. Paternalism does have a backstage rhetoric in which individuals are free to do as they wish, within the limits set by the ruler and sometimes outside them.

Presenting assumptions about the conduct of political life current in 1959 in Orissa is a complicated matter. The front window has a modernity program, which aims to create a society ordered by rationality and intended to "eradicate inequalities of every kind." Behind the front window is another window that contains paternalism's front-stage program based on hierarchy, which is celebrated in showmanship and extravagance; and behind that is a third window in which the freedoms and eccentricities and uncertainties that exist in the back regions of paternalism are visible. Bureaucracy, in practice a hybrid of rationality and paternalism, is more elaborate; it has a front stage of hierarchy and order (the proverbial well-oiled machine), a middle stage where high-up bureaucrats make their own decisions and behave like feudal lords, and a back stage where corruption thrives and the writ of anarchical self-interest runs. Those kinds of freedom are not the governor's; they are usurped, and are not, as in the governor's list, freedoms openly exercised as a matter of right.

Later I will consider how these varied menus were used in practice, and what they had to do with the growing failure of nerve that I think I detected in 1959. The next chapter will describe another set of foundational ideas available at that time: entrepreneurial capitalism or the rhetoric of business. Entrepreneurial capitalism shares some features with the back stages both of paternalism and of bureaucracy, and virtually none with the philosophy of the governor's address.

4

The Rhetoric of Business

Sharp Practice

Not all the maharaja's shopkeepers would have been in jail, and perhaps some among them were not rascals. But an aristocrat's philosophy easily matches *shopkeeper* with *receiver of stolen goods* and other underhand villainies. Notice that nothing bold is imagined in the businessmen's wickedness. They do not face danger, as bandits do; they do not risk their necks; they are merely devious and dishonest. They lack *arete*, being neither brave nor concerned for justice and the common good. Up front at least, aristocracy and trade are mutually repellent, crooks from one point of view, fools or brigands from the other. In the aristocrat's philosophy the spirit of business is the very inverse of public spirit.

Freedom fighters—those on the front stage of India's struggle for independence—mostly had the same idea, inasmuch as many of them were avowed socialists. There had been some dithering earlier, not least because Gandhi had his own idea of what "socialism" should mean, and it did not include centralized planning. Gandhi, in fact, was at an extreme, for he insisted that India's malaise, and the reason why it had succumbed to colonial rule, was the Indian people's avarice, their desire for wealth, and their acceptance of the values of capitalism. At the other extreme there were some, not many, who had a soft spot for capitalism, but they mostly kept quiet about it. The hesitation was formally ended when the 1955 annual meeting of the Congress, held at Avadi, adopted as the party's policy a "socialist pattern of society." The *Second Five-Year Plan*, issued in 1956, has a chapter with that same title, "The Socialist Pattern of

Society," which outlines social goals that are substantially those contained in the governor's 1959 address.

There were reasons for the dithering, other than ideology. India's growing and influential business class had in fact helped bankroll the freedom fight. A few senior politicians were, in principle—including Gandhian principles—uneasy about the directive and centralizing features of socialism. But not many of them made a public issue out of it, nor did the businessmen. The prime minister, Nehru, was turned firmly toward the left, and India set out on its freedom with every public intention of controlling the market and limiting the profit motive to ensure a just distribution of wealth and an allocation of resources according to the needs of a developing economy. The first of India's several five-year plans was issued in 1951. In 1959, any politician who wanted to play the statesman and emphasize that he could rise above personal, parochial, and party interests, spoke earnestly of his desire to "implement the plan."

Nevertheless, as I will show, it was firmly believed in 1959 that private material interests (whether for wealth or for power) all too often displaced moral scruples and a concern for the public good. Gandhi would have agreed. Such pessimistic notions, of course, are found everywhere.

For sure that was the case among the people I knew best, the villagers of Bisipara. They were familiar with sharp practice, being themselves experienced traders. A few poorer ones made a living by hawking rice and various small provisions around neighboring Kond villages. Others carried surplus produce to sell in the weekly markets in Phulbani or Phiringia. Those who could raise capital bought turmeric from Kond growers and sold it to the merchant in Bisipara or to Phulbani middlemen. Everyone knew how to bargain. They also knew how to cheat. They were constantly on the watch against being suckered, or for the chance to sucker someone else. If someone did prosper, they knew he must have been cheating, or had done something else despicable, such as making the folk-Hindu equivalent of our pact with the Devil.[1]

People configured officials in a perfectly patrimonial mode, not as salaried public servants but as owners of a property (the office), able to charge a rent for what they made available. Whether or not one had a right to whatever it was that the official or his minion controlled—a license, a pardon, a pension, an injection in the hospi-

---

[1] This ambience is described in *The Witch-Hunt* (Bailey 1994).

tal, even sometimes a receipt for money paid over—one got it only by paying a fee. Everyone knew that the law forbade bribes, and they grumbled about corrupt clerks and officials, but mostly they were content if the bribe got them what they wanted, and angered only if the official were really corrupt, that is, took the bribe and did not deliver on it.

Bisipara's own Basu Pradhan, a businessman who had advanced to the level of competing for government contracts, the villagers considered part of the system and expert at it. But that expertise did not earn him respect. The reasons are complex. Undoubtedly people were jealous. They would like to have made money that way themselves and, on occasions, they felt that he had stolen what was rightfully theirs. I recall them listening to one of the schoolmasters reading aloud a report issued by the Public Relations Department. It included a list of the monies expended to resurface (with dirt, after the rains) a road that ran near the village. Some of villagers had worked in the labor gang that the contractor (not Basu) recruited, and they were outraged when they compared the total cost of the work with the wages they had received. It was not entirely moral outrage; in truth, they also felt they had been outsmarted.

But something more subtle was going on in the case of Basu. He was a man of the village. He was a Distiller by caste. Distillers in Bisipara have a place in the moral order that made it possible for everyone to live the life that maintained what the maharaja called "God's distinctions." But Basu had violated that order: He had become prosperous beyond the level that was proper for a Distiller. He had defied the community's moral standards and willingly struck out to reach beyond the mark that God had ordained for his sort. The people did not throw him out, of course; they tried to use him, for they were not the kind to forego a possible advantage merely to maintain a principle. But they were not sorry when, as a candidate for the Assembly, he lost his deposit. Basu had marked himself too blatantly as an entrepreneur, someone who put his own interests in front of the public good.

Of course they all did that, when they had a chance. Basu's fault was that he succeeded in the world of new opportunities, and he was a bad person because that new world's morality was different from village morality; it subordinated the community's well-being to the individual's profit. Basu was a businessman. People disliked him because he had proved himself smarter than they were; at the same time they had the luxury of despising him because he was evil and had not stayed in the place that God had determined for Distillers. Given the chance, most of his detractors would have done just what he did.

All businessmen, from the point of view of people who were not in business, were alien in their morality. To work for profit was to take advantage of others and therefore not to work for the public good. This seems to be near enough a universal attitude where business exists, even in cultures that make a fetish out of money-making and free enterprise. People who did make good materially in village India were expected, as old age came on and death approached, to earn themselves spiritual merit by good works. The great philanthropies of America exhibit just the same imagery. Wealth earned through wickedness is spent in charity to expunge the record of evil deeds. The difference is that in traditional Indian reckoning there was nothing heroic or admirable in the act of making money; it was a combination of undeserved luck and double-dealing. Look again at the governor's address; there is not a word in it to suggest that business and businessmen could have any part in creating the perfect society.

Consorting with politicians in 1959, listening to them talk, and reading the Calcutta dailies, I rarely found my attention directed towards businessmen. They existed, of course, even among MLAs, but (with one striking exception) they did not stand out. The left wing's reach-me-down villain was more often the "feudal" landlord than the "capitalist" businessman. There were a few rather shadowy exceptions; for example there was a constant undercurrent of rumor about the baleful influence of mine owners, especially those who were not Oriyas. But, for the most part, the private sector in commerce and industry stayed backstage and the bright lights were directed towards state enterprises. In fact, what people usually complained about was not the influence of big business on public policy but the proclivity of politicians for turning their politics into a money-making enterprise and then pocketing the profits or applying them, illicitly, to winning supporters or buying off opponents.

Politicians and Public Money

An MLA's stipend at that time was two hundred rupees a month. In addition, they received a daily allowance—I think it was twelve rupees—when the house was in session. There was a travel allowance for journeys between Bhubaneswar and their constituency, four annas a mile on public transport, and eight annas for the few who had their own cars.[2] To maintain an office and agents in their constituencies, MLAs had to rely on assistance from the party, which was not always available, especially in the smaller left-wing parties; or they had to shift for themselves.

One can look at the stipend from two directions. The monthly salary of an elementary schoolmaster at that time was thirty rupees; an MLA was paid at almost seven times this rate (and double that when the Assembly was in session). On the other hand, read this comment from one of the wealthier MLAs:

I am not in it for the money, that is certain. I was a minister in the last government, and after paying one hundred rupees to the Assembly party and fifty rupees to the party, and bills for electricity and water and all that, I was getting a clear eight hundred fifty rupees. Who on earth can live on that? I have to entertain. Morarji and Mrs. Gandhi[3] and other people come down and stay with me, and even if they did not, how on earth can one eat in a town like this, any town, on eight hundred fifty rupees a month? I used to bring over one thousand rupees each month from home, just to keep going. What use is two hundred rupees now that I am an ordinary MLA? There are some MLAs that rent out their quarters and themselves live in the servants' room or the garage. To be in politics you have to be a very rich person, or very poor.

I do not know how many MLAs were "very poor" and lived on two hundred rupees and the daily allowance. Certainly there were some, including two of those described in the previous chapter.

"Scratch a politician in Orissa, and most times you find a landlord or a professional person." That was evidently a commonplace, for I heard it from two separate people. It surely was not true of most members who sat for reserved seats, but it was the case for the others, including the two men who said it (one a Communist and

---

[2] A rupee had sixteen annas. The metric system had been adopted at that time but people were still in the habit of dividing a rupee into annas rather than *nua paisa* (one hundred to the rupee).

[3] Morarji Desai was at that time a minister in the Union government. Mrs. Gandhi, Nehru's daughter, was then a member of the Congress Working Committee and the Central Election Committee. I did not ask how often they came to stay with him.

the other towards the left of Congress). The sentence itself is somewhat misleading, because it refers not to the individuals but to their
families, fathers and brothers and other relatives, including those
allied to them through marriage. Certainly few of them were in a
position to "bring over one thousand rupees each month from
home," or felt the need to do so. But neither were they worrying
about where the next meal would come from. When they needed to
raise money, it was not for subsistence or day-to-day household ex-
penditures, but for campaigning or equivalent expenses.

In that arena, money was needed because money certainly
talked. The coverall phrase, "equivalent expenses," indicates that
campaign money did more than buy posters and pay constituency
workers. It was firmly believed that anyone with money, if he used
it skillfully and was matched against someone who did not have
money, was sure to be elected, unless the opponent was a well-
known freedom fighter or a raja.

> Look at . . . ! He stands for different places and he always wins, be-
> cause he can spend money. He boasts he could win any seat. He
> goes there in his airplane, piloting it himself, scatters leaflets,
> lands, and makes a speech. That's how he gets the votes.

The airplane turns out to be a symbol of transience and plays on
deep-set notions both of the untrustworthy stranger and of the per-
fidy that goes with being a success in business:

> . . . has now sat for three seats. [There was a 1946 house elected on
> the old restricted franchise.] He is the party's financier and they
> give him seats where money will work best. The technique is to
> distribute bribes and make big promises. People know he is rich
> and a big man, so he gets elected, but not for the same place twice
> because the promises are not kept. That is no way to run a democ-
> racy. A member should stay put and learn about his constituency
> and what it needs.

How was money used? Certainly some of it was spent in ways
that are legitimate in a parliamentary democracy. Communicating
with voters was expensive. Impressing them or making them feel
good with a tamasha (putting on a show) cost money. Platforms
and pandals had to be built, performers hired, public address systems set up, and so forth. Remember also that the conveniences of
modern mass media—television, radio, mass mailing, a majority of

the electors who are regular newspaper readers—were absent in rural constituencies (where all but 4 percent of the population of Orissa lived). In that situation, the agent or the candidate who had a jeep at his disposal (not to speak of the one man who had his own airplane) started seven leagues ahead of opponents who used a bicycle or their own feet to stump the constituency. (The airplane, of course, wins the blue ribbon.)

Money also was used, people firmly believed, in ways that were not lawful. There was much talk about four annas per vote, but, given the difficulties of communication and the almost total lack of information about where to find the swing vote, it is hard to see how mass bribery on this scale possibly could have worked. Bisipara people had lots of stories about being promised money for votes, but, they said, no one ever delivered, and, in any case, the sensible citizen would have taken the four annas and voted his conscience. They did, however, usually believe that money had been handed over to someone, who, of course, kept it. The parties, they thought, were foolish for wasting money that way.

Romeschandro tells me that Bisipara and all the Konds are solid Ganatantra, because they have faith (*biswas*) in the raja [the Ganatantra leader]. Congress gave [three local men] four or five hundred rupees to buy votes, but they kept the money for themselves. All three of them are shopkeeper-merchants.

There were many stories about "vote banks," a notion prevalent at that time among political analysts. In this image, electors are portrayed as flocks of voting sheep, whose support can be purchased by paying the shepherd. Where the line should be drawn between such a person and a hired constituency worker is not easily determined; no campaigner could afford to ignore people known to have influence among the electors. It was certainly assumed that ideology had nothing to do with political allegiance (with the exception of freedom fighters and rajas, if one counts that kind of loyalty as a form of ideology); the shepherd, the person of influence, put his flock up for sale to the highest bidder. But, once again, the situation can be nuanced. The ordinary cynic, which most people I met were, assumed a direct material personal payment. The person of influence, on the other hand, would talk of material gains in terms of development work in the village—a well, a road, a school, a dispensary—promised by the candidate in return for the vote. Obviously there is no way now, nor was there in 1959, to count up lawful and unlawful acts of persuasion. In any case, as I said earlier, my concern is more with *assumptions* about how the political world worked, than with how it actually did work. To put the point at its mildest, people in Orissa at that time were certainly not in the habit of giving politicians the benefit of the doubt. Here is an extended version of a quotation given earlier:

> Here only the maharajas are free. Every other politician must maintain a spotless private life. Otherwise he goes down. Look how many ministers lost at the next election because people thought they were corrupt.[4]

Here we encounter a paradox. Money talked, people said, let no one doubt it. Corruption was everywhere, they insisted, and it would not have been if it had not been effective. But mostly they liked to tell "biter-bit" stories, occasions when corruption did *not* pay off. Perhaps they had some underlying wish to deny evil its triumph, if only in their fantasies. Perhaps tales of corruption that succeeded had become so hackneyed that they were no longer worth telling.

Stories of this genre begin even before there was universal franchise. Here is one with an Eatanswill flavor, about an election held on a limited franchise in 1936, when, it seems, the rules of electioneering were less strict, or perhaps less strictly enforced.

> I was at a polling station in Cuttack, with some other Congress youths, shouting slogans. The National party (that was the party of rajas and zemindars) used to bring a lorry load of *mahaprasad*[5] from Puri. A voter would be offered some of this and asked to swear that he would vote for the National party. Having sworn, he was given a rupee and offered tea and tiffin.
>
> But we won, so most of them must have taken the money and voted for Congress.

Some of the stories, I suspect, had their beginnings more often in tales than in life and circulated because they were good stories.

---

[4] Of thirteen cabinet members in 1955, two were defeated in the 1957 election. I do not know whether charges of corruption or some other factor—failure to deliver on promises, a stronger opponent, or whatever else—brought them down.

[5] *Prasad* is food offered to the deity and therefore sacred. *Mahaprasad* ("great prasad") in this instance is food that came from Jagannath's temple in Puri.

My agent went to a village and found the [rival party] had promised them ten rupees per vote. So he raised it to fifteen rupees. [These sums are, in the context, astronomical.] This was election day. He said he had sent someone to get enough money from headquarters, and he kept jingling the coins in his pocket. Please wait; the money would soon come. In fact he kept them there until the polls closed. So even if I didn't gain any votes, the other fellow lost them.

The Communists dressed up some of their people in *khadi* [the homespun cotton clothes that were the mark of Congress] and gave them Congress rosettes and sent them around the villages. They sought out the leading Congress person and talked with him in a place where they could be seen. Then, as they left, they let it be known that he had five hundred rupees from the party for distribution. Of course that was a lie. Later, they followed up with their own agents and talked about dishonesty. Sometimes they could break Congress hold on a village.

There also was a rich folklore about the manipulation of candidacies. The 1957 *Report on the Second General Elections in India* contains this paragraph (vol 1, 134):

It has been generally felt that the provision for retirement [from candidacy—permitted up to ten days before polling] also leaves ample scope for abuse inasmuch as more time is available for manoeuvering by a candidate who may be inclined to extract a price from a rival candidate for retiring from the contest. An unfair and unwelcome feature of the matter is that even an honest candidate who has *bonafide* retired from the contest at once becomes subject to a suspicion that he has obtained a consideration for retiring.

Of course these are grey areas, matters of suspicion, as the report says; in fact in Orissa in 1957 out of 646 candidates nominated for the Assembly only nine retired.[6] But the general image of the situation accords well with the conviction that some people entered the political arena solely to make money.

Nowadays I am not engaged in politics. Politics now, as I understand it, is a means of making money. There is no idea of honesty

[6] One hundred twenty-nine nominations were rejected and one seat was uncontested, leaving 507 candidates in the field.

or service or of doing service to the people. The spirit before 1947 is not there any more. The sincere people have left.

Some of the stories are told as tales of straightforward dishonesty, with private gain as the sole and transparent motivation.

That one is an out-and-out touter. He told you he is a social worker and is starting an agitation against liquor sellers? The truth is he just wants a bribe to leave them alone. He was doing the same with the lac dealers, until they started paying him one hundred rupees a month.

The following vignette came from an official, whom I had known in Phulbani. I had asked him: What is a touter?

A touter goes around a village and raises a four-anna subscription and collects—say—fifty rupees. He uses this to put a bribe in the right place and get a grant of, perhaps, five hundred rupees for repairing a well. He then deducts a large amount for traveling and expenses, returns the four-anna subscriptions, and the rest of the money goes God-knows-where but not for the well. Then some unfortunate SDO [subdivisional officer] comes to inspect the well and finds nothing has been done and starts to make a fuss. At once the tout starts a hue and cry that the SDO is oppressing the people, and anonymous postcards are written by the dozen and taken to the village just so they will have its postmark.

Officials, too, were said to be on the take, sometimes in quite complex patterns of leech-on-leech.

The stationmaster used to take twenty-five rupees per truckload [of timber] from the contractor. Otherwise the wagon would be shunted into a siding. Now he has to take fifty rupees because the government anti-corruption squad want twenty rupees.[7]

The timber-dealer in effect was paying a rent to the stationmaster for the right to practice his business. In his turn the stationmaster

[7] The speaker, an official, had a bias against the regime. "When I was a young man, my father-in-law cheated me out of several thousand rupees. He was a respected Congress worker."

paid a rent to the anti-corruption squad, buying himself a license to be corrupt. Perhaps there was another rent-taker above them, most likely a politician. The situation mimics the land-tenure pattern in some parts of Orissa, where rent-receivers were banked one above the other between the cultivator and the state, each proprietor having the right to "taste"or "finger" the land tax and pass it on.

Misuse of the political process for private gain was not confined to humble touters.

> Businessmen like . . . and . . . come into politics because it suits their business interest. They lose nothing when they do, and are not much interested in service. Professional people like myself lose heavily by coming into politics, and there is no legitimate way to make it up. [He had two university degrees, but in fact had spent most of his adult life in politics.]
>
> A lot of enterprises—mining, paper mills—are in private hands. They are permitted to make contributions to parties. That is where Congress gets the money to buy the votes of Jharkhand members. Undercover donations are probably even more. Also police always intervene on the side of management.

A Ganatantra party official, who had been a businessman, placed the initiative with the politicians.

> I did B.A. at Ravenshaw and postgraduate studies in commerce in Calcutta. Then I went into service in [a feudatory state]. Ten years ago I set up a business buying paddy and handloom cloth, but I had a lot of difficulties with Congress politicians. They would not give licenses, and so forth. [He stuck it out until 1955 and then became a full-time administrator for Ganatantra.]
>
> The party in power can bring strong pressure on commercial interests. Any rice mill owner who does not support Congress will not get permits to sell and his business is ruined.

I asked another man, referring to the time of the freedom struggle, if Congress had not always got money from business people.

> Everyone gave, but naturally the rich business people gave more. Now it is those rich people who are controlling the Congress. Lakhs and lakhs of rupees are given by them [a lakh is one hundred thousand]. They say openly that if they give five thousand rupees, it earns a dividend of fifty thousand. It is an investment. If

I, now out of politics, go to ask them for money for my social work, what they give me is a gift. But if Congress goes to them, they give because Congress is in power and in a position to extort.[8]

There also were individuals who did not scruple, it was said, to use high office for private gain.

[A prominent politician] wanted to sell land to a government department for five times its actual worth. [The then chief minister] blocked it. Then he tried again at a lower level, but before the deal was completed the officer concerned was transferred, and his successor restored the value to the market price. Then he was put in charge of the very department and the first thing he arranged was compensation for himself at five times the market value.

[X, a Congress leader who favored socialism] used to say that of course it was necessary for us to take money from the capitalists. Otherwise we could not run a party. But the kind of corruption I am talking about is different.

Other tales, centered on precisely the tactic that the harasser of liquor sellers and lac dealers used, are less sharply defined as wrong, because the extortioner served a political party, not himself.

In each *thana* [the area under the jurisdiction of a police station] three rice procurement agents are licensed. They cannot lose. They put down a security, which is returned to them when they give up the license, and they work on advances from the treasury, and they are allowed a percentage. They increase this by buying fine quality rice as medium, and medium quality as coarse, and then reselling at the higher level. The peasant who has brought the stuff in— maybe ten miles—cannot do much about it. If he argues, the merchant waits. Meantime the peasant has to feed his oxen and himself and that comes out of whatever profit he might have made.

Naturally the agent has to pay something to party funds and to the official in charge to get the license in the first place. Minor parties cannot get money this way, because they are not the govern-

---

[8] Rajagopalachari, sometime Home Minister in the cabinet that governed India between independence and the first general election, wrote some verses (probably around 1952) in which the following appears (Mahtab 1986, 62):
> No congressmen could bear the expense
> Without the help of moneyed friends:
> Help always carries strings held tight.
> Was it for this our long drawn fight?

ment. But they have another method. A communist, for example—they are the experts—goes along and talks with the cheated peasants, and maybe makes a speech or two outside the agent's warehouse, and gets something in the papers. Before long he is getting a visit from the agent's man who says, *babu dakachanti* [The master wants to see you].

In that way the merchant finds himself making contributions to left-wing parties as well.

Public money, predictably, also could be shifted into campaigning.

In 1955 there was a flood. On 6th July there was the breach and government stepped in on 15th. For nine days all relief work was unofficial. One hundred fifty of us students volunteered, standing ready with sandbags. Later we collected seven or eight thousand rupees, buying food and distributing it. We bought it in Cuttack and had some trouble with profiteering. There were other scandals. Some MLAs asked for money for flood relief and then took it to their own constituencies [where, he implies, there had been no floods] to make themselves popular by handing out donations.

So also could the *promise* of public money.

The candidate went around saying that they would know from the results in each voting booth how a village had voted, and if the vote was against Congress, that village would get no grants or development work.[9]

Thus, in a variety of ways, direct and indirect, public money intended to "implement the plan" leaked away in large and small amounts as private gain. Some of that loss was, in the strict sense, private gain, as in the case of the man who made a living by harassing liquor sellers, or the politician who paid himself five times the market value of property he sold to the government. But judgments cannot always be so unequivocal. Much of the money, dubiously extracted from the public purse, trickled back into the democratic process and might be judged a legitimate, if unnecessarily expensive, way of educating the electorate about the political power they now possessed. Certainly these covert levies on public funds en-

---

[9] Returns were published only for constituencies, not polling stations. Knowledge of how the voting went in a particular polling station could only have been hearsay. Systematic exit polls were unknown.

riched the political parties. In doing so they subverted one important democratic ideal, because the money overwhelmingly went to
the party in power, which at that time in Orissa was Congress. The
party in power controlled the administration, which controlled the
allocation of funds for development.[10]

I am presenting assumptions that people made about how development funds were connected with politics and politicians. I certainly do not claim that this pattern was literally and exactly reproduced everywhere. There were honest politicians and honest
administrators. Egregious offenders were sometimes penalized by
the law or by the electorate. Nevertheless, there was a clear notion
that in the political process the public interest came last. This fact,
everyone agreed, was deplorable. But the situation was one of relatives, not absolutes. What was deplorable from one direction was
right and proper from another. There was a neatly regressive pattern of complaint about how funds that properly should go to the
whole were diverted to a part of it. Development funds, which
should be for everyone, might go into the coffers of the Congress
party. If challenged, Congress would say that it best represented the
public interest. Monies, rightfully distributed across the state,
might be diverted to coastal districts. People from the coast would
respond that the state as a whole would benefit because the coastal
region was more productive than the hill region. What should have
gone to my district, my constituency, my village was siphoned

---

[10] Mahtab's memoirs, referring to the government he led between 1957 and
1960, contain this, perhaps disingenuous, comment (1986, 185): "During this period I must record a process of change through which the Congress party was
passing . . . I had long discussion with Sri Ashok Mehta [a former PSP leader
later enrolled in Congress] about financing the Congress party in the elections.
He tried to convince me that because of the policy of socialism the Congress
should not approach rich people for donations, but the Congress government
should intercept certain percentage of the expenditure of the development
plans. He particularly laid stress on the word `interception.' I was surprised to
hear his arguments. [Mahtab then consulted the Home Minister in the Union
government, who did not disavow the policy.] Thereafter I decided not to run
for any provincial election and try to hold any office . . . Huge amount of money
was spent in the elections [1962] and under the leadership of Sri Biju Patnaik
Congress obtained a huge majority in the Orissa legislature."

What to make of this? Mahtab, it seems, saw nothing untoward in rich contributors. That so pragmatic a politician should withdraw from the arena out of
disgust for a practice that he surely knew went on during his own chief minis-
tership, seems unlikely. These ambivalences, by no means Mahtab's alone, will
be examined in the two final chapters.

away, purportedly in the public interest, but actually to benefit some other district, constituency, or village. One thing, however, can be said with certainty: there was a pervasive belief that money and politics together signaled corruption.

Notice how different this assumption is from that of Adam Smith and his invisible hand, or from the Reaganomic version that wealth trickles down to the poor from the well-filled (and deservedly filled) reservoirs of the rich. In Orissa wealth rightfully belonged to the state, not to individuals. There was no notion that entrepreneurs created wealth or made the economy stronger. Quite the reverse; entrepreneurs weakened the economy. Putting in a bribe as an investment to get a greater return, using public money to run a dirty-tricks campaign, cheapening noble causes (anticorruption, antiextortion, antiliquor, and the like) by using them as an excuse for blackmail, were all seen as parasitic activities that impoverished the people, both morally and materially. The politician siphoning money into his pocket or his campaign was siphoning it out of the public treasury, out of funds that might have been used to build a road, or repair a school building, or equip a hospital. That was the assumption. Human nature, it was believed, made people behave in a way that was the perfect inversion of socialist principles and of the philosophy entailed in the governor's address, both of which assume total dedication to the public weal and the prevalence of unimpeded honesty.

Nothing that I recall being said or written in 1959 ever faced, in a realistic manner, the problem of how to pay for democratic institutions in such a way that money ceased to come in through the back door. There were two notions about what should be done, but they were not practical. Hard-liners, like the raja whose crooked minion fainted, believed that public servants could be terrified into being honest. I suppose he thought terror could work on politicians too. Gandhians, on the other hand, spoke of the need for an ethic of service and honesty (as did the left-wing parties, and claimed for themselves a monopoly of such virtues). Whether anything beyond preaching or intimidation could be done, I never heard discussed. Most people were mild pessimists and saw corruption as a hydra-headed monster that could be pruned from time to time by chopping off a head or two; but nothing would ever wipe it out.

In short, the assumption, backstage, was that any sensible government must learn to live with the entrepreneurial spirit, recognizing that most people, most of the time, would put private material interests in front of the public good, if they had the opportunity to do so.

Profit and Preaching

But that assumption, too, must be qualified. It does not mean that everyone acknowledged personal gain to be the only real motivation in politics. Just as hierarchy on the front stage has anarchic individualism backstage, so also "being in it for the money" stands backstage to the ethic of public service, even in the case of businessmen.

Here is one MLA, who had a business background, telling his story. He is the talkative man who helped his scheduled caste colleague sort out the rent problem. The MLA and his brother owned three hundred acres, from which "we are entirely supported." At the time he was "running his forty-second year."

I was a student of chemistry at Waltair in '42 when the Japanese bombarded the coast. I had to give up my studies and return home. I wanted to go to the military and see the world, but my parents would not allow it. I decided I would do something for my people. There were all these weavers and they could not sell their cloth. So I bought from them and sold elsewhere. I was having my share of profit no doubt, and doing a little other business.

Then some poor refugees, Indians from Burma, came to my district and so I asked the collector for money and put them to work building a road. Some forty thousand rupees were involved.

I still have contracts for weavers and the women are involved doing the spinning, as Gandhiji[11] wished. Now we are getting near mechanization [as Gandhi surely would not have wished].

Later I took PWD [Public Works Department] contracts, forming a company, registered class A. I did much in the agency areas, where no one liked to go, building dams and bridges. [He built a dam at Bisipara. By 1952, when I went there, it had already collapsed, disastrously, because, the villagers said, he left the stump of an old mango tree in the ground and so the foundations were not properly consolidated. He did not mention the failure; nor did I.]

---

[11] "ji," or sometimes "jee," is a suffix of respect attached to a proper name.

After '48 I was not succeeding in the contract line. I could not pull on with these PWD people. They want bribes. They want to meddle. They want me to do bad work and then hide it, and when I refuse to squeeze my laborers like that, they expose [frame?] me. They tried to make me pay sales tax twice on some material and I told them that as a matter of principle I could not pull on with them. So I went back to the loom business and stayed with it until I was elected in 1957. The people wanted me. Also my relative is Sri . . . [another MLA].

He had much else to say. He talked about development in his constituency, about schemes for lift irrigation,[12] for starting industries, and for developing a fishing fleet, all of which sounded rather grandiose. He talked of his skill at making contacts, and of the affection his constituents held for him.

I went to a village with some officials. There was some *sankirton* [a devotional performance] and all that going on and they were digging a tank. I took off my shirt and went down with them, and they were thunderstruck and said "You are very big man. You are MLA," and I said, "You are my creators."

He spoke disparagingly of the development bureaucracy, and recounted several cases of corruption. He complained that officials kept their distance from the people. Their servants said, "Why are you coming now? Babu is eating! Babu is sleeping! Come back in three hours! Come back in three days!" Nor did he have much good to say about many of his fellow MLAs. A lot of them were more concerned with their careers than with serving the people and implementing the plan. "There are some who just do not understand why they are here. Majority is of that type." Finally he told me that his mission in life was to preach the Bhagavad Gita, to create love. "All the world is one family," he said, repeating it, like a refrain. Sometimes, he said, he goes to the villages and expounds the Vedas to the people. He liked to quote his version of scripture, for example "No taxation without protection, as Manu says."

Several voices are heard in this text, and they do not all, as I sit back at this distance, seem to accord with one another. But in his person he made them meld—some of them—and when they did not, he seemed to live comfortably with the contradictions. So did

---

[12] An example would be water pumped up through a tube well. The contrast is with canal irrigation, which relies on gravity.

other people. They seemed to accept the notion of equality, as the governor's address and the public-occasion rhetoric of every other politician gave it to them. But hierarchy was there too, much more bred in the bone than was equality, and therefore not needing to be shouted out loud. The talkative MLA (and most of his peers) preached service, endlessly, but it did not take much effort to discern that service to others was often combined with service to oneself.

> In my business as a contractor I was coming into contact with all kinds of people, and I realized their poverty. I thought that in politics I would be better able to do something about their poverty. I would be brought into contact with important people who would be able to do something for them. I could see that things were not being done well, and in politics I could do something about it.

The handloom workers in his region could find no market; he made one for them. The refugees from Burma had no means of support; he organized work for them involving "some forty thousand rupees." But "I was having my share of the profit, no doubt." What kind of man was this? I can imagine a purist Gandhian seeing in him a soul to be saved, almost a touter, hustling for money behind a veil of public service. But did they not all do that? No; some hustled for money, some did not. But all—Gandhi included and despite the rhetoric of humility—hustled for power. Of course they did: having power, they could do good.

> The population is growing fast. Production is not rising at the same rate. I once thought Chinese and Russians had the answer: No opposition allowed. Now I am not sure. I want to get things done. I am sincere. It does not matter who holds power. I am dissatisfied with political life. I get nothing done just now because I have to sit constantly within sound of division bells in case there is another snap vote.

> I have started lift irrigation in my constituency, with motor pumps. Perhaps we can have a second rice crop. At least we will have grass for fodder. Free of charge I have irrigated land, and I have taught people to grow potatoes and now they are getting seven hundred rupees an acre in place of the sixty or seventy rupees they were getting before.

> I also want to develop fisheries. Now I am concentrating on inshore fisheries and hope to get motors for the boats so that they can

spend more time on the fishing grounds. They are very skilled fishermen. I am also going to start deep-sea fishing. I have been to Delhi to see the minister to get a grant for proper trawlers. There is a big internal market. And I can send fish to Japan through an agent in Calcutta.

I also have big contracts for exporting handloom products overseas to Africa.

Big contracts? Trawlers, paid for by the Union Government? Peasants earning ten times on the acre what they earned before he came? Was that all fantasy? I do not know. But for sure that was part of the vision that he and some other people in Orissa had of their future. It is implied in the governor's address. This was, as I have said several times, a brave new world, and the talkative MLA was not the only one who appeared (sometimes) to believe in it.

Was he a socialist? Did he believe in a planned economy? If asked, he surely would have said, like every other good citizen, that he wanted to implement the plan and that, in the end, they all looked to government. The trawlers would be paid for by a government grant or loan; the irrigation that made potato growing possible was not a private venture; nor was the inshore fisheries project. But, whatever he might have said about himself, he was not a socialist. He did not wait for the plans; he anticipated them; and he took advantage of them, including personal advantage (he was having his share of the profit, or intended to do so). I do not think he was a hypocrite. At one level he believed in socialism; at another he believed in free enterprise. He was a fortunate man; he could mix them both (to his own advantage) and never feel himself incapacitated by the contradiction.

He lived with other things that I saw as contradictions but he did not. I could not reconcile the active part of his life with (as I then saw it) the passive. The active part was the businessman, the go-getter, the man who hustled for grants and contracts and looked carefully at the bottom line to see if the venture was a paying one, the man who cut costs on a dam to make sure that he would make a profit—in short, a rational man who adjusted himself to an empirical reality, a man in charge of his own destiny. On the other hand:

For me the only solution is I must meditate to see what is the right thing to do. In 1951 I went to [meditate in] the Himalayas, because I could not see what to do. My mission in life is to preach the Gita,

to create love. Sometimes I go to the villages to preach the Vedas to
the people.

My reaction to this at the time was to mark him down as mildly
schizoid. I had met other Indians like him: they combined severe rationality in their working life with the grossest mysticism. I had
read in the newspapers of ministers in the union government who
never traveled on a plane without first consulting an astrologer
about the risk of dying. Devotion to a guru was not uncommon. I
knew many others, politicians and academics, who were total nonbelievers in anything except the scientific method and what they
saw as normal decency towards other people. But I misjudged
those whom I took to be half-believers; I thought they must live
very confused lives. It was a long time before I realized that the belief in a spiritual imperative indicated neither confusion nor
hypocrisy but stood alongside a belief in paternalism and a belief in
man's essential venality, as another fundamental assumption that
people had about political conduct. That this spiritual imperative
existed was, of course, very obvious. Gandhi was the exemplar.
What I did not realize was how easily it could sit beside beliefs that
I thought incompatible with it (Gandhi thought so too). Implementing the plan, cutting deals, and having one's profit did not rule out
seeking to be at one with the Divinity.

Whether the talkative MLA thought preaching the Vedas was of
intrinsic value, or whether he valued it as something that would en-
dear him to the voters, I cannot say. The individual's mind is impenetrable. But the climate of opinion is not. To dismiss religious
concern for the individual soul as incidental hypocrisy, as I often
did in 1959, was a mistake, because religiosity among politicians
(and others) had a notional reality no less than did paternalism and
venality. People lived comfortably with such incompatibilities, for
the obvious reason that they did not see them as incompatible. I discussed the talkative MLA's strange (to me) combination of entrepreneurial zest and religious mysticism with his brother-in-law.

There is nothing strange in this. Our chief minister [Harekrushna
Mahtab] prays for half an hour every day. Namboodiripad [the
Communist chief minister of Kerala] used astrology to fix date for
taking office. Did you notice [a Communist MLA]'s shaven head?
His father has just died. Spiritual ideas are the motivation for all

other ideas. This is true for every politician I know. Every Hindu who grows up in a family thinks this way.

Later, after I had left Orissa, I came to realize that behind this spiritual imperative lay a foundational philosophy about how the world can be controlled. Celibacy and self-discipline, asceticism, mastery of the passions—*tapas*—creates in the individual a life force that directly influences events in the world. From "experiments in the spiritual field," Gandhi wrote, he derived "such power as I possess for working in the political field." This did not mean setting a good example or being above reproach (one must control oneself before one can control others). Nor did it mean that one works more effectively, when one's conscience is clear. Nor was it a way of talking about sublimated energy. It meant that personal asceticism regulated the course of external events. The ascetic can "compel the environment" (Rudolph and Rudolph 1967, 199). To be spiritual, therefore, was not to be passive; it was to exert control over the real world in a way that was unknown to India's colonial masters.

Perhaps the talkative MLA believed he was doing that; he did not say so. To a nonbeliever such a theory is peculiar, and perhaps that is why none of the people who talked to me in 1959 chose to highlight the link between Gandhian asceticism and events in the real world. (I have more to say about Gandhi's asceticism in the final chapter.)

The Iron-Foundry Man

I had several haunts in the Assembly buildings, besides the chamber itself. One was the office of the civil servant who was the Assembly's assistant secretary, as it happened a descendant of one of those Maratha families that ruled Orissa before 1803. He was very helpful. On one occasion he came to visit me and brought along a friend, who read my horoscope and said that in the future I was likely to write books. The friend turned out to be a plainclothes policeman, ordered to examine my credentials and write a report on my activities. He was somewhat tongue-tied, at a loss how to begin, and the horoscope was their joint reaction to viewing my passport. They began by asking: "Are you perchance knowing the precise hour of your birth?"

Another haunt was the tearoom. The third was the Assembly's library. The library had a single ceiling fan over a huge reading table in the open space between the stacks. The first time I went there I found a dozen or more men sitting around it, some of them with their feet on it, chatting with each other, none reading, some smoking, none of them MLAs, and none looking like country cousins come up to town to confer with their representative. They were the local wide boys, a metropolitan version of the touts described earlier, and sometimes styled that way, disparagingly. I recall the despairing apologies of the librarian about "all sorts of people" finding their way into his library.

I got to know one of them well. He described himself as a businessman.

> To be frank I am trying to do business without having any capital. My main project just now is to make preliminary soundings on behalf of the Russians to let them develop the port of Paradip. I am a relative of [a prominent businessman], but we do not pull on well together. He is a big Cuttack industrialist; he personally finances three or four MLAs to do his business for him in the Assembly. I know MLAs well. Some are politicians, some are businessmen, and some—frankly—are just village touts.

I asked someone else, an MLA, about him, but he did not recognize the name.

> There are many genuine businessmen who come around here from time to time, trying to get things done—grants, permits, licences and things like that. There are also people who hang around trying to see what personal profit they can make. That person must be one of those. This place is so open. Also you have to remember this is not like Delhi. An MLA knows all the important villagers in his constituency and they are coming to see him and everyone can get in.

One day in the tearoom my touter friend introduced me to an MLA-cum-businessman, one seemingly with fewer complexes and less exuberant than the talkative MLA. He was presented as "a big industrialist," a title that at first seemed to embarrass him. For an instant I wondered if the very word was a stigma in the front-stage world of socialism, but that was not so. The probable cause of his embarrassment was the go-between himself. The latter confided to me later that the MLA had engaged his services to help him "start some rolling mills." The MLA said nothing about rolling mills and told me to be careful because the go-between was rumored to be an agent for the Russians and the local communists—"These communists work very hard. They don't lie down." On this first occasion the businessman also seemed, initially, somewhat intimidated by the presence of another MLA, the very ebullient raja who numbered Morarji and Indira Gandhi among his house guests. When the businessman did talk, it was mostly about business and the dead weight of government. It was a diatribe, a trifle incoherent, seeming quite impassioned. This heat, as I discovered later, was out of character. I suspect now it may have been intended to make an impression on the raja.

> I had some friends from Calcutta come down. They wanted to start a business here. They asked to see the secretary [the chief administrative officer] of the [relevant] department but he said he was too busy to talk with them. So I went on their behalf to see the minister in charge of that department, who said that no doubt the secretary was busy, but he would deal with the matter himself. But he did nothing.
>
> Then look at what happens with pilot projects! Government gives ninety percent cost for starting some minor industrial thing. But they never look closely at the experience or qualifications of the person and so more often than not the money is wasted.

The raja was all the time nodding his agreement, and they entered into a gleeful exchange of complaints about measures to set a ceiling on the size of landed estates, agreeing it was all impractical nonsense and, the raja insisted, bad for the people, anyway. They both belonged to the Congress party and I decided I had stumbled upon its right wing. By the end of the conversation they had become quite fraternal, saying how they had long wanted to meet one another. "You must dine with me some time," I heard the raja say.

I interviewed the industrialist about a week later at his MLA quarters. It was nine in the morning and there was a bustle about the place. Two cars were outside, a mechanic working on one of them. (I would be surprised if, rajas excepted, more than a dozen of the 140 MLAs owned a car of their own at that time.) Two of his constituents were squatting on the floor of the room, waiting patiently for his attention. Two other men were there, and received long and detailed instructions about meeting someone. Another man came in to fetch a chair to have its seat recaned. I got the impression of a small-time tycoon. Throughout that year I never ceased to wonder how men of consequence managed to deal with half a dozen entirely unconnected people all in the same room all at the same time. In fact, that was one way of knowing when you were in the presence of a person of consequence. They needed, if not an entourage, at least an audience. One-to-one interaction seemed to make them uneasy. Several people, who chose to be interviewed at my quarters, brought along a couple of hangers-on, who sat there but never spoke during the interview. I soon learned not to involve them; they always deferred to their patron, and he was apt to be miffed if I paid attention to them.

We are three brothers. Eldest lives at home and looks after the land. One is in Calcutta and runs the engineering and iron-mould-ing business. I am here. I am rising forty years old. My father was a small landowner, not big. There is enough land for us to live on. I get best cooperation from brothers. Without them I could not go on.

I did my intermediate degree in commerce at Calcutta and went as apprentice to Martin Burns, six months here, six months there, learned everything. They gave me charge of some labor, and then I left and went to work for government on war disposals. When that department closed I worked as permanent in commerce and sup-ply. I was also having a little business and making money.

I was also doing some underground freedom work during the '42 movement. [I expected him to enlarge on this, but he did not.]

Some friends suggested I stand here in the 1952 election, so I re-signed from government service. I was not in favor of joining any party. In India these parties do nothing but their party politics. But I lost the election. I went back to Calcutta and got a job in USIS [United States Information Service], but I did not like it. So I started the casting and molding business, which is now one of the biggest of its type in India.

In the 1957 election I was persuaded to stand again and I was elected as an independent. People wanted me to stand on the Con-gress ticket. I did not want to be in any party. The Congress candi-date I defeated is my relative.

There were seven of us independents in the Assembly. We de-cided to form a party of independents [!], but it failed because Con-gress began to get hold of the independents and everyone except your friend joined one or the other party. [At that time I had a room in the quarters of the sole remaining independent MLA.]

In 1958 I became a fully fledged member of the Congress party. I could see that there was some malpractice and I could see what sort of men these independents were. So, if that be the case, let me join the Congress, although I am not a party man of any kind. I want to see some government. Let it be XYZ so long as it is government. The other parties could never make a government; that is why I joined Congress.

I do not mind if there is another election. [I interviewed him when the coalition was in the offing, but not yet settled.] I can spend some money and do it properly.

I do not like these opportunist members. One should think of the good of the country. I have not been able to do what I wanted, perhaps because mixing politics and business is a tricky thing. You should not use politics to do your business. Keep them separate. We should not be in it for our own profit. But without a business I would have no money, and to get elected you need money. Having your own money, you are free to do what you think best.

I have a big constituency, two-member. I do a lot of touring. The other member is Congress; I told people to vote against him. Some wrong things were done in the '55 famine relief. There is a committee of inquiry, but there never will be a report from it. But I expect it will scare people off a bit. He is not very active. He has not the courage to fight for what has to be done.

The top leaders in Congress understand me. But some of the old members of Congress dislike people like me who joined later. But I have organized my own support, fifteen or sixteen people who put progress before the interests of the party.

[I asked who represented the left wing in the Congress party.] There may be some who think that way, but they do not come forward. Chief minister [Mahtab] has got them out; they cannot stand against him.

Four features of this discourse should by now be familiar. First, the family of three brothers, although mentioned only once, stands out as the economic unit within which he orders his life. The brothers parcel out the family enterprise—farm, iron works, and politics—among them. Second, money wins elections. Third, when government spends money, that money is often wasted. People are corrupt, and measures against corruption have only a limited effect.

Fourth, there is a clear disdain for the occupant of the reserved seat, an untouchable.

The interview also introduces some partial novelties into the set of assumptions held about how politics were conducted at that time. They become clear in a comparison with the other business-man, the talkative MLA.

The talkative MLA was a large, expansive man, genial, some-thing of a performer, and evidently happy in front of an audience; happy, too, in discoursing on general values and topics that are heart-warming. He took off his shirt and joined the villagers down in the hole where they were digging the tank, and people loved him for it. People loved him anyway, because he was sincere and motivated to serve them and make their life better. He benefited from inverse paranoia, one might say. He had grand schemes to introduce new forms of irrigation, have the government buy deep-sea trawlers, and introduce crops that increased the returns to the grower ten-fold. He thought big, and often, it seemed to me, on the level of wish-list fantasies or campaign promises.

The iron-foundry man was very different. True, like most politi-cians, he professed to have entered the field at the behest of other people. "Some friends" asked him to stand, which suggests a small back room rather than multitudes clamoring in the streets. He toured a lot in his constituency, and while I did not ask him pre-cisely what he did on these tours, my impression is that this was standard constituency-nursing, sorting out people's problems rather than wooing them with grandiloquence and the promise of deep-sea trawlers. He may or may not have been a religious person, but I am sure that on his tours he did not get out of his car and expound the Vedas to his constituents.

There is almost nothing in the interview of the customary guff about serving the people. He came across to me as a political tech-nician, looking on government as a machine designed to produce order and prosperity through a curiously circular process in which ordinary people were parts of the machine and at the same time the consumers of its product. To win an election you did not first have to win their hearts; if you made the appropriate investments, you won the seat, and hearts had nothing to do with it. There was a con-spicuous absence of moral feeling in almost everything that he said, and when he condemned politicians, it was less for wickedness than for foolishness and incompetence. He professed not to care for

ideologies. He wanted a government, any government—"XYZ"—
so long as it worked efficiently.

There was a hint of this when the talkative MLA momentarily reflected on the consequences of having an opposition, and wondered whether things might not be more effectively done, as he
imagined they were in China and Russia, under a one-party system. On that occasion he put the thought behind him, but it was
there, very plainly, in the discourse of the iron foundry man. Without ever talking directly about one-party regimes, he expressed his
dislike of parties. "In India these parties do nothing but their party
politics." Certainly, in 1959, it had become a commonplace in
Orissa that excessive party loyalties stood squarely in the path of
"implementing the plan." Here is another MLA (Congress and not
a businessman):

> One thing you must understand is that opposition here is not like
> the opposition in England. Your opposition is creative: equal par-
> ties, equally based, equally capable. Here the opposition is essen-
> tially negative. There is nothing constructive about them. I have
> talked to them personally. Ganatantra is reaction on the right. It is
> only for political power. Even if they come to power, they
> [Ganatantra and the left wing, PSP and CPI] cannot go on pulling
> together long.

The notion that democracy and efficiency do not sit well together
was often voiced, but, as in the case of the talkative MLA, there was
rarely an unequivocal assertion that democracy should give way.
On occasions it had done so. In the nervous early years following
independence most of the Communists whom I later got to know
(in 1959) had been imprisoned or had gone into hiding. This was
seen by Congress politicians not as abandoning democratic principles, but simply as an emergency measure to prevent democracy
from being destroyed by political chaos. The quotation given above
hints that the fault lies not in the system but in the people running
it. That diagnosis was often made, sometimes with the suggestion
that excesses on the part of the opposition parties, and the conse-
quent heavy-handed reaction from the Congress governments,
were a sign of inexperience and an accident of recent history that
left the Congress so overwhelmingly in power. Given time, the system might stabilize itself.

The iron-foundry man had no interest in long-range speculation about how systems would evolve. One constructed or reconstructed systems; one did not leave them to evolve. Nor was he much interested in what had gone on in the past, even the recent past. His barely concealed instrumentalism with regard to people, and his undemocratic misgivings about the usefulness of opposition parties, together with his entrepreneurial successes, to some extent put him on a margin. Indeed, he made a virtue of being in that position; he could fend for himself. But a close reading of the interview reveals another source of marginality. He had not been, in any noticeable way, a freedom fighter. He made one short reference to "doing some underground freedom work" in 1942, but chose not to elaborate. He also said that he got on well with the leaders of the party he had now joined, and made it clear that he thought them, in particular the chief minister, the kind of realists with whom he could work.[13] He did not get on with some of the "older members" of Congress; presumably they were more ideological. Given his philosophy, it can be deduced that he did not much care.

Neither, I imagine, did he see anything outrageous in the way his political destinies were being worked out, if what is written below is true. I asked another MLA, a charitable, fair-minded man, Gandhian in his demeanor, why he thought the industrialist had given up his independence and joined the ruling party.

> Like everyone else who does that, he needed favors. I do not know exactly what. Maybe he wants to start a business here and needs permits or subsidies. People say there is a big income tax case pending against him—more than two lakhs [two hundred thousand rupees]—and the Congress might help him get his case stopped. Perhaps the case was only started to make him join Congress.

The iron-foundry MLA would without doubt have preferred not to be in trouble with the tax authorities, but, seeing himself as a political entrepreneur, committed to hard bargaining and instrumental realism, he hardly can have been astonished. That was the way the game was played.

---

[13] Chapter and verse for the chief minister's realism will come later.

Pervasive Improbity

Both the raja's disdain for shopkeepers and the governor's address (and, I suppose, the five-year plans) imply an ideal social world in which it is not done to hold out for a price or sell to the highest bidder. Such a world is regulated by notions of service, duty, and the obligations that are attached to status. Interest, advantage, and profit are then aberrations from the moral norm, motivations that should not occur in a well-ordered society. The public interest, the collectivity, is the only legitimate interest and is the measure of what is right and good. A free market, in this philosophy, destroys a fundamental value by inducing people to look to their own private interests.

Yet there was a clear recognition by those I encountered in 1959 that the reality in which they lived had much less to do with morality, as defined above, than with free-market behavior. Venality—the word, which in origin meant putting things up for sale, and now connotes corruption—was all around them. Venality, people assumed, was part of human nature.

But it was deplored and confined to the back stage, the-world-as-it-is, and kept off the front stage, which portrays the should-be world. In this chapter, the spokesman for that front stage has been the man who would launch a fleet of deep-sea trawlers and make seven hundred rupees grow where only seventy grew before. As I described him, I let the spotlight shine on the dam that broke or "I was having my share of the profit, no doubt" and other features that suggest a measure of hypocrisy. Perhaps there was; I do not know what was in his mind. But for sure, what he presents is not the mentality of the raja's shopkeepers, or of the businessman driving hard bargains. He was a visionary. He had an image of the perfect world, in which the deep-sea trawlers stood for unlimited prosperity and the Bhagavad Gita represented moral perfection.

At the same time he was aware not only of the imperfections of the world in which he lived, but also of the reasons why it was imperfect. Party politics took some of the blame because they taught people to concern themselves with narrower interests, while pretending to look to the good of the whole. People, then, are not "sincere," a word in common use at that time to indicate someone concerned for the public good (defined at its widest extent). But party politics were not the root of the problem; the root was a failed morality.[14]

The notion that the solution to Orissa's and India's problems was to identify "good men," and in doing so bypass the party system, was widespread. Here, for example, is a complaint from a feisty Ganatantra MLA, a rani:[15]

> Politics in Orissa are very bad. My husband says party politics cannot be good. Any man will always support his party and then there cannot be justice. People should choose their candidates, and let good people come into politics. Then it would be healthy. But if two rogues stand, then one rogue will be voted in.
>
> This publicity department! So much money is spent just saying what good the government is doing. But doing good is the government's duty. Let the people feel it! Why do they have to spend money telling about it?

I thought at first she had in mind the princes as the natural "good" people and the guardians of morality, but she was thinking on a higher level.

> Also there is not enough religious and moral instruction in our schools. Things can never be good until that is done. One must have faith in God. I say my prayers in my home every day. But what prayers are there in our Assembly? When a person is religious-minded, criticisms are constructive and not just trying to pull down. Guidance—hold my hand and tell me when I am going the wrong way—is better than shouting to other people, "See! Look what he is doing!" But in politics we have to do that. If not, no one hears.

Both the rani and the talkative MLA considered their political world in trouble because people lacked the proper moral feelings. The iron-foundry man, by contrast, blamed a lack of brains and commonsense. Certainly, like the rani, he knew that the right people must be in charge, but the right people were those competent to run the system. The criterion was not devotion to God, or a loving heart, but results—not intentions but achievements. Feelings were a

---

[14] The Gandhian affinities of these sentiments will be considered later.
[15] Her brother was a minister in the Congress government at the time.

secondary matter; in a sense people were secondary too. He was not quite the perfect neoclassical economic man, for he could see further than his own personal profit and, as an engineer, he approved of design and planning and had nothing explicit to say in favor of free markets and free enterprise, as matters of principle. But he did subscribe to the neoclassical economist's notion of the essential non-morality of social systems. So, of course, did all those other people who believed that everyone cheated and everyone looked after themselves. But he was one of the few who saw no point in bemoaning that fact; one lived with it and made the best of it.

The notion that there were no honest politicians, no honest bureaucrats, no one at all in public life, at any level from the village upwards, who would not cheat given the chance to get away with it, was pervasive in Orissa in 1959, but, as I recall, it was not very salient. No major scandals that might have rocked the government or led to resignations or dismissals reached the headlines. Rather, acquisitive self-interest was, as I said, regarded as an unfortunate but quite normal fact of public life. This habit of mistrust has two consequences. First, when people look on their social and political world in that way, they are likely to regard every compromise cynically and think of it as a form of selling out. I will come back to that attitude in the final chapter when I write about Harekrushna Mahtab and his realism.

Second, those who believe that self-interest is active all around them are apt, when presented with instances of honesty and self-sacrifice in public life, to see such qualities as features that really belong to another place or to another age, but hardly at all to theirs. That manner of disenchantment reveals itself in the several narratives about the freedom fight that I will present in the next chapter.

5

The Rhetoric of Struggle

Agitation and Leadership

Two volumes, together containing more than a hundred essays, were published in 1990 to celebrate Cuttack's millennium. Most of the writers (but not all) were in a festive mood, rejoicing in the city's glorious past. A few were unhappy, one in particular (evidently a scion of the Cuttack lobby) who argued that shifting the capital to Bhubaneswar had hurt not only Cuttack but the entire state. The damage that most concerned him was in "the sphere of political leadership." The "creation of charismatic leadership with all-Orissa renown" became impossible after the move; there was a "proliferation of second-class leaders in the body politic." The reason he gives for this decline, and the instances he quotes, are instructive; they exemplify a particular style of thinking about politics that was prevalent in 1959 and still, apparently, survived into 1990.

In 1951 a student from the Engineering school in Cuttack got into a quarrel with the owner of a radio repair shop. This event happened to coincide with the school raising its fees by one rupee. A student agitation followed, a combined protest against the fee hike and the shopman's disrespect; it "destabilized" the Orissa cabinet. Five years later, the agitation over Saraikella and Kharsawan, also led by students, "brought down [the] government."[1] The writer cites these events with evident approval and goes on to say that

---

[1] Dash 1990: in Behera et al. vol. 1, 150–51. Reality was a good deal more complex. For the elections of 1957 Mahtab had replaced Nabakrushna Chaudhuri as the leader of the Orissa Congress. Student rioting probably contributed to the change, but certainly was not its sole cause, as the next chapter will show.

when the government moved to Bhubaneswar, there were no more such happenings. "No such result is seen after Cuttack lost its pre-eminence as there are no common people in Bhubaneswar and those who are there are not interested in such agitations being themselves Government employees. New leaders are not being created and charisma is non-existent."[2]

The components for constructing this image of a political world are simple. There is an authority that is unjust and therefore must be resisted. Legal remedies, if they exist, do not work. Therefore struggle is unavoidable, indeed welcome, because through it are created charismatic leaders. Agitation and disorder make charisma possible, and without them there can be only "second class leaders in the body politic." Bhubaneswar, the writer in effect asserts, has no city mob; therefore it can have no Caesars.[3] This reasoning, which comes from someone described in the list of contributors as an advocate and therefore presumably trained in the law, is at first sight quite bizarre. In fact, it is no more than a somewhat extreme derivative from a rhetoric of struggle habitually used by those who had brought India its independence.

In this chapter I intend to explore several political styles that embrace this rhetoric of struggle. Features that mark each of the different styles will reveal themselves as the narratives unfold.

The Man from Koraput

The first tale perfectly exemplifies the Gandhian ideal of nonviolent resistance; it contains a succinct description of that technique at its well-mannered best. The account is excerpted from a series of wire-recorded conversations with a man who represented a constituency in the district of Koraput in the south of Orissa. He had been a minister in the 1952 Congress government, when Chaudhuri was the chief minister, and was considered an expert on revenue and land tenure issues. People said he was a clever politician, able

[2] Unrest and agitation were a consideration in planning the new capital. In an interview, given almost twenty years later in 1965, the former chief minister, Harekrushna Mahtab, said that they had been reluctant to develop industries in the new capital not only because of dirt and noise, but also because labor troubles might "adversely affect government activity" (Grenell in Seymour 1980, 34).

[3] The argument is weakened somewhat by the fact that a third student agitation, quoted as bringing down a government, took place in 1964, more than a decade after the shift to Bhubaneswar.

to outwit his rivals. But—this was rare—I cannot recall a single comment that branded him as unscrupulous or "insincere," that favorite epithet for putting down a rival. He belonged to a family of Sasan Brahmins, owners of land granted them—he guessed about 1880—by the local ruler in return for "reading *Puranas* in the raja's court." At that time the region was part of Vizagapatam district in the Madras Presidency. In 1936 Koraput became a district in the newly formed province of Orissa.

About the end of March, 1959, during the hot weather, I talked with him in Bhubaneswar. Later, when the rains were beginning, I visited his home in Koraput. Nothing in my notes describes the setting, but I recall a long, low-roofed bungalow, the rooms giving off an enclosed corridor-like verandah at the front. The upper part of the walls, close to the ceiling, were decorated with pictures: some group photographs, several religious paintings, and a poster-like portrait of Gandhi. A youth brought us tea; no one else of the household appeared, although I could hear women's quiet voices somewhere at the back. I did not meet his wife. He had talked about her and about his children when, in Bhubaneswar, he had told me the story of his political life.

It had been raining that day and the ground was wet. He held his dhoti clear of the mud and, as he led the way into a room, put off his wooden sandals. I recall these because he gave me a pair as I was leaving; I had admired them. They are platforms, carved from a single piece of light-colored wood, with an inch-deep ridge running around the edges, like a horseshoe. They are held against one's foot by a single dark teak peg, capped like a mushroom, passed between the toes. He was a Brahmin, and the sandals let him keep his feet out of the wet without polluting his house with leather. For me they were quite impractical; it was like walking on stilts.

I was born in 1910. Due to early marriage, I could not come to college, although I had passed matric in 1929. But I did get a job teaching science—the headmaster wanted me because I was very good at football—and later I got teacher-training qualification. In 1936 I stood on the Congress ticket. It was a zemindari area. There was a lot of extortion by petty officials and the forestry people. People knew nothing about Congress or independence; we made maladministration of the zemindar our ticket. My opponent got about five hundred votes. Congress got four thousand and I was elected. There were sixty people in the Assembly then. It met in Ravenshaw college [in Cuttack]. My first impression was that I was too young to be there. Proceedings were in English and it was not easy for us.

Then war came [1939]. By the wish of Congress we resigned from the Assembly and I came back to my area and for ten months conducted hundreds and hundreds of meetings, explaining what is meant by swaraj [self-government or independence] and making people conscious of their political rights. Gandhiji had selected a list of persons [in the district] to offer personal satyagraha.[4] Biswas Ray was the first; me second; Doctor Sahu third. On three successive days. [This was 1940.] Then others followed.

This is how we did it. First write to the Collector saying what you would do; then publish it in all the newspapers. Police used to come and wait. The satyagrahi goes there with bag and baggage knowing he will go to jail. He stands up and says, "No one is to help the war effort; no one is to give a single penny." Then the police approach and take you to jail. Mr. Wilcox tried my case; nothing to dispute; plead guilty; sentenced to one year's imprisonment or a fine; refuse to pay the fine and go off to prison. I was four or five days in the district jail and then I was taken to the central jail in Berhampur. Others came; forty or fifty Congress members, many MLAs, were in the jail.

In jail we were getting newspapers, books and other things. But somehow I am not good with books, except some of Jawaharlal [Nehru]. But newspapers I always read. At that time I could have successfully quoted 70 percent of the speeches delivered by the Secretary of State for India. Read, reread Gandhi's speeches, Congress speeches. Not much attracted to theory. Only wanted to know certain things, to understand things that would help to deliver speeches, to carry on a debate, to argue.

I stayed in jail from December 1940 to December 1941.

Then the '42 movement came: Quit India. We were arrested August '42 and stayed in jail until near the end of '45. Our movement was to cut down telephone lines; break bridges; not to pay rent [taxes]. Often there was a mêlée. There was firing in two places in my district; a forest guard was killed. About one hundred persons from my district have died altogether. Thirteen persons were sentenced to death and one of them was hanged in Berhampur jail in

---

[4] The literal meaning of this word is "pertinacity in the search for truth." Translated into political action, as on this occasion, it meant nonviolent defiance of government regulations.

1944. We did our best; we helped him to file an appeal. Then there was the Cripps mission and freedom was in sight. All those sentenced to life imprisonment were let out of jail in 1946.

The notes transcribed from talks with this man—what is written above is a fragment—amount to twelve thousand words. No one else was willing to talk at that length. He spoke quietly. He took time to hear and understand my questions. Occasionally he showed emotion but he did not become impassioned. There was no grandstanding. The only segment that came anywhere near bragging occurred when he talked about his mastery of revenue regulations, and even then he played down his own abilities.

In jail Mr. Patnaik and Mr. Pradhan and Naba babu [Nabakrushna Chaudhuri] decided to study the Madras Estates Land Act. Mr Chaudhuri saw us sitting under a banyan tree studying this and he came to us and was pleased and joined us. He is an expert in revenue. He started this Krushak movement, you know, in the nineteen thirties, the peasant movement against the atrocities of zemindars in coastal Orissa. Naba babu used to analyze and amplify and could quote from memory the rules of all the other provinces besides Madras.

Several people had suggested that I should talk with him, and I was introduced to him some time before I had these long conversations. At first I had the impression that he was fighting shy of an interview. Then (I suspect but do not know) I was given a clearance by Nabakrushna Chaudhuri, for whom he had an evident respect and affection. It is obvious to me now, but certainly was not at the time, that quite without intending it, I had become associated with one of the several factions that divided the veterans of the freedom fight. In 1977 I visited Orissa and spent a day with Nabakrushna Chaudhuri and his wife Maloti Devi, both of them old and frail—he was then eighty-two—but gracious and hospitable. I also reencountered the rival leader, Harekrushna Mahtab, and was monumentally snubbed. I will return to this topic later, for it connects with the theme of disenchantment and the babel of political voices.

In that long interview there were a few very discreet references to a falling out between the two Congress leaders in Orissa, so discreet that at the time I did not notice them. I was then much less aware of this dynamic than I have become now, as I read over my notes and put together scattered clues. In 1959 the divide between left and right adhesions within the Congress party was obscured by the huge and obvious chasm between Congress and Ganatantra. Moreover—evidently not listening clearly enough to socialist and communist acquaintances—I unthinkingly assumed a broadly socialist concordance behind the rhetoric of "implement the plan." I did not realize how significant and how longstanding was the three-way policy divergence within Congress: Gandhi's benevolent anarchism, radical left-wing socialism, and, third, that compromise with capitalism which elsewhere has come to be called social democracy.

The Labor Organizer

The second story is that of a socialist MLA. It by no means exemplifies the Gandhian ideal.

My father was head clerk in the collectorate at Balasore, a very powerful position. He was a religious man. A guru used to come to our house and read from the *Puranas*, especially one that tells how after the present age will come the age of religion and there will be no caste system and the ungodly will die. About 1915, when I was three years old, a revolutionary came from Calcutta and was arranging to get arms from the Germans.[5] He was captured and there was a general police search and it was learned that my father had been reading out seditious propaganda (the *Puranas*!) to his clerks and friends. The guru got two years RI [rigorous imprisonment] and my father was dismissed. Then he got a job as assistant manager of the Puri temple. I went to schools at Puri and then to the high school at Balasore.

When I was nine years old I saw Gandhi. When I was fourteen [1926] I met Mahtab who was then chairman of the District Board. I was a boy scout and we used to do good deeds, helping clean out tanks and the like, and Dr. Mahtab took an interest in sanitation work. He also had a press that was producing an Oriya weekly *Prajatantra* and an English weekly called *Adventure*. I had a regular job of selling *Adventure* in the school.

In 1929 the Congress held a provincial conference at Balasore. I volunteered to help. The headmaster, A. S. Ray, an Oxford-returned M.A., forbade participation, and all students withdrew ex-

[5] This incident is described at length in "Exploits of Jatindra Nath Mukherji and his associates in Orissa," Appendix C of Mahtab 1957, vol. 3.

cept me. But my mother died at that time, and the headmaster did not punish me.

In 1930 came the salt campaigns. Students went on strike for three days. Then Gandhi was arrested, and students struck again, and we picketed the school to ensure complete strike. Students were suspended but later allowed back, with some penalties. I had not taken matric but I did not go back. Instead I took charge of one of the salt manufacturing centers. Next year I was arrested for taking part in a no-tax campaign and served four months RI.

Then came the Gandhi-Irwin pact and the movement died down. Congress became a legal organization. Mahtab devoted himself to constructive work in a school where exercises, spinning, and so on were taught. I remained in the active part, making propaganda in the villages, organizing spinning classes, collecting funds, and the like. I helped organize a woman's conference at Balasore, the first of its kind in Orissa. Later there was to be an AICC [All India Congress Committee] open conference at Puri. I worked enrolling members of the reception committee, and setting up an instructor's training camp, training them to march in formation with lathis.

Then came Lord Willingdon [as Viceroy] and Gandhi was arrested, with many others. We organized a big demonstration in Balasore. I was given seven months RI, and went to Patna jail. Since I was under-matric I went as third class prisoner. Dr. Mahtab was there and I joined with him and a group of others studying *Das Kapital.* This was in 1932.

Mahtab, after release, was organizing the school. He and my elder sister's husband persuaded me I should go to Calcutta to continue studies because the school in Balasore would not admit me owing to my political activities. My father was against my going because, he said, Calcutta was a hotbed of politics and I would ignore my studies and become involved. Father was right. I went to work on the labor front, organizing unions between 1934 and 1940.

In 1934 the CSP [Congress Socialist Party] was formed and I joined it the next year. When I recruited people into unions, I also enrolled them in Congress, and we had a solid voting block when it came to Congress provincial elections. We had violent clashes with factory owners. We also had clashes with communists. Then in 1939 there was a clash between Gandhi and Bose and we all supported Bose, but only in Bengal. The rest of the CSP were with

Gandhi. I was in jail several times and then returned to Balasore, where I had charge of training volunteers for individual satya-graha.

I was arrested on August 9, 1942, and remained a security pris-oner until July 1945. Violence outside the jail was directed by Jay Prakash Narayan [a leading member of the socialist wing of Con-gress] and other CSP persons. Inside the jail the movement was condemned as non-Gandhian by orthodox Congress supporters, including Nabakrushna Chaudhuri, who by that time had become Gandhian rather than socialist. Young CSP people in the jail sup-ported the movement, arguing that the violence was against prop-erty, not against persons. There were also communist people in jail, trying to recruit from Congress members. I organized classes there to stop the communist influence.[6]

In one part of the interview he briefly described being beaten up by the police. He also referred to casualties in the '42 movement—a police station burned, villages declaring independence, and more than forty people killed. But many of the violent encounters that he had experienced were not directly with the government (or with factory owners), but with communists on the labor front or within Congress itself. These were clashes that, from the point of view of "orthodox" Congress people (as he called them), were peripheral to the freedom fight, internal dissensions to be deplored, both because they depleted the energies of the freedom movement and because they violated the Gandhian philosophy of nonviolence.

An Oriya Patriot

Another fault line in the Orissa freedom movement becomes ap-parent in the third tale, which is told by the one MLA who, in 1959, held on to his status as an independent.

In 1930, when Gandhi wanted people to join the salt campaign, I was eighteen and I joined the national movement, giving up my studies. I had not yet done my matriculation. In 1931 I was let out of jail and I joined the National School, which was started by Dr. Mahtab at Balasore. It was called a university, although there was

---

[6] In 1939 Nabakrushna Chaudhuri had dissolved the Orissa branch of the CSP because it was being "exploited by the Communist elements" (Mahtab 1959, 34).

actually no arrangement for studies as people study in colleges. The humanities were being taught; and politics and economics. We were molding our lives according to the ideals set by Gandhi. We did our own cooking and cleaning and there was spinning. There were twelve of us. It ran for less than a year. Then, after a round table conference, Gandhiji came back and the movement started again, and again I was in jail. When I came out I did some work with Harijans, but I was not very active in Congress until 1941 when individual satyagraha started and again I went to jail.

In 1931 I had some difference with Congress. A movement [Utkal Sammilani] had started long before for uniting all the Oriya-speaking areas into a separate province. The Orissa Congress announced that this was a device of the British to divert attention of Indians from national freedom. They boycotted a committee which met at Puri to work for Oriya unity. But I went to Midnapur to try to get support of Oriya-speakers there for Orissa unity. I did not resign from Congress, but I did not work actively again until later.

He continued to shape his life "according to the ideals set by Gandhi," and was respected by politicians and others both for his integrity and for his devotion to Orissa and its culture. No one feared him. He had neither the ordinary bully's nor Gandhi's capacity to intimidate.

The Man from Singhbhum

I have no visual recollection of the man who is the subject of this fourth narrative. My notes say that I interviewed him at the end of April, and also had a talk with his younger brother. Rereading the narrative, I am surprised that I have forgotten him, for, by his own account, he had led a colorful and even adventurous life. I also heard some quite harsh comments about him from others, who had been active in politics at that time.

I was born in 1920 in a town in the Oriya-speaking part of Singhbhum district [in Bihar] and I went to school there up to the eleventh grade. Saraikella and Kharsawan are in Singhbhum. I got interested in politics at the age of ten, in the Non-Cooperation days, also Swadeshi movement, picketing liquor shops, and so forth. They had started an Oriya high school in the town and Utkal Sammilani [the Oriya Union movement] once met there. The headmaster was a leading political person from Cuttack.

My father is a landowner. We are Brahmins and the land was given to our family for service of the raja. My father is an important man. Leading Oriyas used to stay at our house. Our house was a political center. All types of leaders were coming; Utkal Sammilani and Orissa Congress as well. I was always seeing politics; that is why I came into politics.

We are seven brothers. We have never known poverty or hardship. In those days foreign education was difficult, but one of my brothers even went to England and got Ph.D. We live in separate messes [households] now, but we have not divided the property. I am strong, but whoever is weaker gets assistance so that his status remains equal. Some cultivate, some are in business, and two brothers are in government service. There is money to educate any child in the family who is worth it.

I was an average student, not stupid, but I never worked hard. I always had a leaning to avoid certificates because there was a movement at that time to reject degrees and certificates. But my parents forced me to stay at school, although I sometimes played truant, organizing meetings and leading this public life. At sixteen I left school. By then I was an active politician. I used to address public meetings and everything. I was never just a worker. From the beginning I was a leader. About '38 I took charge of the whole district as secretary and then as president. But even when secretary I was in control and picked the president. I was dictator in my district, appointed by Gandhi, but having strong leaning towards Subhas Bose and the leftist side.

In '39 [in fact 1940] came individual satyagraha and I courted imprisonment and got one year. I had a good study period in Hazaribagh jail, where there were seven or eight hundred political prisoners. We had political classes. I was going with the Forward Bloc and the anticompromise people.

After one year I was released and went back to my district. Then came '42 movement and I was a confirmed Forward Blocist. We were believing in sabotage and I was entrusted to arrange it in the coastal districts of Orissa. I made sure that our active workers did not court imprisonment, and I went around as a supervisor among the coolies, seeing that aerodrome work [the Americans were building an airfield near Bhubaneswar] was badly done and so forth. I was an associate of the right hand man of Sub-has Bose.

We were three comrades and I got some hint of arrest. Two were caught, but I escaped. I got my brother's English-made clothes and walked into Cuttack railway station and away right under the noses of the CID men [Criminal Investigation Department] who were hanging around the station. I went off to the Tributary States area—to Bonai and places like that. Then they made a raid on us si-multaneously. Subhas Bose's right-hand man was hiding in my brother's house. Everywhere a simultaneous raid, and I was the only one who could escape. Then, on the run, I became the victim of blackwater fever. I thought I was going to die and came home. That was '44 or '45 and the movement had subsided. The police had pity on my condition and did not execute the warrant.

I stood in the '46 elections. In spite of having been the Congress leader in that district I was defeated, because the district was in Bihar and I am Oriya. The Bihari Congress people worked openly against me. But I was not discouraged by defeat. I worked harder, every day organizing the peasant movement against landlords and the prajamandal movement against the rulers of the [tributary] states. I was also organizing the bidi laborers.[7]

I took the prajamandal movement into Saraikella and Kharsawan. It was one of the best-organized movements and Kharsawan [the raja] fled away to Delhi. We were completely nonviolent but every-day we held a demonstration. We went there from our area and the local people joined in. Trainloads of people used to come to the meetings. Then the Kharsawan raja imposed Regulation 144 on me, forbidding me to enter his state and hold public meetings.

So I went to Saraikella. I found them demoralized. I went to the town itself and got myself arrested. Processions of people came from outside villages and I walked seven miles to prison, refusing to ride in a car. Thousands of people followed me on that journey; there was a congregation of twenty-five hundred people. There was hartal.[8] I planned that my people would break open the jail.

---

[7] The prajamandals (lit. subjects' circles or meetings) were the equivalent in the tributary states of the national movement in the British administered dis-tricts.

A bidi is a country cigarette made from uncured tobacco wrapped in the leaf of the kendu tree (ebony, diospyros melanoxylon).

[8] The word hartal means, literally, locking of shops. It is an organized form of protest usually against government. It can also be an act of mourning. An im-portant Gandhian element in the construct, making it different from a strike, is the emphasis on sacrifice or self-inflicted suffering.

My brother took over the leadership. Maloti Devi [the wife of Nabakrushna Chaudhuri] came and addressed a crowd of one hundred thousand people and then the ruler knew the strength of the people and released me. I was in jail for two months. Shortly after I was released the tributary states were merged [January 1, 1948].

Then this Bihar-Orissa controversy came on again. It was a miserable time for me. They [the Bihar authorities] arrested my brother as a communist. They arrested me although I was then secretary of the PCC [Provincial Congress Committee]. It was my father's reputation; they thought we were the Oriya movement in that district. The local Congress people were combining with the ex-rajas and other parties in Bihar to make disturbances and try to prove that Orissa could not keep order in the two states. It was very unfortunate. People were tortured and put in jail. I was kept in jail as an ordinary prisoner[9] and was very sick at the time. Then Patel [the Union Home Minister and a power in the Congress party] intervened, and I was released and externed from the district. I was planning to violate the order, but the Orissa leaders persuaded me to keep quiet, for reasons of health.

[He went for three years to Delhi as a member of the Constituent Assembly. He returned in 1952 and was elected to the Orissa Assembly from a seat in Sambalpur district.]

Sambalpur was very difficult. Congressmen there had either resigned or joined the opposition because of land loss from Hirakud dam. I was associated with labor in that district—Orient Paper Mills and Ranpur Colliery, where I was president of the [Congress affiliated] INTUC union. I had good hold on the INTUC union in those days. Practically my whole agency and all my workers were from that area. In battalions and battalions they were moving about. They have assisted me like anything.

From '52 to '57 I was chief whip, and again after the election. I was Naba babu's man [Nabakrushna Chaudhuri, then chief minister]. Later, when Dr. Mahtab returned as chief minister [1956], I was a much misunderstood man. Mahtab did not use me to find out what members are thinking, which is one of the main tasks of a chief whip. I had gone against his return from

[9] I assume this means that he did not have the privileges and comforts granted to "first-class" (political) prisoners by the British. Class A prisoners had access to books and newspapers. In addition they did "not take food from the general kitchen. They were given rations . . . and attendants to help them . . . their jail-life was not so hard" (Mahtab 1959, 58).

Delhi, because I thought his return would not benefit the party in the coming election. But I had nothing personal against him. But he must have known what I had done. He did not consult me. He had his own channels. That was the time of misunderstandings.

Before then, in those 1956 troubles [about Saraikella and Kharsawan], Naba babu was depending on me and my advice. During the Commission's visit [the States Reorganization Commission] I had gone to Saraikella and Kharsawan to organize a demonstration. The Commission's decision dejected me. Our leaders had hoped we would get justice and they were very depressed. We tendered our resignation and Naba babu had gone to Delhi with the letter of resignation. Then Dhebar came down from Delhi and apologized, all this, all that. We are disciplined Congressmen. We had the alternative of leaving Congress or abiding by the decision. When we did not resign we were much misunderstood by our countrymen [sc. Oriyas]. It did us much harm in the election the next year. Our opponents made much of the Orissa Congress bowing down over this. I did not suffer personally because I had made a great personal contribution to the movement and my family had been concerned in it for a long time. But in Dr. Mahtab's own constituency an unknown man polled well. An unknown fellow against the universal leader of the district [Balasore] and whole Orissa!

I was a disciplined man and obeyed Congress, but I do say that a great injustice has been done to our Orissa.

The tale winds its way through youthful adventure and glorious achievement to an anticlimax of disciplined obedience and diminished power. It is an allegory of disenchantment: freedom caged. There is an irony, too, in the admiration for Subhas Chandra Bose and the Forward Bloc, for Bose too had found himself (on one occasion) disempowered by party discipline.

Bose, a Bengali, was born in 1897 in Cuttack, where he went to school. His father was a member of the Cuttack Bar. Bose attended a college in Calcutta, from which he was expelled for defying the authorities. He was later enrolled in another Calcutta college and earned a degree. His family sent him to England, where he studied for admission to the Indian Civil Service. He passed the exam, was admitted, but then resigned and returned to India, where, about 1920, he joined Congress. In the years that followed he was in and out of detention. In 1928 he worked with Nehru to launch the Socialist Independence for India League. He spent some time exiled in Europe, where he met and developed an admiration for Hitler and for the Italian dictatorship. He returned in 1936. In 1938 he was elected Congress president.

Almost from the beginning of his political career Bose advocated violence and found himself in conflict with the movement's moral leader, Gandhi. He stood for reelection to the presidentship, defying Gandhi's wishes that he yield to another candidate (of Gandhi's choosing), and narrowly won. This was counted a breach of party discipline, and Bose found himself boycotted by his senior colleagues. He unleashed his tongue, saying Congress leaders ran a dictatorship, like Hitler's, and called for demonstrations against them. They suspended him from membership for three years, but invited him back when the war broke out in September 1939. In May of 1939 he had formed his own Forward Bloc party in Bengal and did not return to the Gandhian fold.

Bose and other Forward Bloc members were arrested in 1940, charged with sedition, and imprisoned. Imitating Gandhi, he announced that he would starve himself to death. The authorities released him from prison but placed him under house arrest. He escaped, in disguise, and made his way to Afghanistan, from there to Moscow (Russia was still Hitler's ally), and then to Berlin. He set up Indian-language broadcasts from Germany and helped the Germans recruit into their army an Indian Legion of soldiers captured in north Africa, styling himself *Neta* (the equivalent of *Führer*). In 1943 German and Japanese submarines took him to Tokyo, where he proclaimed himself leader of the provisional government of Free India and took over command of the INA (Indian National Army), which had been recruited from Indian prisoners of war to fight alongside the Japanese against British and British-Indian regiments in Burma. In 1945 the Japanese and the INA surrendered. Bose escaped in a Japanese plane and not long afterward died of the burns he suffered in a crash landing on Formosa.

In the public discourse of politicians in Orissa in 1959 the strategy of violent resistance was not disavowed by everyone (I will come to that later), but it came a bad second to Gandhian nonviolence. No one had much to say about the bitter contest Bose had with Gandhi in 1938 and 1939. No one spoke of his ruthlessness, of his stated ambition to be India's dictator, of his inept military leadership, or of his vastly inflated self-esteem.[10] Indeed, in the decade that followed his death, his image had been blurred and sanitized by association with Gandhi and Nehru, as one of the three national heroes of the freedom fight. Much the most common picture, in homes and shops, was what irreverent persons I knew in Bhubaneswar called "the Holy Trinity." This was a triple portrait, brightly colored, Gandhi center, Nehru on his right, and Bose on his left. I saw versions in which haloes hovered over their heads.

But Bose was certainly not recalled in the tale above (and the one that follows) in the image of a saint. Nor did the speakers see themselves in that manner. Their version of the rhetoric of struggle is that of Bose: a disdain for compromise, an admiration for swift and ruthless action, for the kind of courage that verges on foolhardiness, which is aggressive, which is not dismayed by violence, and, at the same time, which can forward itself by cunning and deceit, capacities anathema to Gandhi. For this last quality an icon is the stratagem used by the hero above, and by the one whose story is about to be told: Like Bose, they saved themselves by putting on a disguise. Gandhi, to my knowledge, never appeared as anything but himself.

The Man from Talcher

The teller of the next tale did not pass himself off as a middle-class man in a London-made suit, but put on a sari and pretended to be a woman. Talking to him, looking at his corporation, robustly middle-aged in his politician's uniform of homespun cotton shirt and dhoti, and balding under his Gandhi cap, I found it hard to imagine.

In the second week of March 1959 I was working in the Assembly library and had gone to fetch a book from the stacks. When I returned to the table where my notes lay, I found a man sitting there, talking to the librarian. I was introduced. "I am very glad to meet you," the man said, "and I am happy that you are watching our proceedings with such interest. I hold two ministries; I am Minister of Tribal and Rural Welfare and I am Minister of Commerce." Then he launched, unstoppably, into a lecture, not much on commerce but a great deal on his other responsibility: tribal population figures, number of special schools for tribals, the meals served there,

---

[10] These judgments are derived from a book about Bose (Toye 1962), which is in the main sympathetic toward him.

the medical arrangements, the syllabus, his wish to preserve tribal cultures (configured mainly as song and dance), his intention to provide useful vocational training (such as spinning and agriculture), and the need to make scholarships available to those who had an aptitude for academic learning. I twice wanted to wedge in a question, but he had the air of one who might lose his place, if stopped, and forget what came next.

Fortunately, when, later, he came to talk about himself and about political issues in general, there was none of this public-relations-prepared-handout manner. He turned out to be a natural storyteller. He also was a confirmed monologuist, liking to have the floor to himself and liking to talk about himself. More directly than most others I interviewed, he presented me with a detailed and extended *apologia pro vita sua.* I listened to him for nearly five hours, one evening in June. From time to time other visitors came into the room, wanting his attention, but he would not be interrupted and shooed them away, saying that I was a world-famous historian, who had come to write about Orissa.

I was born in village Poipal in Talcher State in what is now Dhenkanal district in the year 1910 into a poor peasant family. Both my parents died of cholera when I was three months old.

I read three years in the lower primary school. Then in 1918 came a famine and schooling stopped for two years. In 1921 I passed my third year class in Lower Primary and got admitted to the Upper Primary school in Sipur, which was on the other side of the Brahmani [river]. It was difficult to afford the rice and dal which used to be given then as school fees. I missed a year, and then read nine months of the second year and passed the exam and was given a scholarship, worth three rupees a month, to attend the Middle English school in Talcher town. I passed the two-year course, standing first. There was no money to go on with education and I took training as an *amin* [surveyor]. I was using a plane-table survey in the grounds of the school when I overheard a question that none of the class could answer, and I answered it. The teacher knew me and went straight to the headmaster and persuaded him to give one rupee a month from the Poor Boys' Fund. Messing fee was twelve annas [a rupee had sixteen annas] and I gave up eating tiffin [lunch]. I have never eaten it since, although now, as a minister, I am getting eleven or twelve hundred rupees a month, plus travel allowance, this and that.

I passed matric in 1930 and won a scholarship of ten rupees a month to attend university. From my old high school I got a loan of ten rupees a month. I collected admission fees of sixty-eight rupees from seventy-three people, some as loan, some as gift. I was not too badly off. Rice then sold for thirty to forty seers a rupee and pulses about twenty seers [a seer is roughly two pounds]. I got my intermediate in history, logic, Sanskrit, and Oriya. I did not have much hope to go on for BA, but I tried. I was giving private tuition at six rupees a month; fees were seven rupees a month. I borrowed money. Talcher raja promised ten rupees a month from scholarship fund, but it did not come. I got on well with the hostel superintendent and he arranged a half-freeship for me. So I got one free meal a day and lived on that for the third year. In the fourth year, the promised help from the Talcher raja came through and I got B.A. in 1935, in history, economics, English and Oriya, taking honors in history and economics.

For a short time I was tutor to a child in the Talcher raja's household. Then I got a job in Talcher High School, teaching English and history. In 1936 I went back to Cuttack and got B.Ed. with distinction. Then I went back to teach in Talcher.

What interested me in history, particularly English history, was the overthrow of tyrants. In my own mind, and sometimes talking with senior pupils, and when talking at weekends in the villages, I compared European tyrants with the exactions of Talcher raja and other rulers here. People had to build roads, bridges, culverts, bungalows, provide beaters for the raja's hunting, catch fish for him, catch wild animals like buffalo and elephants for him, provide parties to push and pull cars that could not cross river beds, carry the bags of his officers and the British officers who came touring, build camps for them, provide rice and ghi and pulses for the palace, and give all that was necessary for ceremonies in the raja's household, when forty or fifty guests might come. Even the well-to-do people of the state found themselves acting as servants and butlers on these occasions. So I came into politics, preaching against tyranny in the state.

In 1936–37 Orissa States People's Conference was held in Cuttack and addressed by Dr. P. Sitaramayya. I was invited to be secretary, but I declined because if I had come out openly against the ruler I could no longer gain influence among the people and get them organized. The Conference was sponsored by Congress but was not part of Congress. That year, however, I secretly became a four-anna member of Congress.[11]

Out of the Conference came the Orissa States People's Enquiry Committee, composed of Balwantray Mehta, Lalmohan Patnaik, and Mahtab. Again I was invited to be secretary, but again said no. I worked to gather evidence from Talcher and other states in the area. I sought out people who could give evidence of beatings, other brutality, rack renting, false statements about work done, secret murders, and so forth. The committee came to Angul [a British-administered district] to take evidence. I organized a big gathering for the leaders of our movement in the house of a landlord who was a relative of the raja. Only common people went to Angul. This was a ruse so that Talcher raja could not know who was organizing.

But Talcher government set enquiries going to find out who was behind it, and news had leaked out of the kind of lessons I was giving to students. After the enquiry, committee people were refusing to do the raja's work. Talcher ruler sent for me and told me his son and the police were saying things about me and I should mend my ways. He was keeping the police from hammering me. But then the news got out that I had been threatened by the ruler and I became a hero. Then the campaign against me intensified. They tried to frame me with criminal charges. They bribed an old opium-eating fellow to bring me a watch and a gold ring and ask me to sell them, but I instantly called witnesses and handed the property to the police. They planted stolen property in my room. Once I found a watch hidden in the drain hole and I threw it in the river that ran at the bottom of the school garden.

I had friends in the Talcher CID and I was hearing from them what was being planned. They [the raja's men] were planning to murder me. So I was sleeping in another room under the cot of another master. The sixteen students of the eleventh class used to take turns to act as my watch and bodyguard. This went on for three nights. Then I prepared an application for casual leave to go to Cuttack to have operation for internal piles, and asked my little

[11] Anyone who subscribed to the first article of the Congress constitution, which addressed swaraj and nonviolence, and who paid four annas, could become a voting member of Congress. This form of recruitment was one of the measures that made it possible for Gandhi to transform the national movement into a mass movement.

nephew to hand it in next morning. During the night, with the help of four boys, I escaped and went to Angul and thence to Cuttack.

I was organizer of the Talcher prajamandal and was its first president. We put out a demand sheet for abolition of forced labor and contributions, for responsible government, freedom of press, meeting and speech. I had my base in Angul and was teaching people how to practice civil disobedience in Talcher.

At that time prajamandal agitation was going on in Talcher, Nilgiri, and Dhenkanal. In Dhenkanal it was organized by the left-wing part of Congress, Naba Chaudhuri, Maloti Chaudhuri and others. Violence was encouraged and it became a complete failure. Right wing was led by Mahtab who was adviser to our Talcher prajamandal, and we tried to keep it strictly nonviolent. Civil disobedience was refusing to give forced labor and to pay taxes. We were opening shops to sell at low price and break the monopolies in salt, betel nut and leaf, tobacco and suchlike. fourteen hundred volunteers were working there and they were arrested and put in jail, which had space for ninety. Rations were short and food was served on the floor. There were frequent beatings-up. So I wrote to Gandhi and he said that people should leave the state.

In November, when the paddy was coming ripe, the ruler was foolish enough to seize it. People could do nothing but flee, and they came to eight camps that were organized for them in Angul. Talcher people subscribed six thousand rupees to prajamandal, being assessed one anna for every rupee of tax owed. Outside contributions brought money up to ten thousand rupees. Out of a population of 84,000, 64,000 came to the camps in Angul, bringing cattle and building huts for themselves, all within forty-five days.

Our aim was to publicize difficulties within the states. We were drawing attention to the people's plight. Governor visited and there was much public attention. Miss Agatha Harrison M.P. came and stayed three months with us. A. V. Thakkar came down. The Marwari Relief Society offered more funds. The All India Spinners Association came and organized spinning classes. The Cottage Industries people organized the manufacture and marketing of leaf cups and plates. We had our own schools; we had six hospitals; we had three thanas [police stations]; we had one magistrate, first class. The Assistant Political Agent, saying all his people were here and not in Talcher, came and set up camp with us.

On June 23, 1939 the ruler gave a declaration to our liking and the people were advised to return. Thus they had sacrificed two years of crops because it was difficult to sow the year they went back, the ground not having been properly prepared.

In 1938 a warrant was issued against me and I went underground. After the return of the people to Talcher the Orissa government did not enforce the warrant and I was free to go about, but not to return to Talcher state.

At this point he put his life story on hold in order to give me his reflections on techniques of agitation, explaining why his was successful and some others were not. The Talcher movement, he said, was organized on Gandhian principles of nonviolence and its adviser was Mahtab, a very practical man. The prajamandal in Dhenkanal state was led by the Congress Socialist Party people, in particular Nabakrushna Chaudhuri. Their exodus lasted only two months, and no more than two hundred families were involved. There were thirty-six deaths from police firings, and people quickly became demoralized. In Talcher there was only one death from firing on September 23, when some people refused to help the military get a vehicle out of a river bed. After that, they stopped all incursions of their people from the camps into Talcher.

He was ready to generalize. Three or four months, he said, was the maximum time for keeping up popular enthusiasm and morale. Second, the people must be protected, not exposed to violence. If exposed, they quickly lose morale. Third, the Talcher movement was, relatively, right-wing and moderate, and made sincere efforts to be nonviolent. In this way it had the sympathy of the British officials, of the CID in British territories, and of the military intelligence. The Dhenkanal movement was led by Marxists and forfeited this tacit support, especially when there was a resort to violence. Fourth, the Dhenkanal prajamandal was led by outsiders and there was no one equivalent to himself to be a local leader. Finally Talcher had half-a-dozen educated people to give the movement leadership and lend it steadiness.

I wondered about the last two comments because I knew that Dhenkanal had about three times Talcher's population, but I made no comment and he resumed his narrative. Evidently the ban on him had been lifted and he had been allowed back into Talcher state. It was not long before he changed his mind about nonviolence.

In 1939 there was a Crop Enquiry Committee in Talcher, organized by the Political Agent's office to determine the rent to be paid that year. The Agent went round taking the average of my estimate of what a field would yield—I was speaking for the prajamandal—and the estimate of the raja's agent. We were followed by a crowd of several hundred people. One field was ripe, and I urged it be cut and threshed and then we could see whose estimate was right. The crowd did this and threshed it on the spot, and I was proved right. The officer was very angry with the raja's people, but in the meantime the crowd got out of hand and I was arrested for preaching sedition.

In February 1940 I was arrested again, on various charges, and sentenced to fifty-six years imprisonment. I was expecting to die. They gave us little food; we had fetters all the time; it was insanitary and overcrowded. I was having many young followers outside the jail and there was constant talk of breaking the jail open, but nothing was done. In 1942 came Quit India movement and we were told to do what we could to free India. Gandhiji allowed us all to be his own master. I decided enough with one-sided nonviolence. I would escape and kill the whole Talcher raj family and other raj families and set up an independent state in that area. I began to organize it from inside the jail, bribing the warders to carry out messages. Not all prisoners were with me; younger ones were.

We made a human pyramid—four, three, two—and I climbed up and over the wall and away I went. They discovered my escape within the hour. I wanted to go southwest [towards Angul] but I lost the way and went northwest, which misled those following me. The night before I escaped I had a dream that I would meet a certain man, and I did. I disguised myself as a woman in a sari and fled into the interior into hiding. There was a rumor that I had been killed and the Talcher jail was attacked, but unsuccessfully.

Within seven days I had organized a peasant militia and seized the police station at Kaniha, from where we got more arms and ammunition. I declared independence in Talcher, Dhenkanal, and Pal-Lahara, gained control of all the countryside in Talcher, except the town itself, set up panchayat raj in the villages, burned all the records and state insignia, caused the state officials to flee, and was investing Talcher town. Airplanes were brought on Sep 7 by government, there was machine-gunning, thirteen persons killed, the militia stampeded and fled.

For four months after this I kept up a guerilla war, having three bands of two hundred men each. But by November I knew I was defeated. I decided to flee and join the INA. I was to take twenty men with me, but only five came, and we set off for Calcutta, disguised as coolies. I reached Tatanagar [Jamshedpur in Bihar] and worked as a domestic servant. Then I got to Calcutta and became a cook in a private house. When the mistress was showing me the red eyes, I thought of King Alfred and the cakes. I got in touch with certain INA agents, but those Calcutta people did not trust me and I wound up in a "destitute camp" [this was a time of famine in Bengal]. I worked there teaching children. The camp was visited by A. V. Thakkar, who remembered visiting us in the Angul camps, and I was then accepted as genuine by the INA agents.

I volunteered for suicide squad to travel to Burma and carry information to INA headquarters about troop movements and civil morale in India. I went by train as far as possible, with false papers as a contractor's agent. Then I walked at night, crossing swamps and jungles. Twice I did that journey. I wanted to open a front in Talcher, because Netaji was planning invasion of Orissa and Madras. With three hundred soldiers I could have raised volunteers to capture airfields. But before we could act the INA was in retreat.

There was a reward of ten thousand rupees on my head in Calcutta, alive or dead. But none of my fellow Oriyas betrayed me; most of them were there working as cooks. Three times I was in police custody and three times I escaped. I traveled to many places in India. I met Jay Prakash Narayan in Patna, who sent me to survey places where there had been successful agitations in '42 and find out why they were successful. No one was expecting independence at that time; we were making preparations for the next Quit India movement.

Then I went to Delhi and served in disguise as an office peon with the All India States Peoples Conference. Only Balwantrai Mehta was knowing who I was. At that time they were proposing that rulers should be given some privilege, a second chamber and so on. The Conference was collecting further evidence of misrule to combat this movement. I was sent to collect evidence in Chattisgarh states [Bihar] and in Punjab and in some Bengal states. Once I was almost captured. I had been recognized by a Talcher boy and word got to the police. I was with a Muslim companion and he took me to the Muslim community. I borrowed a burka [the long tent-like garment that Muslim women wear in public] and then walked forty miles in eight hours.

That work finished. Mahtab was advising me to surrender to the warrant, but I refused and said I would lead an army into Talcher if the ruler did not withdraw the warrant. Then in 1945 the old ruler died, and the new ruler was persuaded to withdraw the warrant. That was done in July 1947.

This was the time of the Congress ministry. A committee of the All India States Peoples Conference was formed in Orissa and I was co-opted. We were divided; some being for constitutional agitation against the rulers, and others, like me, for violent action and complete overthrow of the durbars [royal courts]. I organized twenty thousand volunteers in the Dhenkanal area and armed them with lathi, Gandhi cap, and a piece of rope. Rulers resorted to divide and rule and incited the adibasis against prajamandal. Our slogan was that each ruler should be left with his palace, and money enough to maintain one motor, one dog, and one servant. There was anarchy. Rulers appealed to Gandhi, who sent them to Patel [the Union Home Minister], who told them that Congress and prajamandal were not connected and they should deal with problems of law and order themselves.

I will close his narrative at this point and report what else he had to say in my own words. The tale of high adventure and physical hardships manfully endured had been told, up to this point, with a zestful demeanor—sometimes *miles gloriosus*, the proud and boastful soldier, at other times grimly defiant, head bloody but unbowed. It was a tale of adversity overcome and bravery rewarded, telling of a harsh world that many times had made him suffer, but for the most part a world without ambiguity. Villains were villains and friends were friends and the forces of evil (as he saw them) in the end capitulated to courage, determination, and cunning. Chance played its happy part (as when A. V. Thakkar was able to vouch for him to the suspicious INA men). When there was ambiguity, for example in the role of the old Talcher raja who was both a patron and an enemy, he gave it only the slightest notice and quickly returned to the certainty that a posture of unrelenting struggle requires. The entire story up to this point, even the suffering, was evidently one he understood and could look back upon with satisfaction. Had I quoted it, he would have relished Henley's *Invictus*: "I am the master of my fate, I am the captain of my soul . . . "

The Orissa rulers capitulated to Patel in 1947 and their domains were formally merged with the new state of Orissa on January 1, 1948. When he talked about this, the minister's ebullient confidence vanished. There were things that should not have happened, his tone said. Evidently he found it hard to understand why they happened. The glaring contradiction—or change—in his attitude, and his understanding of what worked in politics (from Gandhian non-violence to Forward bloc violence), had caught up with him. When Sardar Patel came down to Orissa in December 1947 to strongarm the rulers and make them drop their plans to form a state of their own in the new India, Dr. Mahtab was leader of the interim government. Mahtab refused to allow him to meet Patel, the minister said bitterly, and poisoned Patel's mind. The rulers themselves also were saying bad things about him and he and his followers received a majestic rebuke from Patel, who said that the former tributary states would not be handed over to a gang of dacoits [bandits].

I have much resentment. Would those rulers have given in to Patel so easily if I had not made them scared for their very lives? I do not respect our leaders here. Have they really suffered as I have? Were they ever beaten? All along they were first class prisoners in British jails. They have never been in a raja's jail. Nor do they know the people. I have ploughed fields and herded cattle. They never have.

They made speeches against me, saying I was a dacoit. But in the end they had to realize that I was the leader of a people's movement and I was co-opted as one of the three councillors from the ex-state areas, having the status of minister.

Now I am a minister and in the cabinet, but I do not have confidence in my leader. He has ruined Congress, putting his nominees into the district and pradesh [statewide] party committees. When he could not push aside nomination of followers of Chaudhuri, he even set up independent candidates to stand against them. Also he hated prajamandals, and he has taken ex-rajas into the party. Without his invitation those people would not have come into Congress. With them there, true supporters are discouraged from staying.

I should have asked him why Dr. Mahtab "hated prajamandals," but I did not. Why should there have been any ambivalence in the postindependence Congress ranks about the prajamandal agitations against the rulers of the tributary states? No ruler in Orissa, so far as I know, was an overt supporter of the Congress before 1947. Therefore prajamandal agitation should have had the wholehearted support of orthodox Gandhian Congress people. I believe it did. There was no difference about the goals. There were differences about the means, as the Talcher man's diagnosis shows. That would plausibly account for the disdain that the minister says he experienced from Patel, who called him a dacoit. But it does not fully account for the animus that, he alleges, Dr. Mahtab displayed towards former prajamandalists, and his apparent readiness to recruit ex-rulers into the Congress party. Other factors were involved, and I will come to them later.

Tales of Adventure

How are the texts to be construed? Did these events in fact happen in that way? Should I take a text as an authentic portrayal of a *real* world? Or was I hearing just the narrator's slanted *perception* of reality? Or, perhaps, he was being manipulative and presenting not what he perceived reality to be, but what he wanted me to see as reality? Or—to put an arbitrary end to this combinatoric excursion—what he wanted me to see as *his* perception of reality?

"If they are politicians," a character remarks in a novel about Orissa (the only one in English known to me), "then naturally they must be liars. It would be foolish to expect them not to be" (Beal 1954, 55). Anyone reading the last two accounts has surely caught a whiff of tall story. I do not mean they made it all up. But the tales likely were told with one eye to their effect on an audience—not me alone, for I think they saw the notebook and the wire recorder as a small gateway into the immortality of the printed word. Anyway, one certainly does not sense a scrupulous attention to detailed factual precision. I could, for example, have wondered about the 100,000 people who came to hear Maloti Devi make a speech in Saraikella in 1946. A good turnout, for sure, since at that time the entire state of Saraikella had a population of 150,000, of whom at least half would have been minors. Again, to assemble a mob of 25,000 people and have them walk seven miles is a claim that invites some skepticism. Who counted them? Some ludicrous questions also suggest themselves. Can anyone walk forty miles averaging five miles an hour wearing a burka? Such seven-league striding must have made people wonder what kind of woman that was.

There are also less skittish questions that I can ask but cannot answer, matters that now hang in the air because I did not follow them up. I wonder, now it is too late, what might have been revealed had I done so. Some probably lead nowhere. What is the significance of that mysterious sentence about having a dream about meeting a man, then in fact meeting him and escaping disguised as a woman in a sari? Others, less trivial, more directly concern particularities than the general images people had of their political world. There were hints, for example, about bad blood between the Talcher raja's two sons, and one side or the other being the young rebel's patron and protector. Perhaps his early years were not such an unremitting struggle against the forces of evil as his tale suggests. Also, in the Singhbhum case, I several times was told that the years on the run as a guerilla fighter might better have been described as years of banditry. The man himself said no more than how those years began (escaping from Cuttack under the noses of the CID) and how they ended (with blackwater fever). How were he and his followers bankrolled while they lived as *maquisards*? But the detailed historical exactness of these tales is not my concern; only the mind sets they reveal.

Clear and obvious differences divide the last two narratives from those that came earlier. The last two are tales of adventure; the speakers are egotists; they present themselves, albeit not in so many words, as supermen, heroes who faced adversity and danger and by their own personal courage, determination, and cunning overcame all obstacles. Book learning was not for the man from Singhbhum; he was too talented as a politician, too clever, to need "certificates." The other man, of humbler origins, was obviously proud of his scholarly achievements, but they were not the main source of his self-esteem.

One indicator of success they both respected (as did many other freedom fighters and, in 1990, the essay writer quoted earlier) was the ability to attract a crowd and stage a protest. The message has two interlinked but different meanings. First, thousands marching to escort the prisoner to jail signify democracy in action; the common people, made politically aware, demonstrating where their values lie. Without the clear sign that popular participation gives, the cause cannot be considered legitimate. Therefore, when three-quarters of Talcher's people not only lend their presence, but do so at considerable cost to their own well-being, then no one should question their sincerity or the rightness of their principles. Six hospitals, three police stations, schools, an inventory of well-known visiting sympathizers: magnitudes count and large numbers sanctify. But, second, there can be another message, which is less complicated because it points to the central personality; this is the message of charisma. What signifies is not the cause in itself, but the leader. Both narrators bore insistent witness to themselves and their own capacity to inspire devotion and enthusiasm.

An element in this charismatic image is an impatient, aggressive, even venomous martyrdom. They have suffered, their stories say, and their sufferings are for the most part direct and physical—insanitary jails, beatings at the hands of the police, fleeing from assassins—pain inflicted by unambiguously villainous people. In one case—the man from Talcher—the Gandhian message of loving one's enemies, even while suffering at their hands, has a small foothold in the first part of his tale, when he explains how nonviolence led to victory in Talcher. But those who supported the Forward Bloc and found their image of the great leader in Subhas Chandra Bose were not at all inclined to preach the political effectiveness of long-suffering. There is an impatience about their rhetoric, about the tales of the swift and direct action they took as freedom fighters. They avoided subtlety and qualification and ambiguity; they did not hobble themselves with Gandhian scruples about means, because the end is what matters and one should go for it directly. They countenanced violence; indeed, they welcomed it and saw it as the only tool that was effective. Why else did the Orissa rulers capitulate (the Talcher man asked), if not because they were being threatened by an army of twenty-thousand men armed with lathis, ropes, and (an irony) Gandhi caps?

This is the vision of a young warrior who lives in a world where honor counts, a virile, unhesitating, active world that sharply distinguishes itself from the old man's ambience of compromise, indirection, caution, long-term planning, and patience. Those features come across as impotence, if not cowardice and treachery. The young man's world has no tomorrow. Action now, and the shortest and most direct road to a goal that is unambiguous and straightforward, displace computation and calculation about what will have to be done after victory is achieved. Victory is itself, in this vision, a sufficient guarantee of bliss to follow.

The most famous of all the freedom fighters, Gandhi, who revered honesty but rejected honor (the kind that goes with swift revenge), who disdained virility, and who was neither young nor a warrior, nevertheless shared some of the young warrior's attributes. Many times he held out against compromise, he took direct action, he believed that one should do now what is right and leave the consequences to God, and he propagated a goal that seemed wonderfully straightforward and unambiguous, swaraj (self-rule). In fact, as the following chapters will show, swaraj was quite ambiguous. For Gandhi, the reformer, the word's prime meaning was "discipline of the self." For the great majority of his followers swaraj was simply freedom from British rule.

CHAPTER

6

Pragmatism and the Gandhians

Sarvodaya

Sarvodaya—"well-being of everyone"—was Gandhi's word, the title of a book he published in 1908. A veteran of the movement, in 1959 a Congress MLA in Orissa, described it like this:

> Congress work is not purely political. It also does some social work. It is a peculiar feature of Congress. First it began to non-cooperate with the British administration. We were not to hate the British people, but only the administration which they put over us. We should think them our friends but realize they were doing wrong things and try to convince them of this. That was the way we were taught to think. Politically, Congress meant noncoopera-tion with the government: do without foreign goods; persuade people not to drink alcohol. But the other aspect of Congress is to do some constructive work; to go to the villages and form pan-chayats to settle cases there. By running to the courts the litigants ruin people. We wanted them to settle cases in the village. Another thing was to fight against the usurpers: zemindars, moneylenders, landlords, government servants. We were to organize people to fight against them. We were to teach people to grow their own cot-ton, and to spin and weave cloth for their own use, and not to buy mill cloth; not to drink liquor; nor to take opium. We were to fight injustice. We encouraged women to come out and know what was happening in the country. All these are constructive works. There are twenty-two items of this kind.

Communists and socialists have no capacity for such work. The only work they do is incite people against the existing government, and tell them things in Russia are much better.

They do not do anything among the people to help them. But nowadays this is true of Congress as well. They do not go to the villages and they do not do constructive work. They are only trying to win seats in the elections. They have no interest in voluntary work; they want remuneration for anything they do.

That thought led him off to dark speculations about foreign influence. He knew young men, just undergraduates and with no more than matriculation, getting four or five hundred rupees a month working on a Soviet-subsidized magazine. Other opposition groups were getting American money through "that Forum for Free Enterprise."

That sour comment points us to the disenchanted years that followed 1947 and to the two remaining political styles, the latter-day Gandhians and those who would bring them down to earth, the practical politicians. They, the realists, are the antithesis not only of the Gandhians but also of the mindless advocate of disruption, whose opinions opened the previous chapter.

Land Reform and Local Government

The man from Koraput, spending his time in jail studying the Madras Estates Land Act, was one of those rare politicians (Chaudhuri was another and so was the independent MLA in whose house I lived) who did not come across to me—nor, apparently, to other people—as in the least given to self-puffery. He evidently valued what he had done, but the tale was told without self-conceit. Much of that long interview consists of a detailed and quite academic analysis of the land reform legislation (removing landlords and establishing local government institutions) that he and Chaudhuri had attempted to pass and implement during the years in which they were in office. In a manner that was quite clinical, the person withdrew behind the problem, the strategies available, and the reasons for success or failure.

In 1952 some members of our party—young and impatient ones, I may call them—believed that the government would not abolish zemindari. There were some dissidents in our party, but the bill was passed. At the time it was said, in answer to a question by a communist member, that implementation would take three years. I did most of it in six months.

We knew that if the zemindars heard that abolition was coming up, they will go to the courts and there will be delays. In Uttar Pradesh when zemindari was abolished they spent one lakh of rupees on fireworks and illuminations. I did it in darkness. I did not inform any of my secretaries. Why should I? It was already the declared policy of the state. I started no files because once clerks know, everybody knows. The chief officers of the Board of Revenue were taken into confidence, and then one fine morning the papers announced the government had abolished zemindari.

Between November 1952 and August 1953 we abolished about 12,000 estates. They say there are 200,000 estates altogether, but many are small, three or four acres, and now 80 percent of landlord area is with government. This is in conformance with Congress resolutions about a socialist society. Also we raised income tax, and in that way lowered compensation paid, because compensation is a function of the net income. We have done a very good thing.

But some of our Congressmen, a few of whom I admire, did not like what we had done. It is difficult to know the reason. Probably it affected some of them, or their relatives. Or they were afraid of what would happen to their votes in the next election, because they believed the zemindars still had a voice. Our Indian people are good people; perhaps it is inherent with us, but it was refined by Mahatma Gandhi. He started countless movements but he never had any hatred towards the British people. Same thing with zemindars. These same zemindars and rajas who have mistreated and tortured the people have secured a large number of votes. People said, "They have come to us and begged for our votes. Let us forgive and forget."

Those who were not happy with the reforms were murmuring behind the scenes, but they did not dare come out; that I have felt. They were persons in government or would later come into government. I will give you no names because I really do not have the evidence for this feeling.

Then, without a pause, this followed:

Chaudhuri and Mahtab are very good friends. They did everything together. When Mahtab babu went to Delhi, Naba babu took over. Later Mahtab began to feel he was no more of Orissa and was not consulted about what was happening here. Indian politicians know how to quarrel very easily. They don't know how to unite. They do not adhere to one another in times of emergency. It is a consequence of getting power—so long without it, and they get intoxicated with it. Mahtab babu, however, was not unhappy as a minister in the central government. Until 1952 they were pretty good friends. I had the full confidence of both of them. But in 1952 the gulf was widening between them.

The man from Koraput had his ideals—the kind of socialism that sees fulfillment in the removal of a rentier class—but he also was a sensible man who believed in getting things done in a practical step-by-step fashion. That belief is revealed in the tale of how the landlords were dispossessed. His version of how to conduct politics is far removed from the youthful, fascist-leaning adventurism of the Forward Bloc sympathizers. At the same time it departs from Gandhi's style insofar as it is concerned with the effective use of power and with practical matters of bureaucratic and legal administration.

The man from Koraput worked with Nabakrushna Chaudhuri, chief minister between 1952 and 1956, on zemindari abolition. They also crafted an Anchal Sasan Act that was to divide Orissa into localities (*anchals*) which would be run by elected councils. In essence, it was an attempt not only to fill the small void left by disempowering the zemindars, but also to devolve power downward from the state capital towards local communities.

The bill was introduced April '53, circulated and redrafted, sent to a select committee on March 5 '54, presented in August, and passed in December '55. We worked to implement it and had planned to introduce it by executive order on October 2nd 1956 [Gandhi's birth anniversary]. But there was a complication over reserved forests. Should they be locally controlled? There was delay.

Then in came this Dr. Mahtab [in 1956].[1] A committee was appointed as to what are the difficulties of implementing. They had three senior retired officers from the Revenue department. I saw

---

[1] The use of a demonstrative ("*this* Dr. Mahtab") codes disapproval. Compare, in the comments that open this chapter, "*that* Forum for Free Enterprise."

the report a few days back [this was the end of March, 1959] but have not studied it closely. I think they are saying the people are not ripe for self government. Main thing is some power would have to be surrendered to the people.

My suspicion is people in power do not want to surrender it. I mean people in the cabinet. Congress would not hold power in some anchals. They fear losing elections. To be frank with you, what Mr. Chaudhuri did when he was here was willingly accepted by his colleagues and was very acceptable and catchy to the mass. The extremists like PSP [socialists] and CPI [communists] could not say he lagged behind. But the middle class and the richer class were naturally against him. But those who came after Mr. Chaudhuri said to themselves, "Well, who are these poor people anyway? They are nothing. The rich will still have their voice in the country. It is better to placate them."

He followed this with a long story about an attempt to protect sharecroppers, telling how the measure they passed was blocked by the Union government in Delhi. "My good god, I tell you their head and heart is not in social reform!" he said, adding, "I have always been interested in the degree of sincerity of people, irrespective of what party they belong to."

That mildly acerbic comment was not his usual style. The following better represents the forbearance that seemed to be his habit.

I saw a report in the newspaper about some minister [in Mahtab's cabinet] not being complimentary about the work of the previous government [also Congress, but Chaudhuri's]. That's not good; I didn't like that. I also feel strongly about the attitude of the superior people towards the backward areas. I tried to move officials on more than one occasion about the adibasis in my district. Either they didn't understand me; or if they did, they didn't do it. I did not want any longer to be associated with parliamentary activities.

So I thought, better not fight. After all, we have given them five years. Let them have a free hand. I would not have been happy with the interference of [my] own party men. If you drive me to Cuttack, I shall not tell you how to use the clutch and the brake; only see that you are not going to Puri.

I don't blame them too much. I know what administration is; what the difficulties are. Therefore I don't find fault with my colleagues. Of course sometimes I feel very unhappy.

The Gift of a Village

When free India was about to become a reality, Gandhi announced that he wanted the Congress to withdraw from politics and become entirely a sarvodaya movement. This was perfectly consonant with the polity that he envisaged: decentralized, agrarian, and having the village as its basic unit. In that scheme the villages are the place where decisions are made and the work of governing is done. But others, practical men both of the political left (Nehru) and of the right (Patel), saw a different kind of polity. India would be a strong, industrialized state, governed as a representative democracy. In that context the Indian National Congress would have no choice but to become the Congress *party*. Those in power quietly wrote off Gandhi's vision as, in the middle of the twentieth century, utopian and utterly impractical. Those not ambitious for power, or willing to relinquish it, saw Gandhian "democracy" as the only ethical (and the only practical) way to create the good society in India and in the world.[2]

One of these true believers was Nabakrushna Chaudhuri. He was a minister in Mahtab's (1946) government, but resigned to found an ashram in Angul district. In 1950, when Mahtab departed to become a minister in the Union government, Chaudhuri returned to party politics, succeeding Mahtab as leader of the Orissa Congress party, and becoming chief minister. In a small way Chaudhuri was my patron. I was introduced to him when I first went to Orissa (in 1952) and received his wholehearted encouragement because (I am convinced) my research at that time was to be done in a rural setting in a backward district. During his tenure as chief minister—effectively ended by the riots of 1956—much of his energy was spent on working for the welfare of the rural poor, on agrarian matters (in particular zemindari abolition), and on the decentralization of power, as the long account of his friend from Koraput testifies.

The person who at that time in India presented himself as the next best thing to Gandhi was Vinoba Bhave. In 1948 there had been communist-led uprisings in Telugu-speaking regions, and some land was forcibly occupied by tenants. Soldiers were sent in to re-

[2] "Gandhiji's conception of democracy is definitely a metaphysical one. It has nothing to do with numbers or majority or representation in the ordinary sense. It is based on service and sacrifice, and it uses moral pressure" (Nehru 1962, 252).

store order. In their wake (in 1951) came Vinoba Bhave. Pitching Gandhian morality (a change of heart) against both communist violence and government-enforced agrarian reform, he initiated a social work campaign called *bhudan* (the gift of land), appealing to landlords to give him, as their "fifth son," a fifth of their land, which then would be distributed to the landless. They gave land (cynics said they gave what they had already lost to squatters), and Bhave went on his way to continue the campaign elsewhere. In ten years he had collected more than a million acres. Toward the end of the decade he graduated to *gramdan* (the gift of a village), in which he asked to be given all the land in the village so that it could then be worked as a cooperative. The movement had an outpost in Koraput. I went there in the hot weather of 1959.

Sarvodaya was the term social workers in Koraput used to name what they were doing. I interviewed one of their leaders, a man from western India, a person of importance who appeared from time to time on the national stage, a politician despite himself. The *mise-en-scène*—on the veranda of a government bungalow where their organization (Vinoba's Akhil Bharat Sarva Seva Sangh) had set up its headquarters—was partly what I had come to expect. As soon as we began to talk, several young men gathered around, keeping a respectful distance and listening attentively, having the air of disciples at the master's feet but not overdoing it. The leader was about sixty, and had the same peasant-like weather-beaten look[3] and clear eyes and air of inner serenity that Nabakrushna Chaudhuri and other Gandhian leaders had. There was no trace of self-importance. Nor was his style that of the regular political bigwig. He seemed to give me his exclusive attention; he listened to my questions and addressed them, sometimes helping me phrase them more clearly. Many of the big men I interviewed were fidgety, polite certainly, but, perhaps unwittingly, giving off signs of impatience, as if there were ten thousand important decisions waiting for them elsewhere. Gandhians mostly were not like that; they made you feel you mattered to them.

He told me how things stood with the Sangh at that time in Koraput. At their peak, he said, two years earlier, they had more than two hundred fifty workers in the district. All but sixty came from outside Koraput, and not one of them spoke the tribal language of

---

[3] Vinoba and his acolytes did a lot of walking in the countryside.

the area. Now they were down to about seventy. Of the thirty original centers ten survived, and later in the year they planned to wind up the work of their organization and hand over the houses, cooperative stores, and all their equipment to local committees. Then he talked at length about the Sangh's difficulties with Orissa's politicians. I will come to that in a moment.

I also talked with a younger leader, out in one of "their" villages. He was transparently honest. There had been problems, he said. For example, in the village in which we were talking the Sangh had appointed as its agent a man who thought himself superior to the local rustics and did not hesitate to let them know it. There were also accusations, both in that village and elsewhere, of embezzlement, of cooperatives being monopolized by dominant families, of funds being diverted to outsiders, of Sangh workers expecting to be fed and to receive homage as if they were zemindars or officials, and of other kinds of misconduct. Villagers had been misled by Sangh agents who told them that if they gave land in gramdan they would get it back and not have to pay taxes any more. There were also problems at the next level upwards. Title to donated land was unclear; as a consequence much of the land given to the movement had not been redistributed. He showed me a large paddy field, almost an acre, which, he said, had not been plowed for several years. Also, even when land was handed over to a cooperative, the uncertain title made it hard for the new owners to obtain agricultural credit. Officials at all levels were unhelpful.

It had not always been so, as I learned when I talked with local people who were hostile to the movement. The trouble started, one of them said, when Maloti Chaudhuri came down in 1952 and incited local tribal people to occupy the property of landlords. The agitators called the movement *Adibasi Sarvodaya*. But they had to backpedal because Chaudhuri, then the chief minister, could not countenance his own wife creating that kind of disorder. So the social workers returned to persuasive methods, and land was duly donated, and then all the misconduct started and local officials, knowing that the chief minister looked kindly on the movement, gave it every help, even to the extent of not reporting or not trying to prevent wrongs and abuses.

But the official goodwill did not last. There were several reasons. The Sangh, after receiving a lot of support from the Congress party, decided that it would be truly Gandhian and no longer involve itself at all in politics. So it advised people that the Gandhian way was consensus and, therefore, they should not engage in party politics and "fifty-one percent democracy." Many Congress politicians were irritated at what they saw as ingratitude, not to speak of the loss of what was in effect a cadre of unofficial party agents. Second, the activities of the Sangh caused headaches for local officials. I recall a conversation with one of them, in which he described the high cost of arranging security and transport for important Sangh workers, not least for Bhave himself, and the legal and administrative chaos that followed the transfer and retransfer of lands. Third, the departure of Chaudhuri in 1956 (to work for the bhudan movement) and the return of Orissa's other chief minister, Mahtab, replaced an enthusiastic supporter with a scornful and implacable opponent. When Mahtab arrived, the Sarva Seva Sangh leader told me, the local collector, who was a keen supporter of Vinoba, was transferred and the new collector took it as his job to wind down gramdan.

The kindest comment I heard about the movement was that its purpose was right, but its organization was hopeless. Even some of those inside the Sangh acknowledged that the Gandhian ideal of staying out of politics could not be combined with effective agrarian reform. Another man (not in the Sangh) said that agrarian reform and economic development were tasks for government agencies, not volunteer social workers. Gramdan people were responsible to no one; but a government official at least had his career and his pension at stake and could be punished. Thus one arrives at the inverse of the Gandhian creed; the invocation of career, pension and punishment assumes rational self-interest and denies both an internal guiding ethic (self-discipline, *swaraj*'s other meaning) and the possibility of unsecured trust.

This reversal in the fortunes of the sarvodaya people in southern Orissa is a small representation of what happened on the larger scene in India in 1947. The practical people took control, but not so decisively that they could silence the Gandhian opposition and build a tacit consensus behind the policy of pragmatism. There was consequently much disenchantment, both with the political process and with politicians. Nor was the situation made less ambiguous by the tactical expedient, up front, of temporizing and continuing to talk reverentially of Gandhi and his values. The realists appropriated Gandhian rhetoric, but often did not act on Gandhian precepts; sometimes they went directly against them. In particular, they did not much hesitate to use violence when they thought it was needed to defend the interests of the state.

A Modernizing Realist

Nevertheless, the realists, who took charge of Orissa in 1946 and again in 1956, were not released from Gandhi's entailments. Some of them did not want to be; for them devotion for Gandhi was internalized, even when they thought much of his program impractical. Virtually all of them, in Orissa and elsewhere in India, whether respecting Gandhi or not, continued to find his residues of practical use. They spoke his language, and proclaimed his values, and wore items of the politician's uniform that had been, so to speak, endorsed by him. They used his rhetoric and his presentational style to appeal to their electors. Those in opposition, communists and socialists and even some Ganatantra people, often did the same.

The practical Congressmen, when they came to power, had to put up with the distrust of constituted authority and the forms of nonviolent resistance that Gandhi had invented and used so successfully against the British. I suspect, also, that they identified in some of their opponents the trait that had caused them quietly to sideline Gandhi: what they saw as excessive and impractical idealism. This was the verdict that the social-democratic crypto-right politicians (such as Mahtab in Orissa or Patel in Delhi) passed on erstwhile left-wing sympathizers (for example J. P. Narayan in Bihar or N. K. Chaudhuri in Orissa). In addition, of course, they also had at their disposal the usual menu of political vices available for nailing an opponent: insincerity, opportunism, parochialism, a lust for power, incompetence, and, worst of all (after 1947), revolutionary tendencies.

My local beau-ideal of the practical modernizing realist, one who was appalled by revolutionary tendencies, was Dr. Mahtab. Mahtab, his allies said, was an able administrator, a devoted friend of Orissa, and an astute politician—above all a practical man, a leader who accepted responsibility. Vallabhai Patel, the strong man who came down from Delhi and cowed the reluctant Orissa princes into acceding to the Union, wrote in a foreword to one of Mahtab's books that he was "a true patriot in that he loves Orissa, but loves India more, a practical statesman and a born leader of men" (Mahtab 1974, iii).

Mahtab's political actions in Orissa were, for the most part, ideologically consistent with one another. In contrast with Chaudhuri (and Gandhi), he was a clear and enthusiastic supporter of industrial development, and in particular of the Hirakud dam. He had a vision of Orissa that approached the imperial, believing, it seems, in big government and in spectacular projects. While Chaudhuri was in office, the construction of the new capital moved slowly. The pace quickened when Mahtab returned. As Mahtab himself tells the tale, when he departed in 1950 to serve in the Union government, the scheme to build a new capital at Bhubaneswar was quietly subverted by the Cuttack lobby; it was not entered into the 1952 Five-Year Plan and therefore not financed. The scheme was restored on his intervention (from Delhi), but construction was not resumed, he claims, until he came back to Orissa in 1956 (Mahtab 1986, 58–59). Mahtab also took an evident pride in the defeat he inflicted on the princes of Orissa, and the part he played in creating a "Greater Orissa" through the incorporation of the princely states in 1948. But less than a decade later he was working to bring ex-rulers into the Congress party. That move can be interpreted in several ways. It was Gandhian forgiveness; or it helped to bring all Oriyas together; or perhaps he needed to "placate" the rulers if he was to stay in office, because they were rich and able to command votes. The price paid, as the man from Talcher indicated, was the disenchanting of Congress supporters, especially those who had been involved in prajamandal agitations (as, paradoxically, had Mahtab himself). They saw him dismissing his best friends to make room for those who had been, and probably still were, his worst enemies. Nonetheless, courting the princes seemed at the time to be the logical thing to do, if the goal was to hold power and keep the government strong.

Mahtab, his enthusiasm for strong government and industrialization notwithstanding, also presented himself as a dedicated Gandhian, who lived his political life in line with the master's principles. He wrote a book about Gandhi.[4] He has already made an appearance in the Gandhian mode in some of the stories told earlier. He was the person who counseled Gandhian tactics and gave the

---

[4] In 1965 Mahtab published a set of lectures that he had given on Gandhian philosophy. The same book, revised and enlarged to include an unfortunate panegyric on Mao's China and its use of Gandhian principles (as Mahtab thought) during the Cultural Revolution, was published again, under a different title, in 1973.

Talcher prajamandal agitations the success that eluded socialist-led violence in Dhenkanal.[5] He organized a National School in Balasore on Gandhian principles. When it was the Congress policy to do so, he stood for local office and took on its responsibilities. In the confused days of wartime (about which more later) he stood firm with the orthodox Gandhians, against both the violence-prone socialists and Forward Bloc people on one side, and, on the other, the Swarajist Congressmen who joined a coalition government in Orissa and supported the war effort unreservedly. When the time came to court arrest, he did so. He constituted, one might say, an outstanding Gandhian role model for the young men of Balasore district, even the one presented earlier who was a leading socialist MLA in 1959.

But he did other things that, one imagines, Gandhi would not have done. His dealings with the rulers of the princely states were quite bare-knuckle. Mahtab was the first chief minister ("premier" or "prime minister" were the titles they used at that time) of the interim Congress government that ruled Orissa from just before independence to the general election of 1952. As an Oriya patriot he was determined, as I said, to bring all the Oriya-speaking areas under the one Orissa government, including those in 1947 still ruled by princes. The rulers had other ideas: at that time they were endeavoring to set up a unit in the new India that would include the Eastern States (principalities later incorporated into Orissa, Bihar or Madhya Pradesh) and might even be linked with the very large and wealthy state of Hyderabad. The book that Mahtab wrote about this episode (mainly a collection of documents) gives himself top credit for thwarting the rulers, both by his persuasive diplomacy in Delhi with Congress leaders and British emissaries from the Labour government, and, tellingly, by the decisive use of exemplary force to intimidate the princes. In Nilgiri, a small tributary state bordering Mahtab's home district of Balasore, a "few adibasi criminals" were encouraged by the ruler's people to "loot and set fire to the houses of the prominent prajamandal leaders." Violence spread and gave Mahtab the excuse to send an armed force into the state to take it over and administer it as an "occupied territory." He wrote proudly:

[5] "The Prajamandal activities in Dhenkanal were under the guidance of Sri Nabakrushna Chaudhuri, whose demand was for a complete surrender of powers by the Darbar to the people, while in some other states, such as Talcher, Pal Lahara, Ranpur and others the working was under the advice and guidance of Sri H. K. Mahtab, who adopted a more conciliatory policy" (Mahtab 1959, 122).

"The way in which Nilgiri was taken over created a flutter among the rulers of the Eastern States. This was really the beginning, and the taking over of Hyderabad was the end" (1974, 27). (The Nizam of Hyderabad, which at that time contained more than fifteen million people, held out for independence within the new India until his state was invaded by the Indian army in September, 1948.)

A year later (1949), still in the midst of turmoil with other disruptive elements (mainly communists, see below), Mahtab published a history of Orissa. His verdict on the reign of King Prataparudra Deva (1504–32), in line with that of the historian Banerji (*see* chapter 2, fn. 17), hints at his philosophy of government and at the way he saw his own place in history.

> . . . administration of the country was very loose during the reign of Prataparudradeva and the state of political stagnation that marks his reign may easily be ascribed to the cult of love which was gradually spreading in Orissa and which reached its climax on the advent of Sri Chaitanya into Orissa. A doctrine that preaches inaction and sentimentalism is harmful to the ordinary man in his daily walk of life and it is simply fatal to the administrator who holds the destiny of millions (1981, 329).

For several years Orissa's few communists had been feeling Mahtab's heavy hand, which at that time did hold "the destiny of millions." From the government's point of view, the communists deserved it. The following selections are taken from a chapter (pages 21–32) in the government publication, *Orissa 1949*. The chapter is disingenuously entitled "The Tasks of Peace (Through firmness and courtesy to law and order)."

> In 1946 activities of anti-social elements were confined to Communists who continued agitation among the ryots [peasants] in Ganjam for reduction in rent and abolition of the [landlord] system. As a result of speeches by Communists . . . some ryots actually carried away the crop without paying their share to the [landlords]. In Puri district, tenants who generally pay half their produce to landlords were advised by the local Communists not to pay more than one third. Preventive action under sections 107 and 145 Cr.P.C. was taken . . . Communist-instigated Press workers of Cuttack went on strike . . . Unruly conduct resulted in the arrest of 43 workers . . . At

Barang police had to disperse several processions and prosecute the leading Communist workers.

In 1947 Communists . . . fomented an agitation to establish the rights of ryots over . . . lands in the Zamindari areas . . . section 144, Cr.P.C. was promulgated and proceedings under section 107, Cr.P.C. were started against the main agitators and ten others . . . In Puri district the Communist-instigated tenants were prosecuted for forcibly entering upon the land of a local Zemindar . . .

[In 1948] The Communists intensified their activities in the districts of Cuttack, Puri, Ganjam and parts of Sambalpur and Balasore . . . The situation deteriorated in May when a large mob armed with lathis and other weapons attacked a Police search party with the result that firing had to be opened resulting in 5 dead and 16 injured . . . The Communists established a firm hold over the sweepers in Puri and successfully instigated them to launch a strike. But with the arrest of the leaders the strike was soon called off.

In the beginning of [1949] the Communists concentrated on the railway employees to bring about a strike which was averted by the arrest and detention of the main instigators . . . The Communists took to large-scale leafleteering in different areas of the Province. A close watch was maintained for Communist workers who had gone underground in furtherance of the party programme and several of their prominent workers were arrested and kept under detention.

This, evidently, is how the zestful agitation, told in the tale of the Talcher man or the Oriya loyalist from Singhbhum, appears from across the tracks where the establishment resides. Surely this also was how each ruler saw the activities of prajamandalists in his state. This, too, was the British government's take on the freedom fighters themselves, including even those like the man from Koraput (or Mahtab himself) who played by Gandhi's rules. Reading this, one better understands the text quoted in the first chapter. Here is part of it again.

The years after 1947 were a deep disappointment. People had been led to believe that freedom would be a millennium that would bring them a new and benevolent kind of ruler. But in fact the new system was beyond their understanding. Equally the Congress workers were out of their depth. They found that with the British gone the system still survived, and they were powerless to bring about the changes they desired.

That lament came from Chaudhuri, a Gandhian, and the change he desired was a moral reformation and a government styled according to Gandhi's benign anarchy. But that is not what Mahtab's dominant faction in the Orissa Congress envisaged. Their goal was more immediate, more practical, much less profound: the people must (be made to) realize that government and its agencies were no longer the enemy.

From an agent of the British Government to oppress and persecute the people, on the 15th August 1947 the Indian Policeman became overnight the sentinel of India's independence. (*Orissa 1949*, 21)

The reasoning and its rhetoric are simple. The leaders of the freedom fight have become the people's chosen representatives and it is wrong to employ against them the techniques of struggle that they themselves had developed to defeat the British. But old habits die hard. If the new nation is to survive, then, paradoxically, its new rulers, who "hold the destiny of millions," have no choice but to employ the methods of suppression that their predecessors had used against them. What other course is open to a responsible leader, when the entire country is in peril? So, those former freedom fighters who cannot break themselves of the habit of protest and do not understand that what was once principled resistance now is sedition must be kept under control and out of power. One should be wary of making a hero out of such virtual dacoits as the Talcher man, habituated to violence and by nature resistant to authority.[6] Mahtab's faction was wary in that particular case, until they realized that they needed him.

---

[6] The minutes of a meeting between some of the rulers and Mahtab, held in 1946, were recorded in two versions (both printed in Mahtab's 1974 book): one written by Mahtab and the other by the ruler of Saraikella. It is reported in the latter version (but not in Mahtab's) that, when the rulers protested against their vilification in "obscene language" by prajamandal leaders, "Mr Mahtab responded that he had no sympathy for such people. One of the absconders from the Talcher State, who met Mr Mahtab at Delhi and asked him to allow him to come back to Orissa, was told that if he landed in Orissa he would be arrested and handed over to the Talcher Darbar" (Mahtab 1974, 136–37). At that time the man from Talcher whose tale was told earlier, was serving "disguised as an office peon" in Delhi. It seems possible that he was the "absconder."

Second, there was no place now, in free India, for revolutionary politics. It is no accident that communists were a main target for the forces of "firmness and courtesy." They were seen as deliberate makers of agrarian and industrial anarchy, a threat to the new state. All left-wing activists soon acquired the same reputation. Before long the focus became even wider, and any nonestablishment political initiative was likely to be regarded as designedly subversive. (Sarvodaya fared slightly better, being judged only unintentionally disruptive.) The left and right division was not new. It had appeared again and again in the days of the Indian National Congress, for example in the episode with Bose in 1938 or, earlier, in the formation of the Congress Socialist Party, but it had been kept in check, partly by Gandhi's resolute rejection of such ideologies and mainly by the presence of the common enemy, the British. By 1948 both those restraints had been removed.

This ideological cleavage has appeared in many contexts in India. One basic form, after independence, pitted distributive justice against productive efficiency. Where should development resources be invested? Should they go to those most in need, when it is known that they will be used less efficiently, perhaps even squandered? The left-wing and the idealist answer is that they should. The practical politician insists that, in general, resources should go to those who will give the best return. Mahtab was a practical politician. Chaudhuri, in the testimony of his friends and by his own admission, in some ways was not; he was a Gandhian. Such men Mahtab soon came to see as spoilers of the good society.

To adopt the intendedly benign Gandhian anarchy was to opt out of the arena of party politics, but not necessarily out of politics altogether. The reason is obvious: sarvodaya, by denying the legitimacy of political contests, challenged not just the party in power but the regime itself. In some instances the challenge was minimal. After 1956 Chaudhuri and his wife ran their ashram and, if there was any threat to the regime, it was indirect, no more than the example they set. But that had not always been the case. From the twenties onward social work could be joined with politics. (Which was the vocation and which the avocation is sometimes hard to determine.) Social workers in the Gandhian style constituted 17 percent of the lower house of the 1952 Delhi parliament (Morris-Jones 1957,120).[7] They were 20 percent of Congress party members,

---

[7] They came third after lawyers (25 percent) and landowners (19 percent). Forty years later other features became salient. I read recently, in a newspaper

19 percent of the socialists, and 42 percent of the communists (Morris-Jones 1957,123). To separate these two callings, as Gandhi wished when India became independent, was decidedly a revolutionary step. But, in fact, social work was not removed from politics; instead it became a challenge to the regime of parliamentary democracy itself.

For many true believers, whether in sarvodaya or anything else, their own example was only a base from which to launch active proselytizing. The notorious example in those years was Vinoba Bhave. At the end of May 1955, Mahtab, then governor of Bombay, wrote a letter to the prime minister, Nehru, asking if he was aware of what was happening in Orissa. Mahtab had heard that "Vinoba Jee was serious about launching an All-India movement of the type of the non-cooperation movement and he would begin it just on the same model as Gandhijee began his non-cooperation movement. He would give a call to all those who were in office to lay down their offices and come down to join his movement." He added that he believed Chaudhuri (at that time still chief minister of Orissa) would accept the invitation and that it was being considered by various other significant persons, including the president of India (1986,173).

Mahtab's memoir, *While Serving My Nation* (1986), consistently portrays Vinoba Bhave as an unfortunate influence on Indian politics, if not an evil one. "I held that Vinoba Bhave unwittingly undid what Gandhiji did and his movement, because of lack of any logic behind it, became hypocritical and superficial show" (108). (By "logic" he must mean any thought as to the practicality or the consequences of the program.) "Bapu [Gandhi] strove for removal of poverty, while Vinobaji is distributing it" (109). "I know the details of Vinobaji's tour in Orissa. It gave me a rude shock to know how much money was spent and how gorgeous arrangements were made by the State" (109). This contempt for Vinoba was extended to other constructive workers: "Gandhiji was let down badly also by the constructive organizations which he had built to secure mansupport for his political activities. Those organizations, from the beginning, developed a kind of self-righteousness and consequently superiority complex and thus were cut [off] from the people and the political current" (1973, 46). Gandhi's idea of constructive work, Mahtab claimed, had been misunderstood and perverted. Con-

---

article on violence in Indian politics, that one third of the members of the Uttar Pradesh legislature had criminal records.

structive workers now saw it as their role "to criticize the Congress Government for not doing things as they suggested." They wanted a free village-based *non-mechanized* economy, which, Mahtab argued, would have played into the hands of "mill-owners" since cottage industries, without machinery and electric power, could not meet people's needs. "I felt sorry that the most practical way of Gandhiji was reduced to a pitiable position by the orthodox constructive workers of the Gandhian days who had developed a self-righteous static mind" (1986, 18).

There were other perversions of Gandhian practical philosophy that Mahtab deplored. Satyagraha, he claimed, had been misunderstood and cheapened. Gandhi, Mahtab wrote, did not anticipate the crackdown that followed his *Quit India!* resolution of 1942, and when asked by followers what they should do, in the event of his imprisonment, had said people "were free to do whatever they could under the circumstances." This, Mahtab explained, was misinterpreted by some as approval for violent action. He goes on:

> But at this distance of time it must be noted that the 1942 movement led by Congressmen has left behind a very wrong expression about the Gandhian technique. Now every agitation is described as Satyagraha. Various kinds of fasting such as "symbolic," "relay fasting" etc. are now going in the name of Non-violent movement. Unfortunately those congressmen, who carried out the so-called "mass action" in 1942 and were ridiculing the non-violence of Gandhiji, subsequently after independence became the protagonists of Gandhian Truth and Non-violence under the leadership of Vinoba Bhave. History will record with deep regret that an effective and efficient technique which Gandhiji evolved not only for the attainment of freedom but also for the redress of wrongs whenever and wherever they are committed in a democratic set-up became completely obsolete in the middle of confusion. Gandhian technique has become a matter of distant history now. It lost all contact with the situation which developed after independence. (1973, 49–50).[8]

---

[8] Mahtab made Vinoba out to be the kind of menace to good government that in fact he was not. Bhudan and still more gramdan left a trail of administrative chaos, but the movements, although in a sense intentionally subversive, were in some respects pacificatory. What influence Vinoba had was used to promote moral rehabilitation and probably served to diminish the threat that class struggle might have been to the regime. Marxists, certainly, recognized Bhave as an unintentional ally of the bourgeoisie. It is ironic that, at the time this second ver-

There is a difference, and not a slight one, in the tone of all this and Chaudhuri's statement about the people being "humbugged." Chaudhuri was saddened that in their ignorance the politicians did wrong things: they did not trust the people; they could not bring themselves to acknowledge their own mistakes. But that did not make them incurable villains. Mahtab, in contrast, saw not only fools but also enemies—malicious, self-interested, "hypocritical" people. Vinoba was a particular menace; so were other constructive workers who placed themselves above the elected representatives of the people; so also—and eminently so—were civil servants who misused authority and backgrounded the politicians. He complained, " . . . planning was left in the hands of erstwhile bureaucrats by the political leadership" (1986, 17). One of his many letters to Nehru addressed this subject. "Towards the end of 1954, I noticed the leadership losing its grip both on the administration and also on the party organization, I felt compelled to write some strong letters to Jawaharlalji, to one of which he replied." Mahtab had written: "Circumstances have conspired to push out all idealism from the active field. . . . I have started many institutions . . . money plays very little part in keeping them up. It is enthusiasm and faith in the work . . . enthusiasm is created if initiative is left with those who work . . . [but if they] feel that their opinion does not count [they lose enthusiasm]." He went on to sympathize with the "poor Congressman" to whom nobody listened and who found himself "pitted against officers who may have been his juniors in the Colleges or who may have been his critics during the days of the political movement." He concluded: "In these circumstances is it fair to criticize the poor man or to expect from him enthusiasm entailing personal sacrifice?" (1986, 92–93).

There are many other expressions of disenchantment in Mahtab's political writings. "A nation without a philosophy is like a ship without a rudder. That is why India appears to be aimless today. Since the national philosophy of Gandhiji has been given up, the old philosophies based on race and religion have come into prominence and that is the reason why disintegrating tendencies on account of caste, religion and language are so much in prominence

---

sion of Mahtab's book on Gandhi was issued, J. P. Narayan was demonstrating in Bihar that the Gandhian style could be used—Mahtab would have said *mis-used*—to destabilize a government (the outcome being Mrs. Gandhi's two-year dictatorship from June 1975 to March 1977).

to-day" (1965, 53). But, as should by now be clear, Mahtab's interpretation of that philosophy was not, at least in some respects, in line with Gandhi's own. Mahtab wrote: "Politics means competition for power. Its sole aim is to hold on to power by suppressing or managing somehow the opposition or to assume power by weakening or destroying those who are in power" (1973, 20). Such verbs as *suppress, weaken* or *destroy* are not in Gandhi's idiom. Consistently, Mahtab argued that Gandhi entered politics only when in 1920 he became president of the All India Home-Rule League. What he did in South Africa was not politics but "social work"—a narrow verdict indeed, when one remembers that the issue there was civil rights for Indians and the adversary was the South African government. Finally, his summary of Gandhi's achievements, although perfectly accurate, by implication inverts the values that Gandhi would surely have preferred: "His work was to forge moral weapons for political action" (1965, 8). That was what Gandhi did, but for sure that was not his sole intention; for him morality was an end in itself, not a means to power.

Mahtab's writings seem to reveal an intellectual and emotional need for enemies; without them his world would make no sense. I do not imply that he invented them; they were real enough. The British put him in prison. The rulers of the princely states endeavored to thwart his grand scheme for "Greater Orissa." Civil servants, I have no doubt, sometimes got in his way, as they do for politicians everywhere in parliamentary regimes. The Cuttack lobby, as I am calling it, tried to scupper his plans for the new capital. Local interests agitated against his other grand design, the Hirakud dam. The Jharkhand party people made him pay for their support "at considerable cost," as he enigmatically put it (1986, 184). He found himself embarrassed in Delhi by the Orissa boundary agitations in the mid-fifties and his party grievously weakened when he returned to take charge of it in 1956. His return was opposed by the former supporters of Chaudhuri; they would have preferred another Congressman, Biswonath Das, to have taken command. Chaudhuri himself, Mahtab claims, wrote "now and then" urging him not to return to Orissa (1986, 183). Then, quite soon after his return, he was maneuvered into accepting a coalition with his princely enemies in the Ganatantra party, and his reign came to a somewhat ignominious end in 1960, when the Orissa Congress was ordered by the Delhi "high command" to withdraw from the coalition. Democracy was suspended in Orissa, which, for a short time, came under "Governor's Rule" (control by the Union government). Not surprisingly, given that record of being shafted, Mahtab's memoirs and other writings exhibit little sign of Gandhian forgiveness.

They show none at all of Gandhi's insistent humility. Letters of thanks, or of praise, or of congratulation from eminent people (Nehru, Mountbatten, Edwina Mountbatten, Stafford Cripps, Dag Hammarskjold, and many others) are proudly reproduced in the 1986 memoirs. So are letters of "blessing" from the Mother at Pondicherry, from a Roman Catholic priest, and from a French lady who was a "spiritualist." Nowhere does he acknowledge things mistakenly, let alone wrongly, done by him. Bad people—civil servants, former princes, Vinoba Bhave and other Gandhian social workers who had not understood the Gandhian message, his rivals in the Congress party—these and many others are castigated, sometimes by name and sometimes indirectly, always with gusto. Even in the closing sentences of his memoirs, telling of the indignities and hardships inflicted on him and Nabakrushna Chaudhuri, both in their late seventies, when, during Mrs Gandhi's "Emergency," the then chief minister of Orissa had them imprisoned, he cannot resist hinting at his own macho excellence and Chaudhuri's failings. "Sri Naba Krushna Chaudhuri, former Chief Minister, suffered partial paralysis in the Baripada prison where he was detained as an ordinary person. I was also to be treated that way in Phulbani jail, but I agitated and took to hunger-strike as a result of which I was given better treatment in the Bhanjanagar jail" (1986, 186). He was kept there for nineteen months.

The Perfect Politician

Mahtab's way to resolve the uncertainties that filled the years after independence was radically different from Chaudhuri's. It should be obvious by now which of those personalities I found, and still find in recollection, the more congenial. There are features, however, in Mahtab's political style that deserve respect. He was a hardheaded realist. In 1956, explaining to an American that Indian socialism was not "the socialism of USSR or China," he wrote, "socialism is a liquid that takes the shape of the cup in which it is put [in India] it is really advanced capitalism . . . " (1986, 135–36). No doubt, this was written partly to suit the audience; but it also represents Mahtab's realistic view of where India was heading at the time. He liked to see things as they are. Morarji Desai, seeming to believe that Bombay was dry because Morarji said it was, provoked his irony. Vinoba, unwilling to acknowledge the futility of bhudan and gramdan, earned his contempt. The same determination to deal with the world as the world really is, and not as one would like it to be, underlay his rewriting of Gandhi's program for village economies, when he argued that to replace hand tools with electric power and machinery would merely be to update, not to overturn, Gandhian principles.

Indeed, Mahtab writes sometimes as if Gandhi had been a hard-headed realist like Mahtab himself, ready to use even a little duplicity to get his message heard and understood. "Whenever he used to think of a problem, he used to say that he was seeking light from within and whenever he used to come to a decision he used to say that God had shown him the way. This was his way of expressing himself and *it went down very well for those for whom it was meant*" (1973, 5. emphasis added). The point is made explicitly on the previous page: "Gandhiji had always in mind the level of development of the mass mind in India as he was addressing himself to millions of unsophisticated people who were far away from the reasoning of the enlightened few." (I will come back to Gandhi and the "unsophisticated" masses in the next chapter.)

I found in my notes a verdict, given by another politician, that sketches, harshly but not without admiration, a negative profile of Mahtab's realism.

> He is the perfect politician. He is without personal loyalties. He is not in the least hindered by ties of sentiment or affection. He would drop a colleague without turning a hair and give the job to someone in the other party. He is also adept in giving meaningless promises, but clever enough to keep his word if it is a real promise.

That ungenerous comment portrays Mahtab as supremely rational, "not in the least hindered by ties of sentiment or affection." By that argument, neither should he have given way to genuine anger nor been moved by sincere hostility. The comment that he would "give the job to someone in the other party" and do so "without turning a hair" points that way. But all the evidence is that Mahtab was the one given to anger (he was writing it down twenty-five years after the events that made him angry); Chaudhuri, the idealist, was not.

Chaudhuri, certainly by the time he embraced bhudan, had become, like Gandhi, *non*rational. The nonrational life is one that is closely governed by immediate moral imperatives, in which potentially complicated calculations of *useful/not useful* are replaced by a straightforward, spiritually-guided, and wholly intuitive apprehension of *right/wrong*. The focus is on purity of means, of right conduct as an end in itself.[9] In other words, the nonrational person follows his or her conscience and is not constantly figuring outcomes, still less asking, "What's in this for me?" Chaudhuri had withdrawn from the place where calculating rationality is an everyday requirement. Opting out of representative politics removed him from the hurly-burly of day-to-day contestation and tactical thinking. I do not imply that ashram life is inactive, mere contemplation; it is a strenuous and disciplined regime of learning, teaching, and service. But an ashram is also, by definition, a place that should be innocent of adversarial posturing; quarrelling is against the rules. First principles are uncontested. Of course there will surely be arguments about exactly what accords with first principles, not to speak of backbiting and political maneuver, as in every community, but on the ashram's front stage there is no place for threats and intimidation, no room for politics as Mahtab defined them: competition for power. One should not constantly to compute the next move, working out what hostile argument the opponent is about to make. There are no arguments, only discussions. The theory of satyagraha, as Gandhi expounded it, maintains that truth itself will prevail, becoming obvious in the course of the discussion. Debaters do not have to think ahead; truth itself is like a beacon and will guide them.

But in less spiritual settings, in the political world which Chaudhuri left and in which Mahtab remained, it is not the vision of truth that guides action but calculations of advantage. *Truth* in Mahtab's political world is not a transcending force that has its own dynamic, uncontrolled by any person, but rather is a manifold thing, one person's "truth" being an infringement on the other person's "truth," and if they join to agree about *the* truth, all that means is that they have struck a bargain. In that arena, the players work out the costs

[9] "The Christian does rightly and leaves the result with the Lord" (Weber 1948, 120).

and benefits of truth's various versions and choose the one that will give them the most advantage. Furthermore, as in all negotiating, intimidation and threats and the tactic of displaying potential or actual outrage are the weapons of choice. Such an encounter is the very inverse of satyagraha: pressure is exerted not by *self*-sacrifice but by convincing the other party that they are the ones who will suffer if they remain intransigent. To speak at the highest level of abstraction, Chaudhuri's world is guided by the hand of God; in Mahtab's, one must strive for what one wants and overcome those who would deny it.

Chaudhuri retreated into a higher morality in pursuit of a goal, the perfecting of human society, that in the end can only be utopian. The reward, for those who find one, must lie in the striving, not the attainment. Mahtab confronted the world as it was; absolute morality of the Gandhian kind was subordinated. I do not suggest that he was evil or unprincipled, only that he identified concrete goals that he considered realizable in the here and now—the new capital, the merger of the princely states, and the Hirakud dam[10]—and resolved the many-voiced uncertainties of the political scene by subordinating everything to those goals, and by attacking "the orthodox constructive workers of the Gandhian days who had developed a self-righteous static mind," along with anyone else who had a design for Orissa and for India that did not accord with Mahtab's own.

Retreat into Good Works

The man from Koraput, looking sadly at the colleagues who replaced him, was not alone in feeling disheartened. Others too, like his friend Chaudhuri, believed that their ideals, if not actively betrayed by wicked men, were being lost in a confusion of opinions and interests and irreconcilable differences about right conduct and the good society. Certainly they gave some indication of feeling helpless, even angry (the anger softened by Gandhian forgivingness), but they were far from falling into Nietzsche's *ressentiment*. As I read their demeanor at the time, and as I now read the words that I recorded, neither a sense of their own impotence nor envy for others afflicted them. For sure they recognized defeat and to some slight degree were cynical, usually targeting the "sincerity" of indi-

[10] He describes the new capital, the Hirakud dam, and the merger of the princely states as his "three pet projects" (1986, 100).

viduals, not people at large. They did not despair of human nature, nor were they oppressed by a sense that human effort was futile. Indeed, they were sincere populists, believing that ordinary uneducated people had moral virtues that too often went unacknowledged by their superiors. Nor did they think that, in a world that never would be set right, nothing could be done except identify the culprits and excoriate them. Of course, that vindictive sentiment was around and frequently voiced when people (but not these two men) talked about the vanquished imperialists or about their present political enemies. But the man from Koraput and his mentor, Chaudhuri, had listened to Gandhi and taken his message. They were constructive and forgiving, not vengeful, more saddened than angered by what they saw being done around them.

The mentor, Nabakrushna Chaudhuri, had retreated into good works. The noun *retreat* has two meanings, withdrawal either from the field of battle or from the everyday world to seek spiritual renewal, and this ambiguity parallels political judgments made at the time. There were people who said that Chaudhuri fled from combat, defeated by forces he could not overcome. I am sure he would have acknowledged that he had not been able, as chief minister, to accomplish what he wanted. But I think he saw his exit from party politics less a defeat than an opportunity to begin the struggle again in a more compelling and constructive fashion. The retreat was a positive move that signalled a Gandhian rejection of power and an advance to the higher moral plane of self-sacrifice and service to others, to sarvodaya. This path he surely considered not only ethically correct but also a perfectly practical strategy: only sarvodaya could put an end to the struggles and the animosities that were built into "fifty-one percent democracy." The good society cannot be imposed from above; it comes naturally into being, by consensus, when individuals are free to realize the natural goodness ("truth") that is within them.

In this frame of mind there is no hint of anomie—of being entirely perplexed by the turn of events, not knowing what to do. Chaudhuri sorrowed over the obstacles that other politicians put in front of his land-reform programs and his attempts to give power to the people, and he was surely distressed by the violence that the boundary disputes provoked, but, strong in the Gandhian faith, he suffered no loss of nerve. He tried not to look for evildoers: institutions, not persons, were at fault. In his own mind he perfectly understood what had happened: the administrative chains set in place by the British still bound the politicians, who then made the mistake of not admitting they were in error and instead "humbugged" the people by telling them they were now free. Some of them also were in error because they put power before service. But adversarial confrontation was not the solution. Nothing would be accomplished by penalizing the politicians. Rather they (and everyone else) should be educated into following the way of truth.

In that manner Chaudhuri resolved the many-voiced uncertainties of the political scene. His way, which was the way of principle, was fundamentally different from Mahtab's pragmatic solution to the same conflict. Each solution carries its own distinct package of consequences, both for individuals and for the society at large. I will consider those consequences, and other matters, in the next chapter.

7

Disenchantment and Compromise

Enantiodromia

By its very nature, true belief in a cause—that it will triumph, come what may—is fragile. First, it must overcome the common human propensity to avoid effort by minding one's own business. Then, once aroused, it is buffeted by an objective world that knows nothing of true believing, does not obey the scriptures, and sooner or later punishes inattention to reality.[1] But hubris blunts the critical faculties and blinds true-believing political enthusiasts to the lessons that adversity otherwise might teach them. That is both their strength and their weakness. In the end, reality must win; there is a nemesis. Things fall apart, and instead of the one great central truth that is everyone's guide and the one hope of salvation, there are many competing truths and would-be certainties. The cause, increasingly unable to shut out a changing and unforgiving reality, gives way, among those whose political ardor has been ignited, to a babel of conflicting ideas and ideologies.

This enantiodromic process—positions moving toward their negation—is not like nature's pendulum (the seasons or the light and dark half of the moon); it is a feature of human activity and a product (albeit unintended) of human decisions. The economist's boom-and-bust cycle is an example, and to make sense of it, one must first understand what is going on in people's minds. The same

---

[1] " . . . an irrational world of undeserved suffering, unpunished injustice, and hopeless stupidity" are Weber's melancholy phrases for the ethical indifference of the world (1948, 122).

is true of the cycle of political morale; it is a mental thing (of course with material consequences). It is marked by two polarities. One extreme is a single predominant true belief and a general readiness to endure hardships and make sacrifices for the cause. That was the way political veterans in Orissa liked to depict their freedom struggle. The other pole is an abundance of conflicting ideologies within a single political arena. In the late 1950s, Orissa politics were moving in that direction.

High morale in a community of true believers requires hostility to be projected onto an external enemy. If victory is won and the enemy removed, unity becomes precarious. In 1905 Rabindranath Tagore, his Bengali nationalist sentiments aroused by a proposal to partition the province, wrote a number of patriotic songs, which celebrated the beauties of Bengal; but he did not in the least demonize the colonial authority (Dutta and Robinson 1996, 144–45). Three years later, following acts of terrorism by Bengalis against the British, he gave reasons for restraint.

> Some of us are reported to be of the opinion that it is mass animosity against the British that will unify India . . . So this anti-British animus, they say, must be our chief weapon . . . If that is true, then once the cause of the animosity is gone, in other words when the British leave this country, that artificial bond of unity will snap in a moment. Where, then, shall we find a second target for animosity? We shall not need to travel far. We shall find it here in our country, where we shall mangle each other in mutual antagonism, athirst for each other's blood. (Dutta and Robinson 1996, 152)

Tagore was right about the consequences: if animosity cannot be retargeted onto another outsider, the pendulum swings back and solidarity gives way to conflict. He was right, too, when he demonstrated that patriotism can, to a degree, be manifested in a positive fashion, without violence and hatred. But the implication that imperialism can be actively contested without arousing negative passions is surely mistaken, alike for him and for Gandhi.[2]

Of course, ideas and ideologies do not contest one another; peo-

---

[2] The proposition that uncalculating adherence to a cause entails an enemy is a logical transformation of the idea that "during the time when men live without a common power to keep them all in awe" there can only be the war "of every man against every man" (Hobbes 1946, 82). The difference is that anger replaces awe as the relevant unifying emotion.

ple do, and in the Orissa that I chose to observe in the 1950s those people were political leaders. Whether leaders stay with outright confrontation, asserting their own true beliefs and denigrating others, or whether they decide to negotiate (that is, to hunt for ideological common ground) or to bargain (to seek the best available outcome for themselves) depends, in part, on how they think their followers will react to compromise. The short and unpleasant truth in this process is that those who display unreasoning outrage usually sell more tickets than those who fair-mindedly concede that the other side might have a case. Compromise comes across as equivocation and a sign of weakness.

In the third book of *The Peloponnesian War* Thucydides has a wonderful description of the vicious incivility that extremes of political outrage occasion. He is writing about the city-states in fifth-century Greece, in particular Corcyra.

> What used to be regarded as a thoughtless act of aggression was now regarded as the courage one would expect to find in a party member; to think of the future and wait was merely another way of saying one was a coward; any idea of moderation was just an attempt to disguise one's unmanly character; ability to understand a question from all sides meant that one was totally unfitted for action. Fanatical enthusiasm was the mark of a real man, and to plot against an enemy behind his back was perfectly legitimate self-defence. Anyone who held violent opinions could always be trusted, and anyone who objected to them became a suspect. To plot successfully was a sign of intelligence, but it was still cleverer to see that a plot was hatching . . . In short it was equally praiseworthy to get one's blow in first against someone who was going to do wrong, and to denounce anyone who had no intention of doing any wrong at all. (1972, 242–43)

Fanatics feed on outrage, and outrage calls for a clearly defined and personified source of evil. In Corcyra, hatreds were focused inward. That is the other end of the pendulum's swing.

After 1947 there was no *single* palpable external enemy in Orissan politics, angers were diverse and mostly turned inward, and there might have arisen a condition—Gandhian ethics notwithstanding—that approached the factionalism of Corcyra. But in the 1950s Orissa came nowhere near that state of chaos. Pragmatism was the mode. I do not think this happened because people told each other they might fall into the Corcyrean pit, that unconstrained strife would end in everyone's destruction. Some of them did talk that way, especially when they pontificated about implementing the plan, and the dire consequences of pursuing sectional interests. But it was said so often that it had become a cliché, and those who heard it rarely became impassioned. Even those who spoke it were not Cassandra-like, prophesying doom; rather they had the manner of a committee chairman getting the standard agreed formalities out of the way before coming to the real business. Many of them had already quietly entered the domain of compromise and were busy making deals, using reason and responsibility, and generally taking care not to throw down gauntlets. They seemed to be serving what they believed to be the public good, staying well short of the Rubicon, partly as a matter of principle and partly because they thought it prudent to do so. That attitude of mind—combining principles with moderation and accepting compromise—is the topic for this final chapter.[3] In many ways it is an inversion of the mentality that had prevailed (so people claimed) during the freedom struggle; many of those who tacitly accepted the new political style, also professed to deplore it.

Distance Lends Enchantment

Was there in fact such a change in their attitude? Did the image they had of lost virtue represent a reality? If not, the enantiodromic process, as described, may be in error because the difference is not between what once was and now is, but between what people would like (what they fantasize) and the reality they live with. The national movement had taught them the joys of service and sacrifice, people said, and in the years immediately following independence, there was a genuine confidence in the future and (with some exceptions) a broad unity of purpose. By 1959, most of that euphoria appeared only on the front stage of public rhetoric (as in the governor's address); in private, a different tale was told. One has to ask whether that difference between public claims and private admissions had not always existed. Perhaps people chose to recall the facade and suppress the reality; perhaps they never had the unity of purpose and true-believing enthusiasm they claimed to remember; perhaps they only imagined a time of willing service and joyful sac-

[3] The Greeks, of course, had a word for that quality of mind: sophrosyne.

rifice; perhaps they were just telling a story to point up their present unease.

It may be that "distance lends enchantment to the view." The people who talked at the end of the 1950s about their frustration were complaining about the here-and-now; time had not edited what was in their minds or on their tongues. When they described the years before 1947, they may have simplified issues and straightened the paths of those who had in reality been deviant, and generally put things in an order that was consistent with the great success they had achieved. The good fight had been fought and deservedly won, and so they constructed an image of the years before 1947 that was just nostalgic fiction. There was no genuine shift from true-believing certitude to disenchantment, only our human tendency, as we grow older, to romanticize the past. Had I been there during the freedom fight, talking over each day's events—Who would not like to have a time-machine?—I might have observed some of the same backbiting, pessimism, and frustration that I did in 1959.

There must be some truth in that, certainly on the issue of unity. The people who spoke into my recorder did not conceal fights within Congress before independence. They recalled Bose, unable to stand against Gandhi, going off to found the Forward Bloc. Congress split over tactics, crucially over the use of violence. There were differences over whether to contest seats in the limited-franchise legislatures that the British introduced in selected areas, or whether to boycott elections altogether. There was a continuing, somewhat muted, division between socialists and others who had a fondness for free enterprise.[4] Those who were both Oriya nationalists and Congress supporters for sure had been caught in a dilemma and spoke freely about it. 1941 and 1942 were particularly difficult years for the Congress. Its socialist wing and the Forward Bloc people urged maximum harassment of the British, not excluding violence. Orthodox Congressmen obeyed Gandhi and wanted nonviolent noncooperation with the war effort. From a third direction, "Pandit Nilakantha Das incurred the displeasure of the Utkal provincial Congress Committee for his propaganda against Gan-

---

[4] In May 1950 Mahtab, then in Delhi, was invited to a "quiet lunch" by Maulana Azad, at that time the minister of education. "He explained to me the political situation in the Centre, how Sardar Patel was resisting the appointment of the Planning Commission, how he was openly in favor of free economy and opposing any planning whatsoever and so on" (1986, 4–5). No one in Orissa, at least when talking policy, came openly out of the capitalist closet.

dhiji's policy of nonviolence and in favour of participation in the military efforts of the British . . . He was expelled from the Congress organization with effect from the 7th August 1941" (Mahtab 1957, vol 4, 71–72).

In 1959 people mentioned some of these divisions but did not dwell on them; even Bose had been inducted into the post-1947 pantheon. Nor, *at that time*, did I hear anyone deplore the violence that broke out in 1942, when Gandhi and many senior leaders were imprisoned and the field was left clear for active saboteurs who wrecked trains and blew up bridges and stormed police stations. All in all, it had become the fashion by 1959 to recall the freedom fight in the image of unity, both in the cause itself and in the person of the leader, Gandhi.[5] Hardly surprising; it takes time, perhaps at least a generation, before people are detached enough to willingly darken the luster of a famous victory.

But that cannot be the whole story. Distance may lend enchantment, but not always; if memories are sour enough, the past remains as bad in recall as when it was the present. Mahtab's five-volume history of the freedom fight, published between 1957 and 1959, is a model of enchantment, tales of glory and adventure that tell of hateful oppressors and heroic self-sacrificing freedom fighters (and admitting to a few renegades). But what Mahtab wrote in his memoirs in 1986, or in the two versions of his Gandhi lectures (1965 and 1973), does not in the least indicate that he was ever likely to look back on the fifties in Orissa, despite his victory over the princes, and the building of the new capital and of the great Hirakud dam, as years of collective endeavor and achievement. Rather, he presented those years as a time when he was continually obstructed by

---

[5] The conscience-saving explanation from socialists, given long after the events, was that they directed violence against things (bridges, telephone lines, police stations, police uniforms, and the like) and not against people. But it is hard to burn down a police station "nonviolently" if the police inside defend it, and the record set out in Mahtab (1957, vol. 4 and 1959) shows significant human casualties on both sides.
Twenty years later Mahtab was open about the hypocrisy of those who engaged in this "mass action" (although reluctant to condemn it—often, in the 1959 volume of the *History of the Freedom Movement in Orissa*, excusing the violence as the result of police provocation or official ineptitude). In his essays on Gandhi (1973, 49–50), he wrote, "Unfortunately those congressmen, who carried out the so-called 'mass action' in 1942 and were ridiculing the non-violence of Gandhiji, subsequently after independence became the protagonists of Gandhian Truth and Non-violence under the leadership of Vinoba Bhave."

the stupidity and selfishness of other people; the glory of achievement he reserved for himself and his few allies.

There is one more thing to be said: If the question stays moot, all is not lost. I think there was high morale among the freedom fighters, dissidents notwithstanding. I also think that in 1947, for all the terrible things that were happening on the Indian subcontinent, there were high expectations. But even if neither was the case, and the past was being painted rosier than people knew it to have been, the problem is still there. In 1959 most freedom-fighters, like their younger colleagues and others who had not been part of the movement or had opposed it, were displaying clear and unequivocal signs of disenchantment with the political process. The present, as they saw it, was anything but rosy. Whatever morale was like earlier, that discontent and that loudly-deplored sense of disunity still have to be explained.

Hard Realities and High Hopes

Assuming the freedom fighters had a unity of purpose, how did they achieve it? Or if they only thought they had it, how did they think they achieved it? Years later, some of them were still exercised by that question in the light of what they had since experienced. Mahtab clearly felt that after independence things did not work out as he would have wished. He thought about the reasons, and in the first version of his essays on Gandhi he wrote (1965, 2):

> In these sixteen years of independence when the first flush of enthusiasm which freedom brought in its trail is wearing out, as it does in all cases of success, and when high hopes raised by the success itself are dashing against hard realities of the circumstances, necessity has arisen to hark back and restudy the method of the Great Leader who pulled the country out of utter despair and put it on the right track to the goal of independence. How could he do it?

Mahtab's conception of political morale, at first sight simple, requires some unfolding. "Hard realities," he implies, bring down "high hopes." In a sense he is right. Hopes are high until experience proves them unrealizable; then people lose their nerve. In another sense, he is not right, if he means that to experience failure and dis-appointment—to be put in jail, to see one's opponents unmoved by what one does and says, or to discover that one's allies and follow-ers have gone their own way—is *ipso facto* to lose hope. The free-dom fighters had frequent encounters with hard reality, particularly with the bureaucratic carapace of the imperial power and its legion of loyal Indian servants. The issue, then, is not experience of adver-sity, but the capacity to be *unimpressed* by that experience: the strength, in other words, to be unrealistic, to ignore contrary evi-dence, to make believe, to have such faith in the leaders and in the cause that defeat becomes unimaginable. If one understands how people blind themselves to adverse experiences, one also under-stands enchantment, and therefore disenchantment, which is no more than accepting adversity as insurmountable and the goal as unattainable.

Gandhi, the "Great Leader," Mahtab suggests, had himself cre-ated the high morale that carried the movement through to inde-pendence. He made swaraj an issue for everyone; without his ef-forts and his communicative skills, the national movement could never have reached down to the common people. That is Mahtab's claim, and it is true. In India's struggle for freedom, Gandhi was the charismatic nonpareil. Nehru wrote this about him:

> For it was clear that this little man of poor physique had some-thing of steel in him, something rock-like which did not yield to physical powers, however great they might be. . . . there was a roy-alty and kingliness in him which compelled a willing obeisance from others. Consciously and deliberately meek and humble, yet he was full of power and authority, and he knew it, and at times he was imperious enough, issuing commands which had to be obeyed. His calm deep eyes would hold one and gently probe into the depths; his voice, clear and limpid, would purr its way into the heart and evoke an emotional response. Whether his audience consisted of one person or a thousand, the charm and magnetism of the man passed on to it, and each one had a feeling of commu-nion with the speaker . . . The language was always simple and to the point and seldom was an unnecessary word used. It was the utter sincerity of the man and his personality that gripped; he gave the impression of tremendous inner reserves of power. (1962, 129–30)

In the twenties and thirties Gandhi dominated the national movement. Nehru, scoffing at a journalist who suggested that Gandhi had become an embarrassment, wrote:

> But without him where was the struggle, where was Civil Disobedience and Satyagraha? He was part of the living movement; indeed, he was the movement itself. So far as that struggle was concerned everything depended on him. (1962, 288)

It was Gandhi, before all others, who gave the movement its popular support.

> His main activity for some years had been Khadi propaganda, and with this object he had taken extensive tours all over India. He took each province by turn and visited every district and almost every town of any consequence, as well as remote rural areas. Everywhere he attracted enormous crowds . . . I do not think any other human being has ever travelled about India as much as he has done. (1962, 191)

Mahtab, no less than Nehru under the spell of Gandhi's personality, was also, like Nehru, a very practical thinker. Charisma is conventionally regarded as an attribute of the person, something magical, a "personality that grip[s];" a leader either has it or lacks it. But Mahtab, while not denying the charisma, believed that Gandhi had a *method* that politicians could "hark back to and restudy." He liked to demystify Gandhi and show him to be hardheaded and calculating (like Mahtab himself). Recall his comment on Gandhi's claim that God guided him. Gandhi repeatedly referred to his "intuition." When Mahtab consulted him about what to do in Orissa and asked what humble workers like himself could do, since they were not gifted with intuition, "Gandhi smiled," and said that the word "judgment" would do as well. The text continues: "To understand Gandhi's leadership properly one is always to keep in mind that he was trying to make the masses move with faith and confidence to achieve the national objective" (1965, 4).

To speak of Gandhi's "method" implies that charisma is to be understood less as a simple quality of the person than as a function of the leader's demonstrated attributes in relation to a cultural and historical context. Those who understand the context and its requirements know how to cultivate the appropriate attributes.

The cultural context in India was not unfavorable to leadership.

Most people I knew in Orissa, from the villagers of Bisipara to Bhubaneswar's intelligentsia, were habituated to thinking of their rulers in Leviathan-like terms. They saw nothing unusual or undesirable in having someone in charge, someone to cope with crises and to settle disputes.[6] In that respect they were the inverse of libertarians; the sentiment of "look to government" and the paternalism in which it resided was second nature to them. If one substitutes "look to a leader," that sentiment was almost everyone's, including (with some ambivalent confusion, to which I will come in a moment) the Gandhian anarchists themselves.

The presentational style must fit the context. Subhas Chandra Bose, as Netaji ("respected leader"), saw himself as a charismatic leader, but he chose the wrong style. India, he wrote, needed "a strong Central Government with dictatorial powers for some years to come . . . Government by a strong party bound together by military discipline" (Toye 1962, 44). He was, as I said, captivated by the example of Hitler and Mussolini. But their mode does not accord with Indian preconceptions of leadership. Conceivably it might have jibed with the warrior kings of India's history—the seventeenth-century Maratha, Shivaji Bhonsle, comes to mind—but I never heard the comparison made. Bose's model is twentieth-century; it makes a fetish out of efficiency, is media-attentive, and endows the leader not with the mildly mystical qualities of representing in his person the body politic, as paternalism does, but with the stark (and very precarious) image of a miracle-worker. If there are no miracles, or if they come inverted as major disasters (as with Hitler and Mussolini), that puts an end to enchantment, and, at least for a time, to whatever philosophy the fallen leader propagated. European-style fascism had no appeal to the ordinary people of India, and not much to the political elite, who took from Europe mostly a meld of nineteenth-century liberalism and this century's socialism. The faith invested in Bose—some of that survived, as the narratives given earlier show, despite the disasters that ended his career and his life—owed more to a style of action (heroic adventuring) than to fascist philosophy.

The mode of leadership that came naturally to paternalists (not Gandhians) was not charismatic but traditional. Legitimacy resided in an office—of collector, or prince, or minister of government. The

---

[6] That does not mean they were unable to show disrespect or contemplate rebellion. Nor did they lack skill at ducking commands when it suited them. See chapter 3.

office legitimized the person through a performance repertoire that did not belong to the incumbent but to the office itself: installation ceremonies, periodic ritualized displays of leadership virtues, and a measure of dignity maintained in everyday interactions. Of course, the personal style of an incumbent might enhance the majesty already granted, or diminish it. But the leader did not create the faith that made his subjects trusting and confident; the faith transcended him. It was fortified by tradition, which was both its strength and its weakness. Long-enduring faith, when it brings adversity, is that much less easily abandoned. On the other hand, such believers find any kind of mind changing difficult, do not adapt readily to new situations, and therefore risk being left behind by events. The Orissa princes were pointed down that road to extinction, although in 1959 their agile remaking of themselves as parliamentarians had given them some years of grace.[7]

Uncertainty calls up a different kind of leader whose personal capacities compel faith. Such faith is usually fragile, not only because it ends at death but also because charismatic leaders eventually must produce results. If they fail, the charisma usually evaporates; if it survives (as in the continued veneration for Gandhi), it is severed from command. The leader continues to be respected, even loved, but no longer decides what is to be done. That was Gandhi's fate even before India won independence.

Gandhi, not surprisingly, meanders across categorical boundaries, combining items, as patches in a patchwork quilt, that one

---

[7] If tradition-bound leaders generally do not fare well in conditions that are new, threaten uncertainty, and do not respond to standard procedures, how did princes succeed in getting themselves elected? Adult suffrage was a novel situation, both for them and for their electors. It was new, certainly, but it did not represent any radical change. Paternalism generally—and faith in princes—was kept steady for ordinary people by the continuing experience of life as it had always been. An election was not a matter of life and death, not a crisis, but more a small commotion that also was an entertainment (a tamasha). "People are no good," the Talcher man said, speaking of those who voted for their former tyrant. But in fact the people were what they had always been, and when they voted for their prince, they were ritually celebrating the only ruler they knew. Paternalism was their sole political style.

On the other hand, where lives were radically upset—among the ruling elite of freedom fighters, the princes themselves, politicians generally, and senior bureaucrats—the legitimacy of paternalism was challenged, and it became only one among several claimants on the fund of available true belief. Even the princes had to dilute paternalism with socialism and, from time to time, enthuse about "implementing the plan."

would not have thought combinable. Paternal, in the broad sense of the word, he surely was. People referred to him as *bapu* (father).[8] But *paternalist* does not suit, if one has in mind princes or authoritarian bureaucrats. There is ample evidence that he was a person of authority who commanded deference,[9] but the only other feature he shared with princes was tapping the reservoir of taken-for-granted Hindu exemplars, and the one he used—the ascetic—was poles apart from the royal style. Asceticism tied him firmly to a vast fundament of Hindu values that uplifted him in the eyes of ordinary people: frugality and the simple life, spirituality, innocence, wisdom, and even the power to work miracles.[10] He was given (by Rabindranath Tagore) the suggestively spiritual title *Mahatma* or "great soul" (in which he claimed to take no pleasure).[11]

His style disavowed power. He did not give orders. (More accurately, he gave advice that was usually received as an order. Nehru remarked that for all Gandhi's courteousness, arguing with him was like "addressing a closed door.") His presentational idiom was the inverse of a Netaji-style dictator. He spoke up when he thought he had been mistaken, which charismatic leaders rarely do. He even took a pride in his own fallibility, admitting he was not consistent in his philosophy, and urging people to believe whatever was his most recent version of the truth. He gloried in the continued growth that a change of mind implies.

> At the time of writing I never think of what I have said before. My aim is not to be consistent with my previous statements on a given question, but to be consistent with truth as *it may present itself* to

[8] Since the common people sometimes called him *ma-bap*—mother-father—perhaps the word should be "parental." An argument is often made that Gandhi's role, both in his public and his private life, is better called "maternal." A persuasive statement of this point of view is made in Bose 1953. See also the brief memoir by his great-niece, *Bapu—My Mother* (Gandhi 1955).

[9] "Gandhiji addressed them [a meeting of Muslims in Allahabad] and after hearing him they looked even more frightened than before. He spoke well in his best dictatorial vein. He was humble, but also clear-cut and hard as a diamond, pleasant and soft-spoken but inflexible and terribly earnest" (Nehru 1962, 46).

[10] More is involved than a frugal life style. A letter, written by Mahtab in 1956, has this passage, "We are passing through a very difficult period. . . . but I have faith in Gandhiji's tapasya. It will not go in vain. Somehow something will get us out of the difficulties" (1986, 178). Tapas, kindled by the practice of asceticism, eliminates sin from the world and makes good things happen.

[11] "Thank God my much vaunted Mahatmaship has never fooled me" (quoted in Bose 1953, 201).

me at a given moment. (*Harijan*, 30 September 1939, emphasis added.)

The subtitle of his autobiography ("My experiments with truth") conveys exactly that unremitting reflexivity and apparently open-ended responsiveness to new ideas.[12]

How could a creed that changed from day to day, offered by a leader more than ready to admit his own mistakes, nevertheless pull "the country out of utter despair and put it on the right track to the goal of independence?" Leaders, more than anyone, must be seen to have faith in themselves and their decisions. They can get away with "I have nothing to offer but blood, toil, tears and sweat," but not with "I listen to one side, and they seem right, and then God! I talk to the other side and they seem just as right, and there I am where I started. . . . God, what a job!"[13] They can even admit failure and offer to get out—Nasser did and so did Castro, and both survived—but they cannot confess to not knowing where to go and what to do. If that is the case, then either Gandhi's meandering "experiments with truth" were not as open-ended and provisional as he made them out to be, or else the philosophy did not have much to do with his hold over the freedom fighters and the Indian masses. Both these propositions are, up to a point, correct.

Gandhi's philosophy had three distinct but connected elements: a recommended form of society; an ethic of service (sarvodaya); and an ethic of nonviolent struggle (satyagraha). (Notice that none of these elements, not even the last, speaks to my main thesis: that impassioned unity is a function of animosity.)

The first element—a blueprint for a nation made up of self-governing villages—died a hard and protracted death after 1947, but it never seemed likely to become a reality, and, for sure, its vision of an archaic nonindustrial society was not what brought the Indian middle classes out of their "utter despair."

Linked closely with the idea of the self-governing village was sarvodaya, "the uplift of all." That too remained on the bannerhead after independence. At first sight, sarvodaya coincided in its aims

[12] He may sound like a pragmatist, suiting his values to the situation. In fact he was far from that. Ideas and policies were tested not against their practicality but in the light of an (apparently ever-changing) "truth." He was, as Nehru said, "a very difficult person to understand."

[13] The first quotation is Churchill's, speaking in the House of Commons in May 1940. The second is President Warren Harding writing (privately) about his frustration with economic problems. It is quoted in Burns 1979, 410.

with the development policies of state socialism (the experiments in Koraput, for example, were intended to promote cooperative farming). But there were quite profound differences in basic assumptions about voluntarism, reflected both in personnel and in methods. The state relied mainly on civil servants and mandatory institutional reform, sarvodaya on social workers and a change of heart in individuals. Sarvodaya was, in Gandhi's view, a missionary endeavor, a religious calling, a command to go out among people and teach them truth and righteousness.

Was sarvodaya the "method" that pulled the country out of "utter despair?" The good feeling that comes from a life of service and sacrifice should certainly get rid of "utter despair." But that was not Gandhi's goal. Sarvodaya was not a way to make those *giving* the service feel good about themselves; it was an end in itself. In any event, the morale raised would be that of the social workers. What of ordinary people? If it was the case that the peasant masses, to the extent that they gave the national movement their support, were in fact responding to Gandhi's appeal to control their acquisitive instincts and think more often of giving than of getting, then certainly sarvodaya would have been the "method" that Mahtab sought. But no one makes that case. Mahtab, I suspect, probably saw the "giving" in a quite unGandhian light, as purely political. He did not pretend that sarvodaya was anything other than a technique for mobilizing popular support among the villagers who benefited from the services provided. It was a tool for gaining peasant support, not an end in itself.

Nehru seems to have thought so too. In September 1932, in one of his many periods in jail, he heard that Gandhi had announced a "fast unto death" to protest a proposal by the government to establish separate electorates for untouchables. An end to untouchability was an important element in Gandhi's constructive work program. But he saw untouchability essentially as a moral problem, to be solved not by institutional change but by a change of heart. Separate electorates would only deepen the divide between untouchables and the rest of Hindu society. Indeed, social reform of any kind must begin with ethics, with religious conviction, not with institutional reform. Nehru, no less aware of the need for change in Indian society, was quite sure that institutional change would have to come first—but only *after* the political battle had been won and independence achieved. Sarvodaya for Nehru was neither a priority nor an end in itself.

I felt annoyed with him for choosing a side-issue—just a question of electorate. What would be the result on our freedom movement? . . . After so much sacrifice and brave endeavour, was our movement to tail off into something insignificant?

I felt angry with him at his religious and sentimental approach to a political question, and his frequent references to God in connection with it. He seemed even to suggest that God had indicated the very date of the fast. What a terrible example to set! (1962, 370)

But then he saw the outcome. On the next page he writes;

Then came the news of the tremendous upheaval all over the country, a magic wave of enthusiasm running through Hindu society, and untouchability appeared to be doomed. What a magician, I thought, was this little man sitting in Yeravda prison, and how well he knew how to pull the strings that move people's hearts! (1962, 371)

Magic indeed! Nehru marveled at (and welcomed) the results but appeared put out by the methods.

I used to be troubled sometimes at the growth of this religious element in our politics, both on the Hindu and the Muslim side. I did not like it at all. . . . Even some of Gandhiji's phrases sometimes jarred upon me—thus his frequent reference to Rama Raja as a golden age which was to return. But I was powerless to intervene, and I consoled myself with the thought that Gandhiji used the words because they were well known and understood by the masses. He had an amazing knack of reaching the heart of the people. (1962, 72)

He continued:

As for Gandhiji, he was a very difficult person to understand, sometimes his language was almost incomprehensible to an average modern. But we felt that we knew him quite well enough to realize that he was a great and unique man and a glorious leader, and having put our faith in him we gave him almost blank cheque, for the time being at least. Often we discussed his fads and peculiarities among ourselves and said, half-humorously, that when Swaraj came these fads must not be encouraged. (1962, 73)

"These fads"—a revealing phrase—are what gave Gandhi his contact with the masses. The asceticism, the clothing, the image of the holy man, above all the technique of intimidating an oppressor by inflicting harm on oneself constitute the "amazing knack of reaching the heart of the people." Nehru, astringently rational, evidently found this difficult to understand.

> What a problem and a puzzle he has been not only to the British Government but to his own people and his closest associates! Perhaps in every other country he would be out of place to-day, but India still seems to understand, or at least appreciate, the prophetic-religious type of man, talking of sin and salvation and non-violence. (1962, 253)

In short, sarvodaya was at best a source of self-respect for the movement's elite (see Nehru on the "chosen race," quoted below). Sarvodaya's "enemy"—ignorance, poverty, selfishness, acquisitiveness, and the like—may have stimulated those who had a vocation for missionary work, but surely was too elusive and impersonal to fire up true-believing enthusiasm in all the freedom fighters. For some of Gandhi's "closest associates" his philosophy evidently was a puzzle. But if the phrase "his own people" is extended to mean the ordinary peasant, what they must have seen was not the social worker but the saint. No doubt they also were glad to have people help them against extortionate landlords and bullying officials. *But it was the messenger and his way of life that made the contact, not the message about service and self-sacrifice.*

Nehru put it like this:

> Gandhiji, indeed, was continually laying stress on the religious and spiritual side of the movement. . . . the whole movement was strongly influenced by this and took on a revivalist character as far as the masses were concerned. (1962, 72)

He did not approve. In May 1933 Gandhi launched another fast. About this Nehru wrote:

> It seemed to me sheer revivalism, and clear thinking had not a ghost of a chance against it. All India, or most of it, stared reverently at the Mahatma and expected him to perform miracle after miracle and put an end to untouchability and get swaraj and so on—and did precious little itself! And Gandhiji did not encourage others to think; his insistence was only on purity and sacrifice. (1962, 373)

If not in sarvodaya, then was the inspiration for true belief found in the philosophy of satyagraha, the nonviolent struggle to find truth? Some of the people who tried to enlighten me in 1959 thought so. They claimed, with repetitive insistence, that Gandhi gave them self-respect, confidence, and the will to endure by teaching them not to hate their enemies, only help them see the truth.

> The essence of non-violence . . . consists in resisting the evil of the wrongdoer so that he is forced to shower punishment upon the non-violent man for his resistance or non-cooperation with evil. If the latter does not bend, then his heroic suffering in a just cause is likely to evoke respect for him in the heart of the wrong-doer, and the process of conversion begins. . . . The way of non-violence thus becomes a way of heroic self-suffering in which the fighter never surrenders his respect for the personality of the opponent, and aims at his conversion rather than destruction. (Bose 1953, 202)

Satyagraha has a curious internal contradiction. Written in the terms of high morality, logically it is amoral. It sets out to do what I am arguing cannot be done: create enthusiasm and faith without focusing on a human enemy. Satyagraha recognizes evil, identifies it, and makes it a target. But it exonerates the evildoer. Recall what the nostalgic Congressman said, "We were not to hate the British people, but only the administration which they put over us. We should think them our friends but realize they were doing wrong things and try to convince them of this." Evil, in other words, must not be personified. Blame the system, not the people; no animosity, no hatred, no witch hunts. But, paradoxically, that supremely moral injunction (to love one's enemies, for in themselves they are blameless) requires a totally nonmoral premise: that all conduct is a function of the structured context. There is no room in that scheme of things for moral choice and moral responsibility. The wrongdoer is not blameworthy. He cannot be judged a good or evil person, because he is not a person. He makes no choices. He is only a machine, programmed to do what the system requires.

But life is more than an exercise in logic, and logical contradictions do not put an end to faith. They can even be a reinforcement; *credo quia absurdum*. In any case, the faithful, by definition, do not deconstruct their own creed. So the question remains: Was satyagraha the element in Gandhi's philosophy that "pulled the country out of utter despair?"

The rule of forgiveness, entailing nonviolence, was potentially a foundation for self-respect. It gave access to a "truth," which had nothing to do with the truth of experience—the hard reality of being beaten with a lathi or dragged off to jail—but was in fact another word for the divine purpose. Truth was not "everything that is the case" but rather what *ought to be* the case, God's design for the world. This philosophy (nonviolence and the search for truth) was one explanation Mahtab offered for Gandhi's success as a leader and for India's present discontents: "A nation without a philosophy is like a ship without a rudder." Before 1947, they had Gandhi's philosophy to guide them. After 1947 they had no guidance and, sixteen years later, they were sliding back into "utter despair." But, as I shall show, Mahtab himself was not guided by that philosophy.

Nonviolence did have a front-stage position in the freedom struggle. A few people internalized it as a moral imperative. Others, like the man from Talcher, appreciated its tactical advantages; violence and casualties, he had noticed in Dhenkanal, could swiftly terminate an agitation. Others were conscious of its limitations. Mahtab himself testified that the method was effective only against a regime that was governed by the rule of law. "There must be rule of law for Satyagraha . . . it cannot operate against a dictatorial Government which does not allow freedom of opinion and action." (1965, 40–41).[14]

Nehru likewise recognized the method's limitations. Gandhi did not.

> That led to the conclusion that the non-violent method was not meant for all contingencies, and was thus neither a universal nor an infallible method. This conclusion was intolerable for Gandhiji, for he firmly believed it was a universal and infallible method. . . . it must function . . . even in the midst of strife and violence. (1962, 209)

But Nehru also gave nonviolence his somewhat dispassionate approval.

> To some extent the revivalist element in our movement carried us on; a feeling that non-violence as conceived for political or eco-

[14] The British must have realized—when faced, for example in 1942, with the opposite—that dealing with nonviolent people was less expensive and less painful than dealing with terrorists.

nomic movements or for righting wrongs was a new message which our people were destined to give to the world. We became victims to the curious illusion of all peoples and all nations that in some way they are a chosen race. Non-violence was the moral equivalent of war and of all violent struggle. It was not merely an ethical alternative, but it was effective also. (1962, 76)

Whether for normative or pragmatic reasons, the principle of nonviolence did have a major influence over conduct in the freedom fight (and, Mahtab claimed, survived in a corrupt form to trouble governments in independent India). Cultural performances that elsewhere incite violence—inflammatory hate-parading speeches, burning effigies, propaganda about atrocities—were not in Gandhi's repertoire. Neither was direct violence in the form of assassinations or the destruction of property, and on one famous occasion in 1922, when "a mob of villagers had retaliated on some policemen by setting fire to the police-station and burning half a dozen or so policemen in it," Gandhi called off the campaign of noncooperation and civil resistance. "This sudden suspension of our movement . . . was resented, I think, by almost all the Congress leaders—other than Gandhiji, of course."[15]

To make the point by understatement, Gandhi endeavored to be a consistently moral person. There were some others, too, who had enough self-discipline to expose themselves to beatings and not strike back. The few Gandhians whom I met had indeed a calm and unaggressive conviction of their own rightness, which, to my surprise, even at this distance I still find impressive rather than objectionable. But I encountered few such people. I cannot see that philosophy alone—nonviolence and the search for truth—being Mahtab's "rudder," still less the "method" that led the country out of "utter despair;" nonviolence could not have been the *prime* mover in raising morale. Most of those who supported the Indian national congress did not do so in order to prove themselves by nonviolent self-sacrifice.

If Mahtab was right, and there was a philosophy that shaped Gandhi's method, it must have had more to it than satyagraha or

[15] Nehru 1962, 81–82. Nehru goes on, "Were a remote village and a mob of excited peasants in an out-of-the-way place going to put an end . . . to our national struggle for freedom? . . . Must we train the three hundred and odd millions of India in the theory and practice of non-violent action before we could go forward?"

the ever-shifting elusive creed that nonstop reflexivity implies. There was, in fact, a firm core of beliefs. One part, which gave the national movement its mass support, was the charisma that Gandhi derived from being a Hindu ascetic. What the common people saw and were attracted by was not an ideology but a style of life. A second part, which appealed in varying degrees to the movement's activists, was, to use Mahtab's phrase, the armory of "moral weapons:" nonviolent civil disobedience and noncooperation with the government, service and the uplift of all, a refusal to hate, an endless capacity for self-suffering, and a resolute struggle to find "the truth"—a distinctively Hindu package that, to repeat Nehru's irony, contained "a new message which our people were destined to give to the world." The third part, which captured the movement's middle-class supporters, was a catalog of purportedly Hindu virtues set in opposition to the values of the colonial power: spiritual against material concerns; an altruistic regard for the community and one's fellows against greed, acquisitiveness, and aggressive entrepreneurialism; and a truly decentralized democracy of village communities as the antithesis of an intrusive, corrupt, and despotic state. These virtues (spiritual concerns, public spirit, and self-government) are the precise *positive* inverts of colonialist negative stereotypes of the Indian character: passivity, soul-centered and therefore selfish religiosity, and a political capacity for nothing between chaos and despotism. Notice that this third tier of the philosophy, which, like the second, is clearly a mechanism for engendering self-respect, identifies qualities that mark, as *un*worthy of respect, the very same opponent for whose person the "fighter [satyagrahi] never surrenders his respect."

The Gandhian devices of nonviolence, sarvodaya, and the struggle to find truth were moral weapons in the fight for independence, alternatives to terrorism or roundtable conferencing. But it is hard to see them as the levers that lifted people out of "utter despair." If they had possessed that force, they might have done what Mahtab wanted when the "hard realities" struck home in the years after independence. But they did not: "Gandhian technique has become a matter of distant history now. It lost all contact with the situation which developed after independence" (1973, 46). Sarvodaya, like nonviolence, became tainted. Mahtab, as the statements quoted earlier demonstrate, considered that the movement's leaders after 1947 were misguided and were putting on a "hypocritical and superficial show" and being pampered by "gorgeous arrangements." The spirit of service also diminished. The very people, it was said, who before 1947 had been ready to sacrifice their all for the cause, after 1947 forgot unity and self-sacrifice, and would exert themselves only for their own advantage. "They have no interest in voluntary work," the old man said, "they want remuneration for anything they do."

People also—Mahtab not least—swiftly regained the capacity to hate the enemy (if they had ever lost it). Mahtab wrote, "In the Indian administration of the British there were only a few Englishmen, all the rest being Indians who loyally served the British. They were participants in repression and suppression of national movement in India" (1965, 49). When he wrote of misguided administrators, or princes, or social workers, anger was more evident than Gandhian forgiveness.

> Incidentally I am constrained to observe that this image [of the freedom fight] was tarnished to a great extent when those who were arch enemies of the fighting Congress and ardent supporters of the British were placed in high position in Government [after 1947]. My predecessor [as governor of Bombay] is an instance in point. He, as a loyal civil servant of the British Government, did his utmost to paint Gandhiji and the Congress in the blackest possible colour before the citizens of the USA where he was deputed to make propaganda about India during the war. We in Ahmednagar Fort used to fret and foam on reading his speeches so much so that once Jawaharlaljee shouted in anger that after release and India obtaining freedom, he would make pinced pie [mince-pie, therefore mincemeat?] out of Girija Shankar Bajpai. (1986, 102)

There are several similar references to the same man in Mahtab's memoirs. Evidently even Gandhi's warmest admirers were quite selective in the parts of his philosophy they allowed to guide them.[16]

What, then, gave the freedom fighters, in all their diversity, faith to unite them in the cause? Of course it was the cause itself, self-rule. Gandhi complicated that word by making it also mean "self-

---

[16] Characteristically, Mahtab did not content himself with plain animosity. He had worked out a possible solution to the problem, although it had come to him too late. He complained that the leaders of the satyagraha movement had not sufficiently looked ahead. "In the whole plan of Satyagraha, there was no arrangement for building a cadre of intellectuals having the experience of field work who would be required at the time of transfer of power to take charge of

discipline," the observation of God's rules for right conduct and control over the emotions as a way of controlling events. For a few dedicated and exceptional people, perhaps that was how they saw the cause they served. But for the great majority of freedom fighters, the dominant meaning of "self-rule" was the departure of the British. A significant mass of freedom fighters, whatever their ideological persuasion—left-wing, right-wing, believers in violence or nonviolence—were ready to subordinate present differences in order to attain the one unifying end, the termination of British rule and in its place self-rule. Simple nationalism did more than Gandhian philosophy to hold the movement together. Nirmal Kumar Bose wrote, "But having been in the thick of it, I often observed that the interest of many workers in satyagraha was not very deep. They were more interested in dealing hard blows on the imperial system which had brought our country to the verge of ruin than in the conversion of the British opponent" (1953, 15). "Hard blows" on the "British opponent"—animosity—provided the fuel that kept morale high, and the catalogue of Hindu virtues and British vices implied in Gandhi's philosophy must, whatever his intentions, have assisted in that process.

It is therefore unlikely that the part of Gandhi's "method" that was contained in his philosophy would ever have been a match for the "hard realities" that followed independence; they were too complex and too diverse, too resistant to any single centering philosophy, and, above all, there was no single target on which the many different antipathies might have been focused. Of course, the test never came because Gandhi was murdered by a Hindu fundamentalist on Jan 30th, 1948, five months after independence. Control of policy, in any case, was by then in other hands.

My writ runs no more . . . No one listens to me any more. I am a small man. True, there was a time when mine was a big voice. Then everyone obeyed what I said; now neither the Congress nor the Hindus nor the Muslims listen to me. Where is the Congress today? It is disintegrating. I am crying in the wilderness.

---

the administration" (1965, 49). He goes on to point out that if the transfer had been violent, the problem would not have arisen; the old administration would have been destroyed. There is a slight note of regret that this did not happen, swiftly countered by the remark that such violence would have been expensive and unGandhian.

That was Gandhi on April 1, 1947, addressing a prayer meeting (quoted in Chatterjee, 1986, 116).

Even Gandhi, the gentlest of this century's great leaders, could not, despite his efforts, avoid having an enemy built into the campaign that enthused his fellow Indians. He struggled hard not to personalize the enemy, insisting that evil resided not in people but in systems, organizations, and ways of life. But the tide of human nature runs strongly in the other direction. In the summer of 1947 India's men-in-the-street provided an awful reminder of the frailty of nonviolence, and the robust human propensity to personalize evil: they murdered half a million of their fellow citizens.

Moderation and Its Causes

The brief but terrible communal violence in the summer of 1947 did not impinge on Orissa and, as earlier descriptions suggest, Oriya politicians in the 1950s exhibited a fair degree of civility. Why were they temperate? What saved them from the miseries of Corcyra?

Diverse opinions need not lead straight to disenchantment. Quite the opposite: those who incline to romanticism see excellence in diversity and are made happy by an abundance of differences. Even those who view the world through the vision of the Enlightenment and its quest for universal order may, in principle, accept diversity as creative, prompting new ideas, leading to a debate that ends in consensus about what should and can be done. But such a consensus, pace Gandhi, does not "present itself" to the debaters as a truth that is inescapable because God wants it so. Still less does it emerge when the antagonists stand rigid in their true belief. Agreement happens when they give in order to get, when they bargain, or when they negotiate. Sometimes they stick at the stage of confrontation, countenancing no other outcome than the destruction of the adversary. Sometimes they regress. Initially they expect to win through confrontation, bending the opponent to their definition of the situation; then, if they come down to bargain, it is because they no longer hope to win outright. But even after a bargain has been struck, the adversarial spirit may remain and the antagonists watch for a chance to start the fight again.

Without doubt there were conflicting opinions in Orissa about what should be done. After 1947 there was no clear goal, or, if goals could be grandiloquently stated (India's greatness, say, or Orissa's prosperity, or the "perfect social and economic justice" of the governor's address, or even "implementing the plan"), it was not clear what those phrases meant, still less how to accomplish whatever it was they signified, or decide which endeavors should have priority. Nothing replaced the beautifully simple and unequivocal goal of an India freed from its alien rulers. There were diverse opinions about the "natural" order of the good society: equality and individual rights (as in the governor's address), hierarchy and duty to the state (Bose as the extreme exponent, the paternalists with a milder version), or a society founded on Gandhi's eclectic moral beliefs. These programs appear unitary and strong when presented as rhetoric, but had any one of them ever been implemented (and therefore unpackaged by an encounter with reality) it would surely have foundered on its own internal confusions. (The one possibility left undiscussed by the politicians at that time, or at least unadvocated, was that dissonance itself, properly handled, might not be so bad. Even those who lived that way, Mahtab, for example, did so from behind the facade of a different ideology.)

1959's dissonance was the product of many voices. There were the parties: Congress, Ganatantra, Praja Socialist, Lohia Socialist (a single MLA), Communists, and Jharkhand. Still heard were discordant strains from within the freedom movement itself: violence against nonviolence, a strong state against benign Gandhian anarchism, socialists against conservatives, Marxists against Gandhians, and the like. Behind the facade of differences about principles and high policy, the voices of more particular interests were heard: Oriya nationalism, hill districts versus the coast, tenants against landlords, the brief renascence of a Tory-like aristocracy in Orissa's politics, and various other concerns. Mahtab summarized them as "disintegrating tendencies on account of caste, religion and language." Those were the conventional fault lines of Indian society, and all three continued to cause disastrous upheavals in independent India.

But in Orissa in 1959, only the last, language, had the capacity to get people into the streets. Religion played a very small part, Muslims being only a fraction of the population (slightly above one percent in the fifties) and everyone else (apart from Christians, who were less than one percent) had no problem with being considered Hindu. Nor was caste a great producer of discord at that time. Primordial loyalties to one's own caste were strong, except in the case of a few individuals in the western-educated elite, but the effect of caste on parliamentary politics in Orissa was much diminished by a Madisonian fragmentation, the multiplicity of divergent interests canceling one another out, and sometimes leading to deals and compromises over the selection of candidates.[17] Indeed, diverse and often conflicting loyalties and obligations made it quite difficult for a politician to be anything but a temporizer. Where should their loyalties lie? Those who spent much of their time balancing the interests of self, family, caste, party, constituency, district, region, state and nation were unlikely to succumb to a true belief, except perhaps as a refuge from the constant uncertainty.[18]

None of the deeper attachments, whether formulated ideologies (socialism, communism, free enterprise, the Gandhian philosophy, and so on) or unarticulated tendencies bred in the bone (paternalism and the principle of hierarchy, or, on the other side, the joy of resistance as a way of life and an end in itself) were fundamentalist enough to displace prudence and clear the ground for true belief. Few people active in politics in Orissa in the fifties behaved like *intensely* true-believing ideologists. Some communists did; but by no means all. In 1959 those I knew, including some who had gone underground or been jailed in 1947 and 1948, played by parliamentary rules inside the house and mostly used Gandhian nonviolent tactics outside it. The same was true of socialists. A few fanatical Gandhians survived, but very few, and they were restrained by the ethic of nonviolence. The great majority of both major and minor players in the political game, although most of them were for sure not unprincipled, knew how to cut a deal. Sometimes they did so in ways that

[17] This was less true of the Orissa educational bureaucracy, in which there was a polarization between Karans and Brahmins. People claimed that careers were made or broken according to whether the Director of Public Instruction was a Karan or a Brahmin.

[18] It may be that the some of Orissa's leaders had a penchant for spiritual matters because therein lay an escape from the uncertainty of everyday life. One wonders, also, how often the astrologer's advice decided not only whether to take a plane trip, but also matters of state, whether a minister should be dismissed or a policy abandoned. One recalls the man who preached the Gita, and the Ganatantra rani who believed in prayer. Mahtab himself gloried in his own spiritual concerns. There is also an extraordinary story of a "disaster of unthinkable proportions," forecast for February 1962 by a Bhubaneswar swami (lining up with astrologers across India) and averted by a monstrous sacrifice organized by a "managing committee" that included a man who had been a leading politician in 1959 and was the editor of one of Orissa's daily newspapers, by the Assembly's speaker, and by another minister of government. *See* Miller 1980, 90.

left them open to disparagement. When the leaders of the coalition spoke grandly of stability and the chance for progress that was now open, the remaining opposition (parties of the left) spoke of "a consolidation of reactionary forces," "a move to perpetuate Congress rule," a ruse "by the chief minister to strengthen his own position inside the Congress party," and "the only motivation behind this unusual coalition is to share power together."

Such dealing, however, was not unambiguously cynical or self-interested. The climate of opinion after 1947 contained contradictory tendencies. There was a perceptible element of idealism, a feeling that this was a new dawn, an opportunity: the British were gone, the controls were in their own Indian hands. That generated at least a simulacrum of fellow feeling (which did prove somewhat fragile when it encountered Mahtab's "hard realities"). There was still in 1959 an overall sense that, at bottom, they ought not to be each other's enemies—not even the princes and the prajamandalists—and they should be able to work out solutions acceptable to both sides.[19] "Implement the plan" was not wholly facade.

On the other hand, they told themselves, for more than a generation they had given their all in the struggle for independence. Now the prize was won, the time had come to hand out rewards.[20] Some of the leaders saw things that way. I am not referring only to the spoils that politicians crave—appointments and the like—but also to larger collective rewards. If India has its freedom, then why not also liberate Oriyas trapped in Saraikella and Kharsawan? Implementing the plan should not mean that my constituency or my district will get the short end of the stick, while others benefit. Considerations of this kind slip easily away from principles in the direction of interests, a shift that conventionally is deplored, but perhaps should not be. Interests are more readily quantified than principles, and are therefore more easily divided, and that makes bargaining easier, and every bargain means that reason has watered down true belief, strengthened critical faculties, and directed attention at the consequences of decisions and actions. A bargain is a move in the direction of reality.

[19] A way of signaling this, frequently used, was to externalize blame for present ills onto what the British had done or neo-imperialists were presently doing.

[20] From a letter written by Nehru to Mahtab in 1954, "Idealism has been powerfully affected by Congress becoming a government and many Congressmen looking forward to preferment."

That calculative sentiment was not new, and it had a predatory side to it. For generations there had been a pervasive notion that government, while surely menacing, was also a cow to be milked. Recall the worldy-wise MLA: "The trouble is [people] do not understand the principles of cooperation. They think it just another government organization that can be cheated when you get the chance." Recall also the pervasive assumption that none but a very few figures in public life could resist the normal human temptation to stack the deck if they got the chance. That design for dishonest living was the trough towards which pragmatists risked drifting when they abandoned the heights of Gandhian absolutist morality. Most of them, I am sure, did not perceive matters that way. Rather they saw themselves steering a rational course between the whirlpool of unrealistic righteousness and the Scylla of plain corruption.

The peculiar distribution of conflicting designs for living itself helped to keep fanaticism within bounds. Not only were there many incompatible designs available, but also customers distributed their purchases across the market. They built up personal political portfolios that contained irreconcilable philosophies, and they changed from one to the other when it suited them. Paternalistic princes used the rhetoric of Gandhian equality or even of socialism. Avowed Gandhians, like Mahtab, knew how to make deals with captains of industry, even with princes. Others, at one time convinced socialists, turned into true-believing Gandhians (for instance Nabakrushna Chaudhuri, who was exceptional because he made that his only position and stayed in it). More than that, within each bred-in-the-bone philosophy (for example paternalism) there was always a back stage where conduct that contradicted frontstage norms was itself the norm. All this is only to spell out what it means to say that there was little space in Orissa politics at that time for intense single-minded true believing.

Much that was acted out on the political stage was done from behind masks. Mahtab preached socialism but was ready to sit down with big business. A communist MLA mounted a vigorous campaign against an extortionate grain dealer and quietly accepted a donation for his party from the dealer. A social worker-politician won a grant to put indigent refugees to work, but was "having his profit." A mask signals, for those who recognize it as a mask, a reality that is alternative to what is being asserted. Thus, the way is opened to private negotiation and a mutual accommodation. Rhetoric, pretence, and even hypocrisy make room for bargaining;

they signal a willingness to stop fronting the scriptures and go backstage where dogma can be put aside and deals made. That this is a normal and usually healthy state of affairs is concealed by life's lie, the indisputable need we have to pretend we are plotting a straight course for ourselves and have a bright star to steer by.

Why was Orissa like that? The "war of every man against every man," or Madison's "propensity of mankind to fall into mutual animosity," suggest that bargaining will not be anyone's *initial* tactic of choice. If Hobbes and Madison are right, all parties would prefer have their own true belief define the situation, because then they get what they want without having to give anything away. Why, then, should anyone bargain? One obvious answer is that they see no realistic possibility of prevailing entirely; since they cannot command, they bargain. What, in Orissa in the fifties, made that happen?

Two historical contingencies intervened, preventing the post-1947 babel from resolving itself into Corcyrean chaos. First, the successor governments in Orissa and elsewhere in India inherited a formidable bureaucratic apparatus for maintaining government-defined law and order. There was, so to speak, an external Leviathan able to hold the lid down by force when the cauldron of true beliefs threatened to boil over. Those who could not bring themselves to compromise, negotiate, and bargain either went out of politics altogether (as Nabakrushna Chaudhuri eventually did), or, if they resorted to violence (as the communists did in 1947 and 1948), they found themselves in jail. Recall the specious phrasing of *Orissa 1949*: "From an agent of the British Government to oppress and persecute the people, on the 15th August 1947 the Indian Policeman became overnight the sentinel of India's independence."

Second, for all the storm and fury over agrarian problems in the early years and later over Saraikella and Kharsawan, there was no breakdown of government and administration in Orissa during the fifties. Political activists indulged themselves in displays of anger and fanatical enthusiasm, as they do everywhere, but for ordinary people the very modest expectations they had of government much of the time were more or less fulfilled. These expectations included a modicum of disorder. There was industrial unrest and strife over displaced villagers at Hirakud and Rourkhela. Student strikes and protests were endemic. There were hartals and political fastings and walkouts and processions and a lot of strident complaining about corruption and development monies siphoned off to finance political parties or fill private purses. There were natural disasters, especially floods (anything but a new experience to the people of coastal Orissa), invariably giving rise to accusations that relief monies had been embezzled or misapplied. But there were no civil wars, no political murders, no terrorism, no managed uprisings in remote areas in the fashion of the Naxalite insurrections that came in the seventies, not even much banditry. The nearest they came to breakdown was the trouble over Saraikella and Kharsawan. There was no accumulation of crises (as in the mid-seventies in India preceding Mrs. Gandhi's short-lived dictatorship), when an ambitious person (in that instance J. P. Narayan and his right-wing backers) might seize the opportunity to stand forth and give the call, "Follow me or disaster will overtake us all!" There was nothing to bring out a spontaneous Leviathan, a dictator. Despite the bad-mouthing and the prophecies of impending doom from those who still thought they might use outrage to win without making concessions, other leaders felt able to turn around and say to each other, "Let's work out what is practical and good for us all." For sure the instinct to find an enemy and carry forward one's own cause still operated, but they also knew how to control their passions and how to maneuver one another into focusing on interests and approaching the whole political enterprise in a give-so-as-to-get frame of mind—hence the Orissa coalition in 1959. Politics, Hobbes and Madison notwithstanding, tend to drift in that direction anyway—compromise—unless steps are taken to keep true beliefs fueled. Ordinary people are usually content to sit in the middle; the leaders push toward the extremes because that is where they can mark out a clear identity for themselves. True believers, of course, consider the tendency to avoid extremes an unmistakable indication of moral decay.

Pragmatism Defined

What kind of people were these pragmatists? The contrary label, "true believer," suggests persons who do what they think is right whatever the consequences, who have principles and a conscience, and perform their duty solely because it is their duty. "Pragmatist," on the other hand, conveys a whiff of opportunism, a lack of principle, and a person guided only by profit—in short, the amoral, self-concerned "economic man," whose behavior is modeled by rational choice theory.

That theory assumes that individuals pursue whatever they believe is of advantage to them and calculate how best to allocate their resources for that purpose: that is, they maximize their utility. The narrowest interpretations of "utility"—and the crassest—are "money" or "power." The 1959 coalition, critics said, was "a move to perpetuate Congress rule" or a ruse "by the chief minister to strengthen his own position inside the Congress party." Second, in a wider sense the word refers to any material benefit. For example, some soldiers joined Bose's Indian National Army because life there, at least before they went into action, was less deadly than in Japanese prisoner-of-war camps. Third, "utility"—that is, the calculating attitude of mind assumed in rational choice theory—may extend beyond material things and encompass principles and values. The governor's "perfect social and economic justice" and his "full freedom of thought, expression, belief and faith" are presented in his oration as true beliefs, intrinsically valued, Weber's "ethic of absolute ends" (1948, 120). "Perfect justice" or "full freedom" are *on that occasion* not up for trading. But in other contexts the same values can be placed in a framework of expected utility; then their status as true beliefs or ethical absolutes diminishes but is not entirely lost. In other words, people are ready to bargain away *some* of their "truth" in the interest of preserving the rest. To act that way is to be pragmatic.

When people compromise over matters of principle they have reexamined a true belief (an ideology) and factored it into a set of preferences. Once that is done, the guiding light is no longer *only* the true belief (socialism, Indian independence, Oriya nationalism, nonviolence, social and economic justice, and so forth) but also pragmatism itself, the principle that requires one to monitor an ideal to see how far (or in what alternative forms) it can be realized, and to find out what will be the costs of doing so. The experience of Mahtab's "hard realities" had exactly that effect on Gandhi's designs for India; it made people look closely at the cost/benefit ratio of his proposals and separate those that still might be implemented (most of them in the domain of social work) from the many that were quietly set to one side (for example, his rustic antistatism).

Such "moral costing"—Weber's "ethic of responsibility"—is the norm in most places at most times, whether for individuals or for collectivities. There are two directions in which to depart from this norm. One is toward the chaos caused by a diversity of uncompromising true beliefs, for example Corcyra long ago or the remnants of Yugoslavia now; its opposite would be toward the true-believing unity and discipline of Nazi Germany, or wartime Britain, or the solidarity that the freedom fighters in Orissa liked to recall. Pragmatism then would seem to hold an intermediate position, itself the contrary of both extremes (babel at one end and, at the other, the single commanding voice). But pragmatism, paradoxically, contains a methodological element that is itself a true belief. "Being reasonable" (giving up a part of one's true belief) acquires the status of an ethical imperative, in which those deserving contempt are those stupidly unwilling to give in order to get. In other words, pragmatism can become itself a moral absolute, a design for living that is intrinsically valued.

Pragmatists, in short, should not be written off as mere opportunists focused on their own narrow sectarian advantage. They are not, so to speak, just in it for the money; they have values, just as single-minded true believers do, but dampened down by reality testing and a concern for consequences. These two features together define pragmatism and distinguish it from other kinds of true belief.

Four Stages

So would the world be perfect if all principled politicians were also pragmatists, emulating Harekrushna Mahtab? Such a world is imaginable but, the enantiodromic model suggests, it could not be permanent, because pragmatism is only one stage in the cycle. It grows out of true belief, which is one of its opposites, and then gives way to another, which is plain corruption. The four phases (which overlap) are: first, a dominant true belief (exemplified in this book by the freedom fight); second, a discordance of contradictory true beliefs and, potentially, the Corcyra scene; third, the emergence of pragmatism, which is a willingness to negotiate (up to a point) over matters of principle; and fourth, corruption, where conscience is no one's guide and a marketplace of sectarian or personal interests dominates the political scene. All these last three stages were emerging, at different levels of growth, in Orissa in the fifties. A fifth stage, in which utter disillusion and a failure of civic nerve lead to a totalitarian "solution" (the S. C. Bose position, or Hitler's), has not yet happened in India, except in Mrs. Gandhi's two-year "emergency" in the mid-1970s.

Let me work through each stage of this cycle again. I begin with true belief.

There is no single comprehensive explanation for why people move into the mode of true belief, disqualifying their intellects, ceasing to ask questions, and giving themselves wholeheartedly to one or another cause. Certainly they do so. Since historical records began, we read of religions inspiring uncritical devotion—that feature is religion's defining element—and mobilizing devotees for political action, frequently violent. As I write, religious fundamentalism threatens to make havoc once again in India.

True belief, however, does not always take that dramatic form. It is in fact a routine experience, and perhaps we should not ask how people get into that mode, but how they ever get out of it. Nonreason permeates everyday life, and we habitually disqualify our intellect and underuse our mental powers. Simple expected-utility models assume a comprehensive no-stone-unturned conscious calculation whenever a decision is made, but that surely makes us far more rational than we are. We do things out of habit, or, if we do think, we take the first likely-looking option and ignore others, or sometimes we are flummoxed, deliberately abandon rationality, and spin a coin to make a decision. More than that, nonreason is entailed every time a reasoned decision is taken. Sooner or later a chain of justification must terminate in an *intrinsic* value, and there is, by definition, no *rational* way to select such a value. Ultimate ends can only be asserted or fought over. Gandhi's philosophy notwithstanding, there are no *moral* truths that "present" themselves, as he put it, and inevitably prevail.[21]

Suspending the critical faculties is a necessity, otherwise there would be no way to get beyond the incessant "why" and actually do something. Life, seen in that frame, is a continuing struggle to terminate questioning and select goals that are moral imperatives, strong enough to drown out the babel of competing claims. But we avoid that struggle much of the time and live without the effort of reasoning; when there is no custom to guide us, we turn to leaders who tell us "the truth" and save us the trouble of puzzling it out for

[21] To think that way—what is right is also what is natural—is to found morality on the impersonal natural world, which, of course, is precisely what every religion, whether spiritual or civic, attempts to do.

ourselves. (The kind of "truth" they are likely to give us is never a compromise, never grey, but pure, simple and unqualified.) In short, true belief is not only an everyday experience but also can be counted part of human nature, a disposition to void our minds of uncertainty by refusing to recognize reality and its problems until hard experience forces them on us. We procrastinate, saying we need not cross the bridge before we come to it, closing our minds to the menace of the unknown.

Formal organizations show a similar inevitable intrusion of non-reason. A rational-choice model, which assumes people in organizations are motivated only by their own interests, logically requires the concept of morality. (I remarked on this earlier when considering the wickedness of princes.) This is the familiar problem of the free loader, the person who takes from the organization without contributing. Someone is required to look after the interests of the organization and prevent it from failing, as did the cooperatives in Koraput, because too many took and too few honored the obligation to give. So the model positions a principal over the agents to restrain self-interested actions that would destroy the collective resource. But each principal is himself an agent, by definition selfishly motivated but likewise disciplined by a principal above him; and so on. *Quis custodiet ipsos custodes?* Where does the series end? It only stops when it is conceded that the basic postulate of rational-choice models is not enough: the concept of a *principal* must in reality encompass a *principle*—that is, the voice of conscience; and conscience is a manifestation of true belief.

This myopia—the refusal to see the need for moral principles—sometimes injects an irony into the discourse of those who use the rational-choice model. In order to define social systems as natural systems, they eliminate the moral actor and assume that utility, narrowly defined as material advantage or "economic opportunities," is the only significant motivation. Therefore, when real people put conscience before advantage, the model's predictions fail. Choice (therefore making room for morality) is then reintroduced through the back door, and the model's failure is explained as the result of human idiocy, perversity, or wickedness.

Everyday life exhibits a procession of actions, taken for a purpose but also taken habitually, without critical thought. This habituation provides a culture that is hospitable to an ethic of absolute ends. Charisma, presentational techniques, and various leadership styles that enchant explain *how* true beliefs are cultivated. *When* there will be an efflorescence is hard to predict. After the event sometimes, in an approximate way, one can understand how and why and when a true belief took hold. In the case of Indian nationalism, for example, one source from which the movement flowed was a decision in 1835 to form an English-educated professional class, "Indian in blood and colour, but English in taste, in opinions, in morals, and in intellect." The decision had consequences that surely were not foremost in the mind of Macaulay, when he wrote that notorious phrase. The educated class made itself familiar with the values that launched nineteenth-century struggles for liberty and national self-determination in Europe, and applied them to its own situation. We also have hypotheses that seek to explain particular situations in which enchantment becomes focused and unified: deprivation and oppression, the search for self-respect, ideas drifting in from other places, charismatic leaders, self-interested calculating leaders exploiting gullible followers, and so forth. But we do not have any comprehensive theory that would apply in every situation, other than the simple notion that human nature makes us eliminate uncertainty by clinging uncritically to a "truth" and, in extreme cases, makes us willing to die—or to kill—to have that "truth" prevail.

The second stage in the cycle is initiated when people begin to realize that the hitherto energizing "truth" is no longer powerful. It may have failed, as happened this past decade with communism in many parts of the world. Or it may have been fulfilled; India won its independence and the cause was ended. Then comes a babel of competing policies, which can lead either to Corcyrean chaos or to the third stage, the ascendence of the pragmatists. Since I have already described the historical conditions that favored their rise in the Orissa of the fifties, I now move to the fourth stage, the demise of pragmatism.

Pragmatism has many weaknesses; its practitioners live in political peril and mostly without much glory, as the disenchanted Mahtab did in the late fifties. Politics and pragmatism are, by nature, at cross purposes. The pragmatist seeks compromise and avoids combat, but politicians, like lawyers, thrive on combat. Pragmatism puts reality (the world as it is) at the head of the list. Politicians, again like lawyers, distort reality if doing so makes them winners. Pragmatism is dull; it has no appeal for the masses. To sell it successfully, the seller must be someone already trusted, someone fortified by tradition or by charisma, best of all someone with a warrior reputation, for example, Eisenhower or Yitzak Rabin. Asking what is practical trims down the prize and invites compromise with other designs; the pristine goal then is diminished, made less complete, less satisfying, and less exciting than it was. Our common metaphor of cold reality quenching the fires of enthusiasm is perfectly apt. Concessions, furthermore, arouse uncertainty, because people wonder where the concessions will stop and they begin to talk about the thin end of the wedge or the camel's nose. On top of all this, advocates of pragmatism must sell their wares in a market where others offer simpler, clearer, and more exciting things (albeit impractical, and not infrequently harmful). That is why pragmatists, like Mahtab, seldom can make an open appeal to the masses, and are themselves vulnerable to rabble-rousers. Pragmatism is bland, humdrum, tedious, seen as a job for bureaucrats and managers, not for leaders. That, too, is the reason why pragmatic deals are often done behind the scenes and presented to the public as if they were something entirely different. Then, falsely labeled, they are easy targets for deconstruction.

If the cover is blown, the pragmatist is stigmatized as unprincipled, without ethical standards, in addition to being timid, dull, and unadventurous. It seems to be our human failing to find honor in mindless true believing. True believers make mistakes, it is said, but at least they have a cause and are not self-serving opportunists, not wheelers and dealers operating in back rooms to make themselves rich. That kind of admiration sometimes attaches itself even to those, like Hitler, who are palpably wicked; villains, if the evil they do is spectacular enough, sometimes become like heroes. Pragmatists, on the other hand, get the same verdict as the maharaja's shopkeepers: they are underhand and unreliable.

There is a simulacrum of truth in this. Pragmatism means bargaining away some parts of a true belief (about socialism, Oriya nationalism, nonviolence, and the like) so as to preserve other parts that matter more. But pragmatism cannot indicate where the concessions have to stop. In fact, they stop when they bump against that part of the true belief that is not for negotiation. As Weber put it, those who act on an ethic of responsibility (calculating consequences and making compromises) sooner or later come to a point where they say "Here I stand; I can do no other" (1948, 127). At that point, morality has taken over from calculation. The risk that pragmatists run is not knowing where that point is, and slipping over into the territory of economic man (or his political equivalent), for whom no ethical stand is of intrinsic value. Holding on to power has then become the guiding value. The coalition in Orissa, critics said, had nothing to do with the public good, implementing the plan, or unifying Orissa; it was no more than "a move to perpetuate Congress rule."

In short, the nemesis that overtakes pragmatists, as their dealing makes deeper and deeper inroads into whatever true beliefs they originally held, is a progressive loss of adherents (especially those whose values or interests have been bargained away) and a growing reputation for ineffectiveness, if not corruption and an exclusive concern for sectional or private interests. That eventually leads to a general failure of nerve and a conviction that, if unchecked, the process will end in everyone's destruction. The scene then is set for a moral revolution, probably the emergence of a prophet proclaiming a cause, and a single dominant true belief. Neville Chamberlain, in the encounter with Hitler, drew the line of "here I stand" but left it too late, and found himself displaced by that mighty embodiment of true belief, Winston Churchill.

The pragmatists' fundamental problem is that they cannot so easily make the tactical use of enmity that is available to nonpragmatic true believers. Compromise dilutes enmity. (Again, the contrast of Churchill with Chamberlain comes to mind.) Of course, pragmatists do have an enemy, or at least someone to despise: the true believers. True believers, for their part, are quite prepared to exterminate pragmatists because pragmatists do not give blind support to the cause, and therefore betray it; but pragmatists cannot reciprocate. If they do, they abandon pragmatism and become true believers themselves, because the only tactic they have is to bargain. Insofar as they compromise, they forego the emotional thrust that comes from personifying an enemy whose existence explains the world's evil and whose extermination provides the one hope of salvation. Pragmatism, in other respects so different, is caught in the same trap as Gandhi's philosophy of nonviolence; it does not sufficiently appreciate the need for enemies.

In all this there is the greatest of ironies. The human habit (what we call second nature) lies somewhere between indifference ("not my business") and moderation, if only because enthusiasm for a cause requires energy and may require sacrifice. Our disposition, as I said, is not to welcome problems and the need to make decisions. In that respect Hobbes, when he envisages the state of nature as a war of all against all, is mistaken. So also is Madison when he talks of "this propensity of mankind, to fall into mutual animosity." It may be the case that "the latent causes of factionalism" are "sown in the nature of man," but they remain latent until stimulated by leaders. As I write, surveys in the United States show that a majority of Americans believe it is not their business to interfere in a woman's decision about aborting a pregnancy. But that moderation (or indifference) remains mostly unvoiced. Benign indifference does not get people into the streets. First they must be politicized; they must be led toward one or the other extreme.

The Argument

Here is the argument again. It has three assumptions. First, when there are many goals and not much agreement about how to set them in an order of priority, antagonists will seek the short route to certainty by holding on to one true belief, thrusting it on other people, and casting the holders of competing beliefs as villains. Second, people, for what reason I do not know, find it easier to stifle doubts if they can be convinced that they have identified an evil that stands in the way of their own version of what is good and true. Third, they do so with more conviction if the evil can be personified, and the persons so identified can be hated.[22]

These are propositions about human nature, and I use them as axioms. Not everyone behaves in this way—Gandhi, obviously, tried not to do so. But they do represent the initial default mode of human interaction in a context of uncertainty and a struggle for power. A secondary default program may intervene if the first produces a stalemate. The antagonists resign themselves to bargaining, and in time the experience of being reasonable may elevate reasonableness and compromise into a Leviathan-like principle of interaction. This lasts until the pragmatists slip downward into plainly corrupt marketplace politics. Then one or other faction among the true believers will produce a revolutionary scripture and make it prevail as the dominant definition of the situation. The cycle has then begun again.

The stunning, unrelenting, media-conveyed and amplified inci-

---

[22] Every day I encounter in the media statements or events or persons that to me are outrageously evil; yet they are interpreted by others as right and just and noble. I, not being Gandhi, write off those who make such judgments as defective human beings who do not merit a place in my moral (and political) community. That point, obviously, is a terminus for rational thought.

vility in American politics today, with which I began this book, is in fact not of much importance, unless it turns out to be a harbinger of Corcyrean-style true-believing factionalism. Verbal hooliganism, to which politicians who expose themselves in the media often contribute, is sustained by greed, audience ratings, show business values, and American commercialism: whatever sells cannot be evil enough to take it off the market.[23] In fact, of course, what sells often is bad, and an eye on the bottom line probably does make some contribution to an already existing propensity for incivility, boorishness, and redneck violence. On the other hand, commercialized incivility is preferable to the Corcyrean extreme, where the malevolence is sincere.

Morality of the Gandhian kind, absolute, unqualified, disengaged from the world, while surely unrealistic, yet attracts an intuitive sympathy and admiration. Once we are jerked out of the normal human condition of indifference, once politicized, we seem to be programmed for true belief. We too readily overlook its dangers. Mahtab's pragmatism was probably the best available design for Orissa in the fifties, an ironic conclusion, given the disagreeable impression his character made on me.

[23] The French, according to a recent PBS commentary, do not run their political campaigns that way. They eschew personalities; that kind of vulgarity is kept for trashy tabloid journalism, as it is in Britain. Americans are worse off because television and the radio are more intrusive than print journalism.

References

Bailey, F. G.
    1960 *Tribe Caste, and Nation*. Manchester: Manchester University Press.
    1963 *Politics and Social Change*. Berkeley: University of California Press.
    1991 *The Prevalence of Deceit*. Ithaca: Cornell University Press.
    1994 *The Witch-Hunt*. Ithaca: Cornell University Press.
Banerji, R. D.
    1980 [1930] *History of Orissa*. Delhi: Bharatiya Publishing House. 2 vols.
Basham, A. L.
    1963 "Some Fundamental Political Ideas of Ancient India." In *Politics and Society in India*, ed. C. H. Philips. London: Allen & Unwin: 11–23.
Beal, H. E.
    1954 *Indian Ink*. London: Harrap.
Behera, K. S., J. Patnaik, and H. C. Das (eds.)
    1990 *Cuttack: One Thousand Years*. Cuttack: Cuttack City Millennium Celebrations Committee. 2 vols.
Beloff, Max (ed.)
    1948 *The Federalist, or, The New Constitution*. Oxford: Basil Blackwell.
Bose, Nirmal Kumar
    1953 *My Days with Gandhi*. Calcutta: Nishana.
Burke, Kenneth
    1969 *A Grammar of Motives*. Berkeley: University of California Press.

Burns, James MacGregor
   1979 *Leadership*. New York: Harper and Row.
Chatterjee, Partha
   1986 *Nationalist Thought and the Colonial World*. London: Zed Books.
Cobden-Ramsay, L. E. B.
   1982 [1910] *Bengal Gazetteers: Feudatory States of Orissa*. Calcutta: Firma KLM.
Dash, Shreeram Chandra
   1980 "Cuttack: The Capital City" in Behera et al., vol. 1, 140–52.
De, S. C.
   1990 "Cuttack Jail in 1859" in Behera *et al.* Vol. 1, 194–97.
Dutta, Krishna, and Andrew Robinson
   1996 *Rabindranath Tagore: The Myriad-Minded Man*. New York: St. Martin's Press.
Epstein, T. Scarlett
   1962 *Economic Development and Social Change in South India*. Manchester: Manchester University Press.
Freud, Sigmund
   1961 [1930] *Civilization and Its Discontents*. Trans. James Strachey. New York: W. W. Norton
Gandhi, Manubhen
   1955 [1949] *Bapu—My Mother*. Ahmedabad: Navajivan.
Gandhi, M. K.
   1944 *Hind Swaraj, or Indian Home Rule*. Ahmedabad: Navajivan.
Grenell, Peter
   1980 "Planning the New Capital of Bhubaneswar." in Seymour 1980: 31–66.
A Handbook of Orissa.
   1958 Bhubaneswar: Government of Orissa, Public Relations Department.
Hobbes, Thomas
   1946 [1651] *Leviathan*. Oxford: Blackwell.
Hunter, W. W.
   1872 *Orissa*. London: Smith, Elder 2 vols.
Lewis, W. Arthur
   1962 Foreword in Epstein 1962.
Mahtab, Harekrushna
   1957 (ed.) *History of the Freedom Movement in Orissa*. Orissa: State Committee for Compilation of History of the Freedom Movement in Orissa. 4 vols.
   1959 (ed.) Vol. 5 of the above.

1965 *Lectures on Gandhian Philosophy*. Annamalainagar: Annamalai University.

1973 *Gandhi: The Political Leader*. Cuttack: Cuttack Students' Store.

1974 [1949] *Beginning of the End*. Cuttack: Cuttack Students' Store.

1981 [1949] *The History of Orissa*. Cuttack: Cuttack Students' Store.

1986 *While Serving My Nation*. Cuttack: Vidyapuri.

Miller, David

1980 "Religious Institutions and Political Elites in Bhubaneswar." in Seymour 1980, 83–95.

Morris-Jones, W. H.

1957 *Parliament in India*. London: Longmans, Green.

Nehru, Jawaharlal

1962 [1936] *An Autobiography*. Bombay: Allied Publishers.

O'Malley, L.S.S.

1933 [1906] *Bihar and Orissa District Gazetteers: Cuttack*. Patna: Government Printing.

Orissa 1949. Cuttack: Government of Orissa, Public Relations Department.

Orissa Review. Bhubaneswar: Government of Orissa, Public Relation Department.

Pradhan, Atul Chandra

1990 "Cuttack under British Rule" in Behera et al., vol. 1, 128–39.

Report on the Second General Elections in India.

1957 2 vols. Delhi: Government of India, Election Commission.

Rudolph, Lloyd I., and Susanne Hoeber Rudolph

1967 *The Modernity of Tradition*. Chicago: University of Chicago Press.

Seymour, Susan (ed.)

1980 *The Transformation of a Sacred Town: Bhubaneswar, India*. Boulder, Colo.: Westview Press.

Thucydides

1972 *The Peloponnesian War*. Trans. Rex Warner. Harmondsworth: Penguin.

Toye, Hugh

1962 *Subhash Chandra Bose (The Springing Tiger): A Study of a Revolution*. Bombay: Jaico.

Weber, Max

1948 [1919] "Politics as a Vocation" in Gerth H.H. and C. Wright Mills, *From Max Weber: Essays in Sociology*. London: Routledge and Kegan Paul: 77–128.

Index

Gandhi's notions of, 91; Mahtab on, 170. *See also* Congress Socialist Party
Socialists (PSP), 3, 39, 43, 127, 150, 166, 200
States Reorganization Commission, 36, 134
Swaraj, ix, 125, 149, 158, 183
Swarajist Congressmen, 161, 181

Tagore, Rabindranath, 177, 187
Talcher state, 136–148, 160–61, 193
Tapas, 111, 187 fn.10
Thucydides, 178
Toye, Hugh, 185
Traders. *See* Businessmen
Tributary states, 35–38, 67, 132–33, 161. *See also* Paternalism; Praja-mandal; *entries for individual states*
True belief, xi–xiii, 8, 176–79, 205–12; defined, 5; in Orissa, 199–204; and Sarvodaya, 155; and Satyagraha, 192–98. *See also* Compromise; Ethic
Trust, x; and bureaucrats, 85; in

politicians, xiv, 50, 96, 105, 121, 209; in government, 20, 61, 159; and rajas, 66, 168; and Sarvodaya, 158; in the people, 3–4, 168

Union government, 35–37, 154
Untouchables, 50–52, 116, 130; and Gandhi, 189–90. *See also* Scheduled castes
Utkal Sammilani. *See* Oriya Union Movement

Violence, xi, xiii, 36–38, 128–29, 135–36, 144–45, 148, 161–63, 181 fn.5, 197–98; in Corcyra, 178. *See also* Quit India movement, Satyagraha

Weber, Max, xiii fn.l, 172 fn.9, 176 fn.l, 205, 210
Women in politics, 12, 55, 120, 128, 150

Zemindars, 68, 98, 124, 150–53, 163

p208   True belief part of human nature

p9 The exotic fallacy

p173 Corcyra